AFGHANS

FOR ALL SEASONS • BOOK 4

"To everything there is a season," the Bible tells us, and the passing of time reminds us of this truth. A season for celebrating life and pausing to relish the scent of fresh flowers. A season for honoring our nation and spending leisurely afternoons swimming or sailing. A season to appreciate Nature's brilliance and give thanks for the bounty we enjoy. And a season to relax by the warmth of the hearth in the company of friends and family. Each time of the year is captivating in its own unique way, as the afghans in this enchanting book prove. Four sections use the art of crochet to chronicle the glorious nuances of the seasons in 49 exquisite throws. Gorgeous full-color photographs will inspire you to create your own crocheted masterpiece, while the clear, concise instructions you've come to expect from Leisure Arts will make it easier than you ever dreamed. So what are you waiting for? Turn the page to embark on your yearlong journey through the splendor of crocheted comfort!

LEISURE ARTS, INC., and OXMOOR HOUSE, INC.

EDITORIAL STAFF

Vice President and Editor-in-Chief: Sandra Graham Case
Executive Director of Publications: Cheryl Nodine Gunnells
Director of Designer Relations: Debra Nettles
Senior Publications Director: Susan White Sullivan
Publications Director: Mary Sullivan Hutcheson
Editorial Director: Susan Frantz Wiles
Photography Director: Lori Ringwood Dimond
Art Operations Director: Jeff Curtis

PRODUCTION
Managing Editor: Valesha M. Kirksey
Senior Technical Editor: Lois J. Long
Instructional Editor: Sarah J. Green

EDITORIAL
Associate Editor: Kimberly L. Ross

ART
Art Publications Director: Rhonda Hodge Shelby
Art Imaging Director: Mark Hawkins
Lead Graphic Artist: Diana Sanders
Production Artists: Karen F. Allbright and Faith Lloyd
Staff Photographer: Russ Ganser
Photography Stylists: Janna Laughlin and Cassie Newsome
Publishing Systems Administrator: Becky Riddle
Publishing Systems Assistants: Clint Hanson, Myra S. Means, and
  Chris Wertenberger

BUSINESS STAFF

Publisher: Rick Barton
Vice President, Finance: Tom Siebenmorgen
Director of Corporate Planning and Development: Laticia Mull Dittrich
Vice President, Retail Marketing: Bob Humphrey
Vice President, Sales: Ray Shelgosh
Vice President, National Accounts: Pam Stebbins
Director of Sales and Services: Margaret Reinold
Vice President, Operations: Jim Dittrich
Comptroller, Operations: Rob Thieme
Retail Customer Service Managers: Sharon Hall and Stan Raynor
Print Production Manager: Fred F. Pruss
Director of Photography, Public Relations, and Retail Marketing:
  Stephen Wilson

Afghans For All Seasons, Book 4
Published by Leisure Arts, Inc., and Oxmoor House, Inc.

Hardcover ISBN 1-57486-280-4
Softcover ISBN 1-57486-281-2

10 9 8 7 6 5 4 3 2 1

TABLE OF CONTENTS

Spring

Spring is a season of wonder. As nature dons her cloak of green, the whole world seems to come alive with fresh beauty. Let this spirit of renewal inspire you to crochet a light-and-lovely afghan in blithe spring hues. You'll adore the lively selection in the following pages, including two small afghans, just right for a brand-new baby or a favorite toddler.

LADY'S CHOICE

This enchanting coverlet is a lady's first choice for style, comfort, and elegance. A ruffled lace pattern edges the rosy wrap for a feminine effect.

Finished Size: 51¹/₂" x 63¹/₂" (131 cm x 161.5 cm)

MATERIALS
Brushed Acrylic Worsted Weight Yarn:
  50 ounces, 2,535 yards
    (1,420 grams, 2,318 meters)
Crochet hook, size I (5.5 mm) **or** size needed
  for gauge

GAUGE: In pattern, 2 repeats = 4³/₄" (12 cm);
    8 rows = 3¹/₂" (9 cm)

Gauge Swatch: 5"w x 3¹/₂"h (12.75 cm x 9 cm)
Ch 16 **loosely**.
Work same as Afghan Body for 8 rows.
Finish off.

AFGHAN BODY
Ch 121 **loosely**.
Row 1 (Right side): Sc in second ch from hook and in next ch, skip next ch, 3 dc in next ch, ch 1, 3 dc in next ch, ★ skip next ch, sc in next ch, ch 1, skip next ch, sc in next ch, skip next ch, 3 dc in next ch, ch 1, 3 dc in next ch; repeat from ★ across to last 3 chs, skip next ch, sc in last 2 chs: 138 sts and 33 ch-1 sps.
Note: Loop a short piece of yarn around any stitch to mark Row 1 as **right** side.
Row 2: Ch 2 (**counts as first hdc**), turn; hdc in same st, ch 3, sc in next ch-1 sp, ch 3, ★ (hdc, ch 1, hdc) in next ch-1 sp, ch 3, sc in next ch-1 sp, ch 3; repeat from ★ across to last 5 sts, skip next 4 sts, 2 hdc in last sc: 50 sps.
Row 3: Ch 3 (**counts as first dc**), turn; 2 dc in same st, sc in next ch-3 sp, ch 1, sc in next ch-3 sp, ★ (3 dc, ch 1, 3 dc) in next ch-1 sp, sc in next ch-3 sp, ch 1, sc in next ch-3 sp; repeat from ★ across to last 2 hdc, skip next hdc, 3 dc in last hdc: 136 sts and 33 ch-1 sps.
Row 4: Ch 1, turn; sc in first dc, ch 3, (hdc, ch 1, hdc) in next ch-1 sp, ch 3, ★ sc in next ch-1 sp, ch 3, (hdc, ch 1, hdc) in next ch-1 sp, ch 3; repeat from ★ across to last 4 sts, skip next 3 sts, sc in last dc: 51 sps.
Row 5: Ch 1, turn; sc in first sc and in next ch-3 sp, (3 dc, ch 1, 3 dc) in next ch-1 sp, ★ sc in next ch-3 sp, ch 1, sc in next ch-3 sp, (3 dc, ch 1, 3 dc) in next ch-1 sp; repeat from ★ across to last ch-3 sp, sc in last ch-3 sp and in last sc: 138 sts and 33 ch-1 sps.

Rows 6-120: Repeat Rows 2-5, 28 times; then repeat Rows 2-4 once **more**; do **not** finish off.

EDGING
Rnd 1: Ch 1, turn; 2 sc in first sc and in next ch-3 sp, sc in next ch-1 sp, (3 sc in each of next 2 ch-3 sps, sc in next ch-1 sp) across to last ch-3 sp, 3 sc in last ch-3 sp, 2 sc in last sc, † place marker around last sc made for st placement; working across end of rows, sc in first row, 2 sc in each of next 2 rows, (sc in next 2 rows, 2 sc in each of next 2 rows) across to last row, sc in last row †; working in sps and in free loops of beginning ch (*Fig. 17b, page 141*), sc in first ch, place marker around sc just made for st placement, sc in same ch and in each sp and each ch across to last ch, 2 sc in last ch, repeat from † to † once; join with slip st to first sc: 604 sc.
Rnd 2: Ch 1, do **not** turn; 2 sc in same st, (sc in each sc across to next marked sc, 3 sc in marked sc) 3 times, sc in each sc across and in same st as first sc; join with slip st to first sc: 612 sc.
Rnd 3: Ch 5 (**counts as first dc plus ch 2**), (dc in same st, ch 2) twice, skip next 2 sc, ★ (dc in next sc, ch 2, skip next 2 sc) across to center sc of next corner 3-sc group, (dc, ch 2) 4 times in center sc, skip next 2 sc; repeat from ★ 2 times **more**, (dc in next sc, ch 2, skip next 2 sc) across, dc in same st as first dc, ch 2; join with slip st to first dc: 216 dc and 216 ch-2 sps.
Rnd 4: Slip st in first ch-2 sp, ch 1, (sc, ch 5) 3 times in same sp and in next ch-2 sp, sc in next ch-2 sp, ch 5, ★ [(sc, ch 5) twice in next ch-2 sp, sc in next ch-2 sp, ch 5] across to next corner 4-dc group, (sc, ch 5) 3 times in each of next 3 ch-2 sps, sc in next ch-2 sp, ch 5; repeat from ★ 2 times **more**, [(sc, ch 5) twice in next ch-2 sp, sc in next ch-2 sp, ch 5] across to last ch-2 sp, [sc, (ch 5, sc) twice] in last ch-2 sp, ch 2, dc in first sc to form last ch-5 sp: 340 ch-2 sps.
Rnds 5-7: Ch 1, sc in last ch-5 sp, (ch 5, sc in next ch-5 sp) around, ch 2, dc in first sc to form last ch-5 sp.
Rnd 8: Ch 1, sc in last ch-5 sp, ch 5, (sc in next ch-5 sp, ch 5) around; join with slip st to first sc.
Rnd 9: Slip st in first ch-5 sp, ch 1, sc in same sp, (3 dc, ch 3, sc in third ch from hook, 3 dc) in next ch-5 sp, ★ sc in next ch-5 sp, (3 dc, ch 3, sc in third ch from hook, 3 dc) in next ch-5 sp; repeat from ★ around; join with slip st to first sc, finish off.

TRIM

Rnd 1: With **right** side facing and working around posts of dc on Rnd 3 of Edging, join yarn with sc around any dc *(see Joining With Sc, page 140)*; ch 3, (sc around next dc, ch 3) around; join with slip st to first sc, finish off.

Rnd 2: With **right** side facing and working around posts of same dc as Rnd 1 of Trim, join yarn with sc around any dc; ch 3, (sc around next dc, ch 3) around; join with slip st to first sc, finish off.

GARDENER'S PLEASURE

Flourishing with an abundance of soft green, this meadow-inspired afghan is sure to freshen your décor. Strips of clusters add a lovely texture that evokes the lush spring countryside.

Finished Size: 48" x 64" (122 cm x 162.5 cm)

MATERIALS
Worsted Weight Yarn:
    Lt Green - 24 ounces, 1,645 yards
      (680 grams, 1,504 meters)
    Green - 17¹/₂ ounces, 1,200 yards
      (500 grams, 1,097.5 meters)
    Crochet hook, size H (5 mm) **or** size needed
      for gauge

GAUGE: Each Strip = 4" (10 cm) wide

Gauge Swatch: 2"w x 4¹/₄"h (5 cm x 10.75 cm)
Foundation Row: (Ch 3, work Cluster in third ch from hook) 4 times.
Rnd 1: Work same as Rnd 1 of First Strip.

STITCH GUIDE

> **CLUSTER** (uses one ch)
> ★ YO, insert hook in ch indicated, YO and pull up a loop, YO and draw through 2 loops on hook; repeat from ★ 2 times **more**, YO and draw through all 4 loops on hook (*Figs. 10a & b, page 139*).

FIRST STRIP
Foundation Row (Right side)**:** With Green, (ch 3, work Cluster in third ch from hook) 57 times: 57 Clusters.
Note: Loop a short piece of yarn around first Cluster made to mark Foundation Row as **right** side and bottom edge.
Rnd 1: Ch 3, work Cluster in ch at base of last Cluster made, ch 3, ★ (slip st, ch 2, work Cluster) in ch at base of next Cluster, ch 3; repeat from ★ across to last 2 Clusters, work Cluster in ch at base of next Cluster, place marker in last Cluster made for st placement, ch 3, slip st in ch at base of last Cluster, ch 3, working on opposite side of Foundation Row, work Cluster in ch at base of next Cluster, ch 3, **[**(slip st, ch 2, work Cluster) in ch at base of next Cluster, ch 3**]** across to last 2 Clusters, work Cluster in ch at base of next Cluster, place marker in last Cluster made for st placement, ch 3; join with slip st to top of last Cluster made on Foundation Row, finish off: 114 ch-3 sps.

Rnd 2: With **right** side facing, join Lt Green with sc in same st as joining (*see Joining With Sc, page 140*); ch 3, sc in same st, † (ch 3, sc in next ch-3 sp) twice, (dc in next Cluster, ch 3, sc in next ch-3 sp) across to next marked Cluster, ch 3, skip marked Cluster, sc in next ch-3 sp, ch 3 †, (sc, ch 3, sc) in next slip st, place marker around last ch-3 made for st placement, repeat from † to † once; join with slip st to first sc: 118 ch-3 sps.
Rnd 3: Slip st in first ch-3 sp, ch 3 **(counts as first dc)**, 4 dc in same sp, sc in next ch-3 sp, ch 3, sc in next sc, ch 1, sc in next ch-3 sp, ch 3, (2 sc in next ch-3 sp, ch 3) across to within 2 ch-3 sps of marked ch-3 sp, sc in next ch-3 sp, ch 1, sc in next sc, ch 3, sc in next ch-3 sp, 5 dc in marked ch-3 sp, sc in next ch-3 sp, ch 3, sc in next sc, ch 1, sc in next ch-3 sp, ch 3, (2 sc in next ch-3 sp, ch 3) across to last 2 ch-3 sps, sc in next ch-3 sp, ch 1, sc in next sc, ch 3, sc in last ch-3 sp; join with slip st to first dc.
Rnd 4: Ch 1, sc in same st and in next dc, (sc, ch 2, sc) in next dc, sc in next 2 dc, (sc, ch 2) twice in next ch-3 sp, place marker around last ch-2 made for joining placement, (sc, ch 2) twice in each sp across to within 2 sps of next 5-dc group, place marker around last ch-2 made for joining placement, (sc, ch 2) twice in next ch-1 sp, (sc, ch 2, sc) in next ch-3 sp, skip next sc, sc in next 2 dc, (sc, ch 2, sc) in next dc, sc in next 2 dc, (sc, ch 2) twice in each sp across to last ch-3 sp, (sc, ch 2, sc) in last ch-3 sp; join with slip st to first sc, finish off.

REMAINING 11 STRIPS
Work same as First Strip through Rnd 3: 118 sps.
Rnd 4 (Joining rnd): Ch 1, sc in same st and in next dc, (sc, ch 2, sc) in next dc, sc in next 2 dc, (sc, ch 2) twice in next ch-3 sp, place marker around last ch-2 made for joining placement, (sc, ch 2) twice in each sp across to within 2 sps of next 5-dc group, place marker around last ch-2 made for joining placement, (sc, ch 2) twice in next ch-1 sp, (sc, ch 2, sc) in next ch-3 sp, skip next sc, sc in next 2 dc, (sc, ch 2, sc) in next dc, sc in next 2 dc, (sc, ch 2) twice in next ch-3 sp, sc in next ch-1 sp, ch 1, holding Strips with

wrong sides together and bottom at same end, slip st in marked ch-2 sp on **previous Strip**, ch 1, sc in same sp on **new Strip**, ch 2, sc in next ch-3 sp, ch 1, ★ skip next ch-2 sp on **previous Strip**, slip st in next ch-2 sp, ch 1, sc in same sp on **new Strip**, ch 2, sc in next sp, ch 1; repeat from ★ across to next marked ch-2 sp on **previous Strip**, slip st in marked ch-2 sp, ch 1, sc in same sp on **new Strip**, (ch 2, sc) twice in last ch-3 sp; join with slip st to first sc, finish off.

RESTFUL RETREAT

Curl up with this lovely azure afghan and a favorite book for a restful retreat from reality. Rows of crossed stitches make this striped cover-up especially quick to create.

Finished Size: 51" x 64" (129.5 cm x 162.5 cm)

MATERIALS
Worsted Weight Yarn:
   Ecru - 26 ounces, 1,785 yards
     (740 grams, 1,632 meters)
   Light Blue - 11¹/₂ ounces, 790 yards
     (330 grams, 722.5 meters)
   Dark Blue - 11 ounces, 755 yards
     (310 grams, 690.5 meters)
Crochet hook, size I (5.5 mm) **or** size needed
   for gauge

GAUGE: In pattern, 5 Cross Sts = 4" (10 cm);
     4 rows = 3" (7.5 cm)

Gauge Swatch: 4³/₄"w x 3"h (12 cm x 7.5 cm)
With Ecru, ch 19 **loosely**.
Work same as Afghan Body for 4 rows.

Note: Each row is worked across length of Afghan. When joining yarn and finishing off, leave an 8" (20.5 cm) length to be worked into fringe.

STITCH GUIDE

CROSS STITCH (abbreviated Cross St)
Skip next tr, tr in next tr, ch 1, working in **front** of tr just made (*Fig. 18, page 141*), tr in skipped tr.

AFGHAN BODY
With Ecru, ch 241 **loosely**; place marker in third ch from hook for st placement.
Row 1 (Right side): Tr in sixth ch from hook, ch 1, working in **front** of tr just made (*Fig. 18, page 141*), tr in fourth skipped ch, ★ skip next 2 chs, tr in next ch, ch 1, working in **front** of tr just made, tr in first skipped ch; repeat from ★ across to last ch, dc in last ch; finish off: 158 tr.
Note: Loop a short piece of yarn around any stitch to mark Row 1 as **right** side.
Row 2: With **wrong** side facing, join Light Blue with slip st in first dc; ch 3 **(counts as first dc, now and throughout)**, work Cross Sts across, dc in next ch; finish off: 79 Cross Sts.

Row 3: With **right** side facing, join Ecru with slip st in first dc; ch 3, work Cross Sts across to last dc, dc in last dc; finish off.
Row 4: With **wrong** side facing, join Dark Blue with slip st in first dc; ch 3, work Cross Sts across to last dc, dc in last dc; finish off.
Row 5: With **right** side facing, join Ecru with slip st in first dc; ch 3, work Cross Sts across to last dc, dc in last dc; finish off.
Row 6: With **wrong** side facing, join Light Blue with slip st in first dc; ch 3, work Cross Sts across to last dc, dc in last dc; finish off.
Row 7: With **right** side facing, join Ecru with slip st in first dc; ch 3, work Cross Sts across to last dc, dc in last dc; finish off.
Rows 8-67: Repeat Rows 4-7, 15 times; at end of Row 67, do **not** finish off.

EDGING
FIRST SIDE
Row 1: Ch 1, turn; sc in first 2 sts, ★ ch 1, skip next ch-1 sp, sc in next 2 sts; repeat from ★ across.
Row 2: Turn; slip st in first sc, ch 3, (slip st in next ch-1 sp, ch 3) across to last 2 sc, skip next sc, slip st in last sc; finish off.

SECOND SIDE
Row 1: With **wrong** side facing and working in free loops of beginning ch (*Fig. 17b, page 141*), join Ecru with sc in marked ch (*see Joining With Sc, page 140*); sc in next ch, ★ ch 1, skip next ch, sc in next 2 chs; repeat from ★ across.
Row 2: Turn; slip st in first sc, ch 3, (slip st in next ch-1 sp, ch 3) across to last 2 sc, skip next sc, slip st in last sc; finish off.

Holding 4 strands of Ecru and 4 strands of corresponding color yarn together, each 17" (43 cm) long, add additional fringe in end of each wrong side row across short edges of Afghan (*Figs. 22b & d, page 142*).

INNOVATIVE

Make a bold statement with our innovative wrap. Variegated yarn and a lush fringe give this fashionable throw an exciting visual texture that demands a second glance.

Finished Size: 47¹/₂" x 63" (120.5 cm x 160 cm)

MATERIALS
Worsted Weight Yarn:
  Ecru - 40 ounces, 2,265 yards
    (1,140 grams, 2,071 meters)
  Variegated - 18 ounces, 1,090 yards
    (510 grams, 996.5 meters)
Crochet hook, size I (5.5 mm) **or** size needed
  for gauge

GAUGE: In pattern, 10 sts = 3¹/₄" (8.25 cm);
      10 rows = 3" (7.5 cm)

Gauge Swatch: 10³/₄"w x 3"h (27.25 cm x 7.5 cm)
With Ecru, ch 34 **loosely**.
Work same as Afghan Body for 10 rows.

Note: Each row is worked across length of Afghan. When joining yarn and finishing off, leave an 8" (20.5 cm) length to be worked into fringe.

AFGHAN BODY
With Ecru, ch 194 **loosely**.
Row 1 (Right side)**:** Sc in second ch from hook and in each ch across; finish off: 193 sc.
Note: Loop a short piece of yarn around any stitch to mark Row 1 as **right** side.
Row 2: With **wrong** side facing, join Variegated with sc in first sc *(see Joining With Sc, page 140)*; ★ ch 1, skip next sc, sc in next sc; repeat from ★ across; finish off: 97 sc and 96 ch-1 sps.
Row 3: With **right** side facing, join Ecru with sc in first sc; [working **behind** next ch-1 *(Fig. 18, page 141)*, dc in skipped sc one row **below**, sc in next sc] twice, (working in **front** of next ch-1, dc in skipped sc one row **below**, sc in next sc) twice, ★ (working **behind** next ch-1, dc in skipped sc one row **below**, sc in next sc) 8 times, (working in **front** of next ch-1, dc in skipped sc one row **below**, sc in next sc) twice; repeat from ★ across to last 2 ch-1 sps, (working **behind** next ch-1, dc in skipped sc one row **below**, sc in next sc) twice; finish off: 193 sts.
Row 4: With **wrong** side facing, join Variegated with sc in first sc; ★ ch 1, skip next dc, sc in next sc; repeat from ★ across; finish off: 97 sc and 96 ch-1 sps.

Row 5: With **right** side facing, join Ecru with sc in first sc; working **behind** next ch-1, dc in skipped dc one row **below**, sc in next sc, (working in **front** of next ch-1, dc in skipped dc one row **below**, sc in next sc) 4 times, ★ (working **behind** next ch-1, dc in skipped dc one row **below**, sc in next sc) 6 times, (working in **front** of next ch-1, dc in skipped dc one row **below**, sc in next sc) 4 times; repeat from ★ across to last ch-1 sp, working **behind** last ch-1, dc in skipped dc one row **below**, sc in last sc; finish off: 193 sts.
Row 6: With **wrong** side facing, join Variegated with sc in first sc; ★ ch 1, skip next dc, sc in next sc; repeat from ★ across; finish off: 97 sc and 96 ch-1 sps.
Row 7: With **right** side facing, join Ecru with sc in first sc; (working in **front** of next ch-1, dc in skipped dc one row **below**, sc in next sc) 6 times, ★ (working **behind** next ch-1, dc in skipped dc one row **below**, sc in next sc) 4 times, (working in **front** of next ch-1, dc in skipped dc one row **below**, sc in next sc) 6 times; repeat from ★ across; finish off: 193 sts.
Rows 8-10: Repeat Rows 4-6.
Row 11: With **right** side facing, join Ecru with sc in first sc; (working **behind** next ch-1, dc in skipped dc one row **below**, sc in next sc) twice, (working in **front** of next ch-1, dc in skipped dc one row **below**, sc in next sc) twice, ★ (working **behind** next ch-1, dc in skipped dc one row **below**, sc in next sc) 3 times, (working in **front** of next ch-1, dc in skipped dc one row **below**, sc in next sc) twice; repeat from ★ across to last 2 ch-1 sps, (working **behind** next ch-1, dc in skipped dc one row **below**, sc in next sc) twice; finish off: 193 sts.
Row 12: With **wrong** side facing, join Variegated with sc in first sc; ★ ch 1, skip next dc, sc in next sc; repeat from ★ across; finish off: 97 sc and 96 ch-1 sps.
Row 13: With **right** side facing, join Ecru with sc in first sc; (working **behind** next ch-1, dc in skipped dc one row **below**, sc in next sc) 6 times, ★ (working in **front** of next ch-1, dc in skipped dc one row **below**, sc in next sc) 4 times, (working **behind** next ch-1, dc in skipped dc one row **below**, sc in next sc) 6 times; repeat from ★ across; finish off: 193 sts

Continued on page 14.

12

Row 14: With **wrong** side facing, join Variegated with sc in first sc; ★ ch 1, skip next dc, sc in next sc; repeat from ★ across; finish off: 97 sc and 96 ch-1 sps.

Row 15: With **right** side facing, join Ecru with sc in first sc; (working **behind** next ch-1, dc in skipped dc one row **below**, sc in next sc) 5 times, (working in **front** of next ch-1, dc in skipped dc one row **below**, sc in next sc) 6 times, ★ (working **behind** next ch-1, dc in skipped dc one row **below**, sc in next sc) 4 times, (working in **front** of next ch-1, dc in skipped dc one row **below**, sc in next sc) 6 times; repeat from ★ across to last 5 ch-1 sps, (working **behind** next ch-1, dc in skipped dc one row **below**, sc in next sc) 5 times; finish off: 193 sts.

Rows 16-18: Repeat Rows 12-14.

Row 19: With **right** side facing, join Ecru with sc in first sc; (working **behind** next ch-1, dc in skipped dc one row **below**, sc in next sc) twice, (working in **front** of next ch-1, dc in skipped dc one row **below**, sc in next sc) twice, ★ (working **behind** next ch-1, dc in skipped dc one row **below**, sc in next sc) 3 times, (working in **front** of next ch-1, dc in skipped dc one row **below**, sc in next sc) twice; repeat from ★ across to last 2 ch-1 sps, (working **behind** next ch-1, dc in skipped dc one row **below**, sc in next sc) twice; finish off: 193 sts.

Rows 20-154: Repeat Rows 4-19, 8 times; then repeat Rows 4-10 once **more**.

Row 155: With **right** side facing, join Ecru with sc in first sc; (working **behind** next ch-1, dc in skipped dc one row **below**, sc in next sc) twice, (working in **front** of next ch-1, dc in skipped dc one row **below**, sc in next sc) twice, ★ (working **behind** next ch-1, dc in skipped dc one row **below**, sc in next sc) 8 times, (working in **front** of next ch-1, dc in skipped dc one row **below**, sc in next sc) twice; repeat from ★ across to last 2 ch-1 sps, (working **behind** next ch-1, dc in skipped dc one row **below**, sc in next sc) twice; finish off: 193 sts.

TRIM
FIRST SIDE
Row 1: With **wrong** side facing, join Ecru with sc in first sc on Row 155; sc in next dc, ch 1, ★ skip next sc, sc in next dc, ch 1; repeat from ★ across to last 3 sts, skip next sc, sc in last 2 sts; finish off: 98 sc and 95 ch-1 sps.

Row 2: With **right** side facing, join Ecru with slip st in first sc; ch 1, (slip st in next ch-1 sp, ch 1) across to last 2 sc, skip next sc, slip st in last sc; finish off.

SECOND SIDE
Row 1: With **wrong** side facing and working in free loops of beginning ch *(Fig. 17b, page 141)*, join Ecru with sc in ch at base of first sc; sc in next ch, ch 1, ★ skip next ch, sc in next ch, ch 1; repeat from ★ across to last 3 chs, skip next ch, sc in last 2 chs; finish off: 98 sc and 95 ch-1 sps.

Row 2: With **right** side facing, join Ecru with slip st in first sc; ch 1, (slip st in next ch-1 sp, ch 1) across to last 2 sc, skip next sc, slip st in last sc; finish off.

Holding 4 strands of Ecru and 2 strands of Variegated yarn together, each 17" (43 cm) long, add additional fringe in every other row across short edges of Afghan *(Figs. 22b & d, page 142)*.

FOND MEMORIES

Inspire fond memories of days gone by with this exquisite comforter. Lacy shell panels link delicate floral motifs for a touch of old-fashioned elegance.

Finished Size: 47" x 70" (119.5 cm x 178 cm)

MATERIALS
Worsted Weight Yarn:
   42 ounces, 2,820 yards)
      (1,190 grams, 2,578.5 meters)
Crochet hook, size J (6 mm) **or** size needed
      for gauge
Yarn needle

GAUGE SWATCH: One Flower Motif = 7" (17.75 cm)
Work same as Flower Motif.

STITCH GUIDE

> **PICOT**
> Ch 2, sc in Front Loop Only of second ch from
> hook *(Fig. 15, page 140)*.

FLOWER PANEL (Make 3)
Panel is made by joining 10 Flower Motifs.
FIRST MOTIF
Ch 6; join with slip st to form a ring.
Rnd 1: Ch 2, 4 dc in ring, ch 1, slip st in ring, (ch 2, 4 dc in ring, ch 1, slip st in ring) 3 times: 4 Petals.
Rnd 2: Ch 2, working **behind** Petals, slip st in ring between second and third dc of first Petal, ch 2, slip st in ring between fourth dc and slip st of same Petal, ★ ch 2, slip st in ring between second and third dc of first Petal, ch 2, slip st in ring between fourth dc and slip st of same Petal; repeat from ★ 2 times **more**: 8 ch-2 sps.
Rnd 3: Ch 5, 4 tr in first ch-2 sp, ch 2, slip st in same sp, (ch 5, 4 tr in next ch-2 sp, ch 2, slip st in same sp) around: 8 Petals.
Rnd 4: Ch 2, working **behind** Petals, slip st in ch-2 sp between second and third tr of first Petal, ch 3, (slip st in ch-2 sp between second and third tr of next Petal, ch 3) 7 times; join with slip st to first slip st: 8 ch-3 sps.
Rnd 5: Slip st in first ch-3 sp, ch 1, sc in same sp, ch 5, (sc in next ch-3 sp, ch 5) around; join with slip st to first sc: 8 ch-5 sps.
Rnd 6: Ch 8, slip st in first ch-5 sp, ch 8, slip st in same sp, (ch 8, slip st in next sc, ch 8, slip st in next ch-5 sp, ch 8, slip st in same sp) around, ch 4, tr in first st to form last ch-8 sp: 24 ch-8 sps.

Rnds 7-10: Slip st in last ch-8 sp made, (ch 5, slip st in next ch-8 sp) around, ch 2, dc in first slip st to form last ch-8 sp.
Finish off.
SECOND MOTIF
Rnds 1-9: Work same as First Motif Rnds 1-9.
Rnd 10 (Joining rnd): Slip st in last ch-8 sp made, ch 2, holding **First Motif** with **right** side facing, slip st in and ch-8 sp on **First Motif**, ch 2, slip st in next ch-8 sp on **Second Motif**, (ch 2, slip st in next ch-8 sp on **First Motif**, ch 2, slip st in next ch-8 sp on **Second Motif**) 4 times; ch 5, (slip st in next ch-8 sp on **Second Motif**, ch 5) around; join with slip st to first slip st, finish off.

PATTERN STITCH

> **Row 1** (Right side): Work Shell in next sc, sc in center dc of next Shell, work Shell in next sc, sc in center dc of next Shell, work Shell in next sc.
> **Row 2:** Sc in center dc of next Shell, work Shell in next sc, sc in center dc of next Shell, work Shell in next sc, sc in center dc of next Shell.

LEFT SHELL PANEL
Note: Right edge of Left Shell Panel is joined to first Flower Panel, beginning at bottom Motif and working in 7 ch-8 sps along each Motif.
Ch 31; with **right** side of Flower Panel facing, skip 6 ch-8 sps from Second Motif, join yarn with slip st in next ch-8 sp on First Motif.
Row 1 (Right side): Ch 4, skip first 6 chs, [dc in next ch, ch 1, (dc, ch 1, dc) in same ch **(Shell made)]**, skip next 2 chs, sc in next ch, skip next 2 chs, work Shell in next ch, skip next 2 chs, sc in next ch, ch 5, skip next 4 chs, sc in next ch, skip next 2 chs, work Shell in next ch, skip next 2 chs, sc in next ch, skip next 2 chs, work Shell in next ch, dc in last ch.
Row 2: Ch 5, turn; work Pattern Stitch Row 2, ch 4, slip st in next ch-8 sp on Flower Panel.
Row 3: Ch 2, turn; work Pattern Stitch Row 1.
Row 4: Ch 5, turn; work Pattern Stitch Row 2, ch 2, slip st in next ch-8 sp on Flower Panel.
Row 5: Turn; work Pattern Stitch Row 1.
Rows 6-9: Repeat Rows 4 and 5 twice.
Row 10: Ch 5, turn; work Pattern Stitch Row 2, ch 4, slip st in next ch-8 sp on Flower Panel.
Row 11: Ch 3, turn; work Pattern Stitch Row 1.

Row 12: Ch 5, turn; work Pattern Stitch Row 2, ch 5, slip st in first 3 chs on Flower Panel.

Row 13: Ch 5, turn; sc in first ch-5 sp, work Pattern Stitch Row 1.

Row 14: Ch 5, turn; work Pattern Stitch Row 2, ch 4, sc in last ch-5 sp, ch 2, slip st in last 3 chs of next ch-8 sp on Flower Panel.

Row 15: Ch 3, turn; sc in first ch-4 sp, work Pattern Stitch Row 1.

Row 16: Ch 5, turn; work Pattern Stitch Row 2, ch 4, slip st in next ch-8 sp on Flower Panel.

Rows 17-137: Repeat Rows 3-16, 8 times; then repeat Rows 3-11 once **more**.

Row 138: Ch 5, turn; work Pattern Stitch Row 2, ch 5, slip st in next ch-8 sp on Flower Panel.

Row 139: Ch 3, turn; work Pattern Stitch Row 1.

Row 140: Ch 5, turn; work Pattern Stitch Row 2, ch 6, slip st in last slip st; finish off.

SHELL PANEL

Note: Each Shell Panel is worked between two Flower Panels, beginning at bottom Motif and working in 7 ch-8 sps along each Motif.

With **right** side of both Panels facing, skip next 6 ch-8 sps from Second Motif on first Flower Panel, join yarn with slip st in next ch-8 sp, ch 36, slip st in seventh ch-8 sp on second Flower Panel.

Row 1 (Right side): Ch 4, skip first 6 chs, work Shell in next ch, skip next 2 chs, sc in next ch, skip next 2 chs, work Shell in next ch, skip next 2 chs, ch 5, skip next 4 chs, sc in next ch, skip next 2 chs, work Shell in next ch, skip next 2 chs, sc in next ch, skip next 2 chs, work Shell in next ch, ch 4, skip last 67 chs, slip st in last slip st.

Row 2: Ch 6, turn; work Pattern Stitch Row 2, ch 4, slip st in next ch-8 sp on second Flower Panel.

Row 3: Ch 2, turn; work Pattern Stitch Row 1, ch 2, slip st in next ch-8 sp on first Flower Panel.

Row 4: Ch 4, turn; work Pattern Stitch Row 2, ch 2, slip st in next ch-8 sp on second Flower Panel.

Row 5: Turn; work Pattern Stitch Row 1, slip st in next ch-8 sp on first Flower Panel.

Rows 6-9: Repeat Rows 4 and 5 twice.

Row 10: Ch 4, turn; work Pattern Stitch Row 2, ch 4, slip st in next ch-8 sp on second Flower Panel.

Row 11: Ch 3, turn; work Pattern Stitch Row 1, ch 2, slip st in next ch-8 sp on first Flower Panel.

Row 12: Ch 5, turn; work Pattern Stitch Row 2, ch 5, slip st in first 3 chs of next ch-8 sp on second Flower Panel.

Row 13: Ch 5, turn; sc in first ch-5 sp, work Pattern Stitch Row 1, ch 5, slip st in first 3 chs of next ch-8 sp on first Flower Panel.

Row 14: Ch 5, turn; sc in first ch-5 sp, ch 4, work Pattern Stitch Row 2, ch 4, sc in last ch-5 sp, ch 2, slip st in last 3 chs of next ch-8 sp on second Flower Panel.

Row 15: Ch 3, turn; sc in first ch-4 sp, work Pattern Stitch Row 1, sc in next ch-4 sp, ch 4, sc in next ch-5 sp, ch 2, slip st in last 3 chs of next ch-8 sp on first Flower Panel.

Row 16: Ch 3, turn; sc in first ch-4 sp, ch 4, work Pattern Stitch Row 2, ch 4, slip st in next ch-8 sp on second Flower Panel.

Rows 17-137: Repeat Rows 3-16, 8 times; then repeat Rows 3-11 once **more**.

Row 138: Ch 5, turn; work Pattern Stitch Row 2, ch 5, slip st in next ch-8 sp on second Flower Panel.

Row 139: Ch 3, turn; work Pattern Stitch Row 1, ch 4, slip st in next ch-8 sp on first Flower Panel.

Row 140: Ch 6, turn; work Pattern Stitch Row 2, ch 6, slip st in last slip st; finish off.

RIGHT SHELL PANEL

Note: Left edge of Right Shell Panel is joined to third Flower Panel, beginning at bottom Motif and working in 7 ch-8 sps along each Motif.

With **right** side of Flower Panel facing, skip 6 ch-8 sps from Second Motif, join yarn with slip st in next ch-8 sp on First Motif, ch 35.

Row 1 (Right side): Work Shell in sixth ch from hook, skip next 2 chs, sc in next ch, skip next 2 chs, work Shell in next ch, skip next 2 chs, sc in next ch, ch 5, skip next 4 chs, sc in next ch, skip next 2 chs, work Shell in next ch, skip next 2 chs, sc in next ch, skip next 2 chs, work Shell in next ch, ch 4, skip last 6 chs, slip st in last slip st.

Row 2: Ch 6, turn; work Pattern Stitch Row 2.

Row 3: Ch 5, turn; work Pattern Row 1, ch 2, slip st in next ch-8 sp on Flower Panel.

Row 4: Ch 4, turn; work Pattern Stitch Row 2.

Row 5: Ch 5, turn; work Pattern Stitch Row 1, slip st in next ch-8 sp on Flower Panel.

Rows 6-9: Repeat Rows 4 and 5 twice.

Row 10: Ch 4, turn; work Pattern Stitch Row 2.

Row 11: Ch 5, turn; work Pattern Stitch Row 1, ch 2, slip st in next ch-8 sp on Flower Panel.

Row 12: Ch 4, turn; work Pattern Stitch Row 2.

Row 13: Ch 5, turn; work Pattern Stitch Row 1, ch 5, slip st in first 3 chs of next ch-8 sp on Flower Panel.

Row 14: Ch 5, turn; sc in first ch-5 sp, ch 4, work Pattern Stitch Row 2.

Row 15: Ch 5, turn; work Pattern Stitch Row 1, sc in next ch-4 sp, ch 4, sc in next ch-5 sp, ch 2, slip st in last 3 chs of next ch-8 sp on Flower Panel.

Row 16: Ch 3, turn; sc in first ch-4 sp, ch 4, work Pattern Stitch Row 2.

Rows 17-138: Repeat Rows 3-16, 8 times; then repeat Rows 3-12 once **more**.

Row 139: Ch 5, turn; work Pattern Stitch Row 1, ch 4, slip st in next ch-8 sp on Flower Panel.
Row 140: Ch 6, turn; work Pattern Stitch Row 2, slip st in same st; do **not** finish off.

EDGING
TOP

Turn; sc in first st, ch 4, ★ † slip st in center dc of next Shell, ch 5, slip st in next ch-5 sp, work Shell in next slip st, slip st in next ch -5 sp, ch 5, slip st in center of next Shell, ch 5 †, slip st in next ch-6 sp, ch 5, skip next slip st, (slip st in next slip st, skip next ch, ch 2, skip next ch, slip st in next ch, skip next ch) 5 times, slip st in next slip st, ch 5, slip st in next sp, ch 5; repeat from ★ 2 times **more**; then repeat from † to † once.

LEFT SIDE

Slip st in next ch-5 sp, work Picot, slip st in same ch-5 sp, (work Picot, slip st in next ch-5 sp) across, (slip st, ch 2, sc) in end of last row.

BOTTOM

Working across beginning ch, ★ † slip st in next Shell, work Shell in next sc, slip st in next Shell, ch 5, slip st in next ch-4 sp, ch 5, slip st in next Shell, work Shell in next sc, slip st in next Shell, ch 5 †, slip st in next ch-6 sp, ch 5, skip next slip st, (slip st in next slip st, skip next ch, slip st in next ch, ch 2, skip next ch, slip st in next ch, skip next ch) 5 times, slip st in next slip st, ch 5, slip st in next ch-6 sp, ch 5; repeat from ★ 2 times **more**; then repeat from † to † once.

RIGHT SIDE

(Slip st in next ch-5 sp, work Picot) across; join with slip st to first sc; finish off.

17

TOUCHED BY NATURE

Cascading flowers form a brilliant border for this graceful coverlet. The purple posies are crocheted as-you-go for a distinct style that's sure to invite compliments.

Finished Size: 52" x 75" (132 cm x 190.5 cm)

MATERIALS

Worsted Weight Yarn:
  Purple - 50 ounces, 2,825 yards
    (1,420 grams, 2,583 meters)
  Off-White - 10 ounces, 565 yards
    (280 grams, 516.5 meters)
Crochet hook, size J (6 mm) **or** size needed
  for gauge
Spilt ring markers (optional)

GAUGE: 9 dc and 5 rows = 3" (7.5 cm)
        Each Flower Panel = $13^5/8$" (34.5 cm) wide
        Each Grass Panel = $5^5/8$" (14.25 cm) wide

Gauge Swatch: $5^5/8$"w x 3"h (14.25 cm x 7.5 cm)
Work same as Grass Panel, page 23, through Row 5.

Note: As a convenience to you, we suggested using split ring markers to mark Leaf and stitch placement. They can be easily attached to the stitch indicated. A 2" (5 cm) scrap piece of yarn can also be used.

STITCH GUIDE

Note: To work a stitch with several yarn overs, YO **tightly** as many times as instructed. When working the loops off, be careful not to allow too much slack in the loops on the hook. Practice this a few times until you have an uniform stitch without a large loop at the end.

FRONT POST TREBLE CROCHET
  (abbreviated FPtr)
YO twice, insert hook from **front** to **back** around post of st indicated *(Fig. 9, page 139)*, YO and pull up a loop (4 loops on hook), (YO and draw through 2 loops on hook) 3 times.

BACK POST TREBLE CROCHET
  (abbreviated BPtr)
YO twice, insert hook from **back** to **front** around post of st indicated *(Fig. 9, page 139)*, YO and pull up a loop (4 loops on hook), (YO and draw through 2 loops on hook) 3 times.

FRONT POST DOUBLE TREBLE CROCHET
  (abbreviated FPdtr)
YO 3 times, insert hook from **front** to **back** around post of st indicated *(Fig. 9, page 139)*, YO and pull up a loop (5 loops on hook), (YO and draw through 2 loops on hook) 4 times.

BACK POST DOUBLE TREBLE CROCHET
  (abbreviated BPdtr)
YO 3 times, insert hook from **back** to **front** around post of st indicated *(Fig. 9, page 139)*, YO and pull up a loop (5 loops on hook), (YO and draw through 2 loops on hook) 4 times.

FIRST LEAF
YO 6 times, working **behind** previous rows, insert hook in marked st indicated, YO and pull up a loop, remove marker, (YO and draw through 2 loops on hook) 6 times (2 loops on hook), YO 5 times, insert hook in same st, YO and pull up a loop, (YO and draw through 2 loops on hook) 5 times (3 loops on hook), YO 5 times, insert hook in same st, YO and pull up a loop, (YO and draw through 2 loops on hook) 8 times.

SECOND LEAF
Note: On **right** side rows, work in **front** of previous rows, inserting hook from **back** to **front** in stitch indicated and on **wrong** side rows, work **behind** previous rows, inserting hook from **front** to **back** in stitch indicated.
★ YO 6 times, insert hook in marked st indicated, YO and pull up a loop, (YO and draw through 2 loops on hook) 6 times; repeat from ★ 2 times **more**, YO and draw through all 4 loops on hook, remove marker.

BOTTOM PETAL
YO 6 times, insert hook from **back** to **front** in dc indicated, YO and pull up a loop, (YO and draw through 2 loops on hook) 6 times.

Continued on page 20.

HALF FLOWER

Working in **front** of 5 dc just made, work Bottom Petal in skipped dc **below** last ch-1 made (2 loops on hook), work Bottom Petal in next skipped dc 2 rows **below** (3 loops on hook), (work Bottom Petal in next skipped dc 3 rows **below**) twice (5 loops on hook), work Bottom Petal in next skipped dc 2 rows **below** (6 loops on hook), work Bottom Petal in next marked dc on previous row, remove marker, YO and draw through all 7 loops on hook, ch 1 **loosely** to close.

TOP PETAL

Note: On **right** side rows, work in **front** of previous rows, inserting hook from **back** to **front** in stitch indicated and on **wrong** side rows, work **behind** previous rows, inserting hook from **front** to **back** in stitch indicated. YO 6 times, insert hook in closing ch-1 of Half Flower, YO and pull up a loop, (YO and draw through 2 loops on hook) 7 times.

FLOWER PANEL (Make 3)

With Purple, ch 43 **loosely**.

Row 1 (Right side): Dc in back ridge of fourth ch from hook *(Fig. 2b, page 137)* and each ch across **(3 skipped chs count as first dc, now and throughout)**: 41 dc.

Row 2: Ch 3 **(counts as first dc, now and throughout)**, turn; dc in next dc and in each dc across.

Row 3: Ch 3, turn; dc in next 17 dc, place marker in last dc made for Leaf placement *(see Markers, page 140)*, work FPtr around next dc *(Fig. 9, page 139)*, skip dc just worked around, dc in last 22 dc: 40 dc and one FPtr.

Row 4: Ch 3, turn; dc in next 21 dc, work BPtr around next FPtr, ch 1, skip FPtr just worked around and next dc, dc in last 17 dc; do **not** finish off: 39 dc, one BPtr, and one ch-1 sp.

Row 5: Ch 3, turn; dc in next 16 dc, skip next ch-1 sp, work 2 FPtr around next BPtr working second FPtr **above** first FPtr, skip BPtr just worked around, dc in last 22 dc: 39 dc and 2 FPtr.

Row 6: Ch 3, turn; dc in next 21 dc, place marker in last dc made for Leaf placement, work BPtr around next FPtr, skip FPtr just worked around, dc in next FPtr, work BPtr around FPtr just worked into, skip next dc, dc in next 4 dc, work First Leaf in marked dc 3 rows **below**, skip next dc from last dc made, dc in last 11 dc: 38 dc, 2 BPtr, and one Leaf.

Row 7: Ch 3, turn; dc in next 14 sts, skip next dc, work FPtr around next BPtr, dc in same BPtr just worked around and in next dc, work FPtr around next BPtr, ch 1, skip BPtr just worked around and next dc, dc in last 21 dc: 38 dc, 2 FPtr, and one ch-1 sp.

Row 8: Ch 3, turn; dc in next 20 dc and in next ch-1 sp, work BPtr around next FPtr, place marker in BPtr just made for Leaf placement, skip FPtr just worked around, dc in next 3 sts, work BPtr around FPtr just worked into, skip next dc, dc in next dc, place marker in dc just made for Leaf placement, dc in last 13 dc: 39 dc and 2 BPtr.

Row 9: Ch 3, turn; dc in next 12 dc, skip next dc, work FPtr around next BPtr, dc in BPtr just worked around and in next 3 dc, ch 1, work FPtr around next BPtr, skip BPtr just worked around and next dc, dc in next 5 dc, work Second Leaf in marked dc 3 rows **below**, skip next dc from last dc made, dc in last 15 dc: 37 dc, 2 FPtr, one ch-1 sp, and one Leaf.

Row 10: Ch 3, turn; dc in next 19 sts, skip next dc, work BPtr around next FPtr, dc in FPtr just worked around, dc in next ch-1 sp and in next 5 sts, work BPtr around FPtr just worked into, skip next dc, dc in next 4 dc, work First Leaf in marked dc 2 rows **below**, skip next dc from last dc made, dc in last 7 dc: 38 dc, 2 BPtr, and one Leaf.

Row 11: Ch 3, turn; dc in next 10 sts, skip next dc, work FPtr around next BPtr, dc in BPtr just worked around and in next 8 sts, work FPtr around BPtr just worked into, skip next dc, dc in next dc, place marker in last dc made for Leaf placement, dc in last 18 dc: 39 dc and 2 FPtr.

Row 12: Ch 3, turn; dc in next 17 sts, skip next dc, work BPtr around next FPtr, dc in FPtr just worked around and in next 4 dc, work First Leaf in marked BPtr 4 rows **below**, skip next dc from last dc made, dc in next 4 dc, work BPtr around next FPtr, skip FPtr just worked around, dc in last 11 dc: 38 dc, 2 BPtr, and one Leaf.

Row 13: Ch 3, turn; dc in next 8 dc, ch 1, skip next dc, dc in next dc, work FPtr around next BPtr, skip BPtr just worked around, dc in next dc, ch 1, skip next dc, dc in next 8 sts, work 2 FPtr around next BPtr working second FPtr **above** first FPtr, skip BPtr just worked around and next dc, dc in last 17 dc: 36 dc, 3 FPtr, and 2 ch-1 sps.

Row 14: Ch 3, turn; dc in next 11 dc, work Second Leaf in marked dc 3 rows **below**, skip next dc from last dc made, dc in next 3 dc, skip next dc, work BPtr around next FPtr, dc in FPtr just worked around, work BPtr around next FPtr, skip FPtr just worked around, dc in next 5 dc, place marker in last dc made for Petal placement, dc in next dc, ch 1, skip next dc, dc in next dc, dc in next ch-1 sp and in next dc, work BPtr around next FPtr, skip FPtr just worked around, dc in next dc, dc in next ch-1 sp and in next dc, ch 1, skip next dc, dc in last 7 dc: 35 dc, 3 BPtr, one Leaf, and 2 ch-1 sps.

Row 15: Ch 3, turn; dc in next 4 dc, ch 1, skip next dc, dc in next dc, dc in next ch-1 sp and in next 3 dc, work Half Flower, working **behind** Half Flower, skip next BPtr from last dc made, dc in next 3 dc, dc in next ch-1 sp and in next dc, ch 1, dc in next 4 dc, work FPtr around next BPtr, skip BPtr just worked around, dc in next dc and in next BPtr, work FPtr around BPtr just worked into, skip next dc, dc in next dc, place marker in last dc made for Leaf placement, dc in last 14 sts: 36 dc, 2 FPtr, one Half Flower, and 2 ch-1 sps.

Row 16: Ch 3, turn; dc in next 13 dc, skip next dc, work BPtr around next FPtr, dc in FPtr just worked around and in next 2 dc, work BPtr around next FPtr, place marker in BPtr just made for Leaf placement, skip FPtr just worked around, dc in next 4 dc, work Top Petal, skip next ch-1 sp from last dc made, dc in next 5 dc, ch 1, skip Half Flower, dc in next 5 dc, work Top Petal, skip next ch-1 sp from last dc made, dc in last 5 dc: 36 dc, 2 BPtr, 2 Top Petals, and one ch-1 sp.

Row 17: Ch 3, turn; dc in next 4 dc, work Top Petal, skip next st from last dc made, dc in next 5 dc, dc in next ch-1 sp and in next 5 dc, work Top Petal, skip next st from last dc made, dc in next 3 dc, skip next dc, work FPtr around next BPtr, ch 1, skip BPtr just worked around, dc in next 4 sts, work FPtr around BPtr just worked into, skip next dc, dc in last 13 dc: 36 dc, 2 FPtr, 2 Top Petals, and one ch-1 sp.

Row 18: Ch 3, turn; dc in next 6 dc, work Second Leaf in marked dc 3 rows **below**, skip next dc from last dc made, dc in next 4 dc, skip next dc, work BPtr around next FPtr, dc in FPtr just worked around, dc in next 4 dc and in next ch-1 sp, dc in next FPtr, work BPtr around FPtr just worked into, skip next dc, dc in next 3 sts, work Top Petal, skip next dc from last dc made, dc in next 9 dc, work Top Petal, skip next dc from last dc made, dc in last 6 sts: 36 dc, 2 BPtr, 2 Top Petals, and one Leaf.

Row 19: Ch 3, turn; dc in next 7 sts, work Top Petal, skip next dc from last dc made, dc in next 2 dc, work Top Petal, skip next dc from last dc made, dc in next dc, work Top Petal, skip next dc from last dc made, dc in next 5 sts, place marker in last dc made for Leaf placement, skip next dc, work FPtr around next BPtr, dc in BPtr just worked around and in next 8 sts, work FPtr around BPtr just worked into, skip next dc, dc in last 11 sts: 36 dc, 2 FPtr, and 3 Top Petals.

Row 20: Ch 3, turn; dc in next 10 dc, work BPtr around next FPtr, skip FPtr just worked around, dc in next 4 dc, work Second Leaf in marked BPtr 4 rows **below**, skip next dc from last dc made, dc in next 5 sts, work BPtr around FPtr just worked into, skip next dc, dc in last 18 sts: 38 dc, 2 BPtr, and one Leaf.

Row 21: Ch 3, turn; dc in next 16 dc, skip next dc, work 2 FPtr around next BPtr working second FPtr **below** first FPtr, skip BPtr just worked around, dc in next 8 sts, ch 1, skip next dc, dc in next dc, work FPtr around next BPtr, skip BPtr just worked around, dc in next dc, ch 1, skip next dc, dc in last 9 dc: 36 dc, 3 FPtr, and 2 ch-1 sps.

Row 22: Ch 3, turn; dc in next 5 dc, place marker in last dc made for Petal placement, dc in next dc, ch 1, skip next dc, dc in next dc, dc in next ch-1 sp and in next dc, work BPtr around next FPtr, skip FPtr just worked around, dc in next dc, dc in next ch-1 sp and in next dc, ch 1, skip next dc, dc in next 6 dc, work BPtr around next FPtr, skip FPtr just worked around, dc in next FPtr, work BPtr around FPtr just worked into, skip next dc, dc in next 4 dc, work First Leaf in marked dc 3 rows **below**, skip next dc from last dc made, dc in last 11 dc: 35 dc, 3 BPtr, one Leaf, and 2 ch-1 sps.

Row 23: Ch 3, turn; dc in next 14 sts, skip next dc, work FPtr around next BPtr, dc in BPtr just worked around and in next dc, work FPtr around next BPtr, skip BPtr just worked around, dc in next 4 dc, ch 1, skip next dc, dc in next dc, dc in next ch-1 sp and in next 3 dc, work Half Flower, working **behind** Half Flower, skip next BPtr from last dc made, dc in next 3 dc, dc in next ch-1 sp and in next dc, ch 1, dc in last 5 dc: 36 dc, 2 FPtr, one Half Flower, and 2 ch-1 sps.

Continued on page 22.

Row 24: Ch 3, turn; dc in next 4 dc, work Top Petal, skip next ch-1 sp from last dc made, dc in next 5 dc, ch 1, skip next Half Flower, dc in next 5 dc, work Top Petal, skip next ch-1 sp from last dc made, dc in next 4 dc, work BPtr around next FPtr, place marker in BPtr just made for Leaf placement, skip FPtr just worked around, dc in next 3 sts, work BPtr around FPtr just worked into, skip next dc, dc in next dc, place marker in last dc made for Leaf placement, dc in last 13 dc: 36 dc, 2 BPtr, 2 Top Petals, and one ch-1 sp.

Row 25: Ch 3, turn; dc in next 12 dc, skip next dc, work FPtr around next BPtr, dc in BPtr just worked around and in next 3 dc, ch 1, work FPtr around next BPtr, skip BPtr just worked around and next dc, dc in next 3 dc, work Top Petal, skip next st from last dc made, dc in next 5 dc, dc in next ch-1 sp and in next 5 dc, work Top Petal, skip next st from last dc made, dc in last 5 dc: 36 dc, 2 FPtr, 2 Top Petals, and one ch-1 sp.

Row 26: Ch 3, turn; dc in next 5 sts, work Top Petal, skip next dc from last dc made, dc in next 9 dc, work Top Petal, skip next dc from last dc made, dc in next 3 sts, skip next dc, work BPtr around next FPtr, dc in FPtr just worked around and in next ch-1 sp, dc in next 5 sts, work BPtr around FPtr just worked into, skip next dc, dc in next 4 dc, work First Leaf in marked dc 2 rows **below**, skip next dc from last dc made, dc in last 7 dc: 36 dc, 2 BPtr, 2 Top Petals, and one Leaf.

Row 27: Ch 3, turn; dc in next 10 sts, skip next dc, work FPtr around next BPtr, dc in BPtr just worked around and in next 8 sts, work FPtr around BPtr just worked into, skip next dc, dc in next dc, place marker in dc just made for Leaf placement, dc in next 3 sts, work Top Petal, skip next dc from last dc made, dc in next 2 dc, work Top Petal, skip next dc from last dc made, dc in next dc, work Top Petal, skip next dc from last dc made, dc in last 9 sts: 36 dc, 2 FPtr, and 3 Top Petals.

Rows 28-112: Repeat Rows 12-27, 5 times; then repeat Rows 12-16 once **more**; do **not** finish off: 36 dc, 2 BPtr, 2 Top Petals, and one ch-1 sp.

Row 113: Ch 3, turn; dc in next 4 dc, work Top Petal, skip next st from last dc made, dc in next 5 dc, dc in next ch-1 sp and in next 5 dc, work Top Petal, skip next st from last dc made, dc in next 4 dc, ch 1, skip next BPtr, dc in next 4 sts, work FPtr around BPtr just worked into, skip next dc, dc in last 13 dc: 37 dc, one FPtr, 2 Top Petals, and one ch-1 sp.

Row 114: Ch 3, turn; dc in next 6 dc, work Second Leaf in marked dc 3 rows **below**, skip next dc from last dc made, dc in next 4 dc, skip next dc, work BPtr around next FPtr, dc in FPtr just worked around, dc in next 4 dc and in next ch-1 sp, dc in next 5 sts, work Top Petal, skip next dc from last dc made, dc in next 9 dc, work Top Petal, skip next dc from last dc made, dc in last 6 sts: 37 dc, one BPtr, 2 Top Petals, and one Leaf.

Row 115: Ch 3, turn; dc in next 7 sts, work Top Petal, skip next dc from last dc made, dc in next 2 dc, work Top Petal, skip next dc from last dc made, dc in next dc, work Top Petal, skip next dc from last dc made, dc in next 15 sts, work FPtr around BPtr just worked into, skip next dc, dc in last 11 sts: 37 dc, one FPtr, and 3 Top Petals.

Row 116: Ch 3, turn; dc in next 10 dc, work BPtr around next FPtr, skip FPtr just worked around, dc in next 4 dc, work Second Leaf in marked BPtr 4 rows **below**, skip next dc from last dc made, dc in last 24 sts: 39 dc, one BPtr, and one Leaf.

Row 117: Ch 3, turn; dc in next 26 sts, ch 1, skip next dc, dc in next dc, work FPtr around next BPtr, skip BPtr just worked around, dc in next dc, ch 1, skip next dc, dc in last 9 dc: 38 dc, one FPtr, and 2 ch-1 sps.

Row 118: Ch 3, turn; dc in next 5 dc, place marker in last dc made for Petal placement, dc in next dc, ch 1, skip next dc, dc in next dc, dc in next ch-1 sp and in next dc, work BPtr around next FPtr, skip FPtr just worked around, dc in next dc, dc in next ch-1 sp and in next dc, ch 1, skip next dc, dc in last 25 dc: 38 dc, one BPtr, and 2 ch-1 sps.

Row 119: Ch 3, turn; dc in next 22 dc, ch 1, skip next dc, dc in next dc, dc in next ch-1 sp and in next 3 dc, work Half Flower, working **behind** Half Flower, skip next BPtr from last dc made, dc in next 3 dc, dc in next ch-1 sp and in next dc, ch 1, dc in last 5 dc: 38 dc, one Half Flower, and 2 ch-1 sps.

Row 120: Ch 3, turn; dc in next 4 dc, work Top Petal, skip next ch-1 sp from last dc made, dc in next 5 dc, ch 1, skip next Half Flower, dc in next 5 dc, work Top Petal, skip next ch-1 sp from last dc made, dc in last 23 dc: 38 dc, 2 Top Petals, and one ch-1 sp.

Row 121: Ch 3, turn; dc in next 22 dc, work Top Petal, skip next st from last dc made, dc in next 5 dc, dc in next ch-1 sp and in next 5 dc, work Top Petal, skip next st from last dc made, dc in last 5 dc: 39 dc and 2 Top Petals.

Row 122: Ch 3, turn; dc in next 5 sts, work Top Petal, skip next dc from last dc made, dc in next 9 dc, work Top Petal, skip next dc from last dc made, dc in last 24 sts.

Row 123: Ch 3, turn; dc in next 25 sts, work Top Petal, skip next dc from last dc made, dc in next 2 dc, work Top Petal, skip next dc made, dc in next dc, work Top Petal, skip next dc from last dc made, dc in last 9 sts: 38 dc and 3 Petals.
Rows 124 and 125: Ch 3, turn; dc in next dc and in each st across.
Finish off.

GRASS PANEL (Make 2)

With Off-White, ch 19 **loosely**.
Row 1 (Right side): Dc in back ridge of fourth ch from hook and each ch across: 17 dc.
Rows 2 and 3: Ch 3, turn; dc in next dc and in each dc across.
Always skip stitch in **front** of a Back Post stitch and **behind** a Front Post stitch throughout Grass Panel.
Row 4: Ch 3, turn; dc in next 7 dc, work BPtr around next dc, dc in last 8 dc: 16 dc and one BPtr.
Row 5: Ch 3, turn; dc in next 8 sts, place marker around last dc made, dc in last 8 dc.
Row 6: Ch 3, turn; dc in next 8 dc, work BPdtr around next BPtr 2 rows **below**, dc in last 7 dc: 16 dc and one BPdtr.
Row 7: Ch 3, turn; dc in next 7 sts, work FPtr around next dc, work FPdtr around marked dc 2 rows **below**, remove marker, dc in last 7 dc: 15 dc, one FPtr, and one FPdtr.
Row 8: Ch 3, turn; dc in next 7 sts, work BPtr around next FPtr, dc in next dc, work BPdtr around next BPdtr 2 rows **below**, dc in last 6 dc: 15 dc, one BPtr, and one BPdtr.
Row 9: Ch 3, turn; dc in next 8 sts, place marker around last dc made, dc in next dc, work FPdtr around next FPdtr 2 rows **below**, dc in last 6 dc: 16 dc and one FPdtr.
Row 10: Ch 3, turn; dc in next 8 sts, work BPdtr around next BPtr 2 rows **below**, dc in next dc, work BPdtr around next BPdtr 2 rows **below**, dc in last 5 dc: 15 dc and 2 BPdtr.
Row 11: Ch 3, turn; dc in next 7 sts, work FPtr around next dc, work FPdtr around marked dc 2 rows **below**, remove marker, dc in next dc, work FPdtr around next FPdtr 2 rows **below**, dc in last 5 dc: 14 dc, 2 FPdtr, and one FPtr.
Row 12: Ch 3, turn; dc in next 7 sts, work BPtr around next FPtr, dc in next dc, work BPdtr around next BPdtr 2 rows **below**, dc in next 2 dc, work BPdtr around next BPdtr 2 rows **below**, dc in last 3 dc: 14 dc, 2 BPdtr, and one BPtr.
Row 13: Ch 3, turn; dc in next 8 sts, place marker around last dc made, dc in next dc, work FPdtr around next FPdtr 2 rows **below**, dc in next 2 dc, work FPdtr around next FPdtr 2 rows **below**, dc in last 3 dc: 15 dc and 2 FPdtr.

Rows 14-114: Repeat Rows 10-13, 25 times; then repeat Row 10 once **more**: 15 dc and 2 BPdtr.
Row 115: Ch 3, turn; dc in next 8 sts, work FPdtr around marked dc 2 rows **below**, remove marker, dc in next dc, work FPdtr around next FPdtr 2 rows **below**, dc in last 5 dc: 15 dc and 2 FPdtr.
Row 116: Ch 3, turn; dc in next 9 sts, work BPdtr around next BPdtr 2 rows **below**, dc in next 2 dc, work BPdtr around next BPdtr 2 rows **below**, dc in last 3 dc: 15 dc and 2 BPdtr.
Row 117: Ch 3, turn; dc in next 9 sts, work FPdtr around next FPdtr 2 rows **below**, dc in next 2 dc, work FPdtr around next FPdtr 2 rows **below**, dc in last 3 dc: 15 dc and 2 FPdtr.
Row 118: Ch 3, turn; dc in next 10 sts, work BPdtr around next BPdtr 2 rows **below**, dc in last 5 dc: 16 dc and one BPdtr.
Row 119: Ch 3, turn; dc in next 10 sts, work FPdtr around next FPdtr 2 rows **below**, dc in last 5 dc: 16 dc and one FPdtr.
Row 120: Ch 3, turn; dc in next 12 sts, work BPdtr around next BPdtr 2 rows **below**, dc in last 3 dc: 16 dc and one BPdtr.
Row 121: Ch 3, turn; dc in next 12 sts, work FPdtr around next FPdtr 2 rows **below**, dc in last 3 dc: 16 dc and one FPdtr.
Rows 122-125: Ch 3, turn; dc in next dc and in each st across.
Finish off.

ASSEMBLY

Alternating Panels and beginning and ending with a Flower Panel, join Panels as follows:
With **wrong** sides and bottom edges together, working in end of rows through **both** thicknesses, join Purple with slip st in Row 1; ch 1, working from **left** to **right**, work reverse sc in same row (*Figs. 14a-d, page 140*), work 2 reverse sc in next row, work (reverse sc in next row, 2 reverse sc in next row) across to last row, (work reverse sc, slip st) in last row; finish off.

EDGING

With **right** side facing, join Purple with slip st in any corner st; ch 1, working from **left** to **right**, work reverse sc evenly around; join with slip st to first st, finish off.

23

TRANQUIL RIPPLE

Snuggle up in a sea of green with our tranquil ripple afghan. Worked in a combination of cluster stitches, this contrasting wrap is as calming as a lakeside picnic in early spring.

Finished Size: 52" x 65" (132 cm x 165 cm)

MATERIALS
Worsted Weight Yarn:
  Green - (64 ounces, 3,615 yards)
    (1,820 grams, 3305.5 meters)
  Dk Green - (16 ounces, 905 yards)
    (450 grams, 827.5 meters)
  Crochet hook, size I (5.5 mm) **or** size needed
    for gauge

GAUGE: In pattern,
    one repeat (point to point) = 6¹/₂" (16.5 cm);
    8 rows = 5" (12.75 cm)

Gauge Swatch: 13"w x 6¹/₂"h (33 cm x 16.5 cm)
Ch 63 **loosely**.
Work same as Afghan for 6 rows.
Finish off.

STITCH GUIDE

CLUSTER (uses one st)
★ YO, insert hook in st indicated, YO and pull up a loop, YO and draw through 2 loops on hook; repeat from ★ once **more**, YO and draw through all 3 loops on hook (*Figs. 10a & b, page 139*).

TR CLUSTER (uses one st)
★ YO twice, insert hook in st indicated, YO and pull up a loop, (YO and draw through 2 loops on hook) twice; repeat from ★ once **more**, YO and draw through all 3 loops on hook (2 legs made) (*Figs. 10a & b, page 139*).

SPLIT CLUSTER
First Leg: ★ YO, insert hook in st indicated, YO and pull up a loop, YO and draw through 2 loops on hook; repeat from ★ once **more** (3 loops remaining on hook).
Second Leg: ★ YO, insert hook in st indicated, YO and pull up a loop, YO and draw through 2 loops on hook; repeat from ★ once **more**, YO and draw through all 5 loops on hook.

ENDING CLUSTER (uses one st)
★ YO, insert hook in st indicated, YO and pull up a loop, YO and draw through 2 loops on hook; repeat from ★ once **more**, YO and draw through all 7 loops on hook (*Figs. 10a & b, page 139*).

SPLIT FRONT POST DOUBLE CROCHET
  (*abbreviated Split FPdc*)
First Leg: YO, insert hook from **front** to **back** around post of second leg of previous Cluster (*Fig. 9, page 139*), YO and pull up a loop, YO and draw through 2 loops on hook (2 loops remaining on hook).
Second Leg: YO, insert hook from **front** to **back** around post of first leg of next Cluster, YO and pull up a loop, YO and draw through 2 loops on hook, YO and draw through all 3 loops on hook.

COLOR SEQUENCE
(1 Row Green, 1 row Dk Green) twice (*Fig. 19, page 141*), ★ 5 rows Green, 1 row Dk Green, 1 row Green, 1 row Dk Green; repeat from ★ throughout, 1 row Green.

AFGHAN
With Green, ch 243 **loosely**.
Row 1 (Wrong side): Work (Cluster, ch 2, First Leg of Split Cluster) in sixth ch from hook, ★ † [skip next 2 chs, work (Second Leg of Split Cluster, ch 2, First Leg of Split Cluster) in next ch] 3 times, skip next 2 chs, work (Second Leg of Split Cluster, ch 2, tr Cluster, ch 2, First Leg of Split Cluster) in next ch, [skip next 2 chs, work (Second Leg of Split Cluster, ch 2, First Leg of Split Cluster) in next ch] 4 times, skip next 2 chs †, work First Leg of Split Cluster in next ch (5 loops on hook), skip next 2 chs, work (Ending Cluster, ch 2, First Leg of Split Cluster) in next ch; repeat from ★ 6 times **more**, then repeat from † to † once, YO, insert hook in last ch, YO and pull up a loop, YO and draw through 2 loops on hook, drop Green, with Dk Green, YO and draw through all 4 loops on hook: 80 ch-2 sps.
Note: Loop a short piece of yarn around **back** of any stitch to mark **right** side.
Following Color Sequence, change colors in same manner throughout.

Continued on page 26.

Row 2: Ch 1, turn; pull up a loop in same st, work Second Leg of Split FPdc, sc in ch-2 sp **behind** st just made, ★ † (sc in next ch-2 sp, work Split FPdc, sc in same sp as last sc made) 4 times, sc in same tr Cluster and in next ch-2 sp, (work Split FPdc, sc in same sp as last sc made and in next ch-2 sp) 4 times, work First Leg of Split FPdc †, skip next Cluster, work Second Leg of Split FPdc, sc in unworked ch-2 sp **behind** st just made; repeat from ★ 6 times **more**, then repeat from † to † once, insert hook in last Cluster, YO and pull up a loop, YO and draw through all 3 loops on hook: 225 sts.

Row 3: Ch 2, turn; skip next 2 sc, work (Cluster, ch 2, First Leg of Split Cluster) in next Split FPdc, ★ † [skip next 2 sc, work (Second Leg of Split Cluster, ch 2, First Leg of Split Cluster) in next Split FPdc] 3 times, skip next sc, work (Second Leg of Split Cluster, ch 2, tr Cluster, ch 2, First Leg of Split Cluster) in next sc, skip next sc, [work (Second Leg of Split Cluster, ch 2, First Leg of Split Cluster) in next Split FPdc, skip next 2 sc] 4 times †, work First Leg of Split Cluster in next Split FPdc (5 loops on hook), skip next 2 sc, work (Ending Cluster, ch 2, First Leg of Split Cluster) in next Split FPdc; repeat from ★ 6 times **more**, then repeat from † to † once, YO, insert hook in last st, YO and pull up a loop, YO and draw through 2 loops on hook, YO and draw through all 4 loops on hook: 80 ch-2 sps.

Repeat Rows 2 and 3 until Afghan measures approximately 65" (165 cm), ending by working Row 3 and completing color sequence; finish off.

Holding 6 strands of Green together, each 16" (40.5 cm) long, add fringe in spaces across short edges of Afghan *(Figs. 22a & c, page 142)*.

DAYDREAM

Wrap yourself in this dreamy comforter and spend the day building castles in the sky. Made with bulky weight yarn, this airy afghan is light as a cloud — and oh-so quick to stitch!

Finished Size: 45^1/$_2$" x 60" (115.5 cm x 152.5 cm)

MATERIALS
Bulky Weight Brushed Acrylic Yarn:
    34 ounces, 1,530 yards
       (970 grams, 1,399 meters)
Crochet hook, size I (5.5 mm) **or** size needed
    for gauge

GAUGE: In pattern,
    (2 dc, ch 1, 2 dc) 3 times = 4^1/$_2$" (11.5 cm);
    6 rows = 4" (10 cm)

Gauge Swatch: 5" (12.75 cm) square
Ch 19.
Work same as Afghan for 7 rows.
Finish off.

AFGHAN
Ch 154.

Row 1 (Right side): Working in back ridges of beginning ch *(Fig. 2b, page 137)*, (2 dc, ch 1, 2 dc) in sixth ch from hook, ★ skip next 4 chs, (2 dc, ch 1, 2 dc) in next ch; repeat from ★ across to last 3 chs, skip next 2 chs, dc in last ch: 121 dc and 30 ch-1 sps.
Note: Loop a short piece of yarn around any stitch to mark Row 1 as **right** side.

Row 2: Ch 1, turn; sc in first dc, ch 3, dc in next ch-1 sp, ch 3, skip next 2 dc, ★ sc in sp **before** next dc, ch 3, dc in next ch-1 sp, ch 3, skip next 2 dc; repeat from ★ across, sc in next ch: 61 sts and 60 ch-3 sps.

Row 3: Ch 5 **(counts as first dtr, now and throughout)**, turn; (2 dc, ch 1, 2 dc) in next dc, ★ skip next sc, (2 dc, ch 1, 2 dc) in next dc; repeat from ★ across to last sc, dtr in last sc: 122 sts and 30 ch-1 sps.

Row 4: Ch 1, turn; sc in first dtr, ch 3, dc in next ch-1 sp, ch 3, skip next 2 dc, ★ sc in sp **before** next dc, ch 3, dc in next ch-1 sp, ch 3, skip next 2 dc; repeat from ★ across to last dtr, sc in last dtr: 61 sts and 60 ch-3 sps.

Row 5: Ch 5, turn; (2 dc, ch 1, 2 dc) in next dc, ★ skip next sc, (2 dc, ch 1, 2 dc) in next dc; repeat from ★ across to last sc, dtr in last sc: 122 sts and 30 ch-1 sps

Repeat Rows 4 and 5 until Afghan measures approximately 60" (152.5 cm) from beginning ch, ending by working Row 5.
Finish off.

Attach one tassel to each corner of Afghan *(Figs. 23a & b, page 142)* and trim the ends.

BABY'S JOYFUL ARRIVAL

Celebrate a joyful arrival with a precious baby blanket. Pretty in pink and white, this tiny throw is just the right size for Baby's crib.

Finished Size: 32" x 47" (81.5 cm x 119.5 cm)

MATERIALS
Sport Weight Yarn:
Pink - 12$\frac{1}{2}$ ounces, 1,140 yards
(360 grams, 1,042.5 meters)
White - 11$\frac{1}{2}$ ounces, 1,045 yards
(330 grams, 955.5 meters))
Crochet hook, size F (3.75 mm) **or** size needed
for gauge

GAUGE: In pattern, from point to point = 4" (10 cm);
7 rows = 2$\frac{1}{4}$" (5.75 cm)

Gauge Swatch: 8"w x 4$\frac{1}{2}$"h (20.25 cm x 11.5 cm)
With Pink, ch 46.
Work same as Afghan for 10 rows.

STITCH GUIDE

BEGINNING SC DECREASE
Pull up a loop in first st **and** in next st or sp, YO and draw through all 3 loops on hook (**counts as one sc**).

SC DECREASE
Pull up a loop in each of next 2 sts, YO and draw through all 3 loops on hook (**counts as one sc**).

DOUBLE SC DECREASE (uses next 3 sts)
Pull up a loop in next st, skip next st, pull up a loop in next st, YO and draw through all 3 loops on hook (**counts as one sc**).

DC DECREASE (uses next 2 sts)
★ YO, insert hook in **next** st, YO and pull up a loop, YO and draw through 2 loops on hook; repeat from ★ once **more**, YO and draw through all 3 loops on hook (**counts as one dc**).

DOUBLE DC DECREASE (uses next 3 sts)
YO, insert hook in next st, YO and pull up a loop, YO and draw through 2 loops on hook, YO, skip next st, insert hook in next st, YO and pull up a loop, YO and draw through 2 loops on hook, YO and draw through all 3 loops on hook (**counts as one dc**).

AFGHAN BODY

With Pink, ch 178.
Row 1 (Right side): Working in back ridges of beginning ch (*Fig. 2b, page 137*), dc in third ch from hook and in next 9 chs, (dc, ch 1, dc) in next ch, dc in next 9 chs, ★ work double dc decrease, dc in next 9 chs, (dc, ch 1, dc) in next ch, dc in next 9 chs; repeat from ★ across to last 2 chs, dc decrease: 169 dc and 8 ch-1 sps.
Note: Loop a short piece of yarn around any stitch to mark Row 1 as **right** side.
Row 2: Ch 1, turn; work beginning sc decrease, ★ † ch 2, skip next dc, (sc in next dc, ch 2, skip next dc) 4 times, (sc, ch 2) twice in next ch-1 sp, skip next dc, (sc in next dc, ch 2, skip next dc) 4 times †, work double sc decrease; repeat from ★ 6 times **more**, then repeat from † to † once, sc decrease: 89 sc and 88 ch-2 sps.
Row 3: Ch 1, turn; work beginning sc decrease, sc in ch-2 sp just worked into, ★ † 2 sc in each of next 4 ch-2 sps, 3 sc in next ch-2 sp, 2 sc in next 4 ch-2 sps, sc in next ch-2 sp †, pull up a loop in ch-2 sp just worked into **and** in next ch-2 sp, YO and draw through all 3 loops on hook, sc in ch-2 sp just worked into; repeat from ★ 6 times **more**, then repeat from † to † once, pull up a loop in ch-2 sp just worked into **and** in last sc, YO and draw through all 3 loops on hook; finish off: 177 sts.
Row 4: With **wrong** side facing, join White with slip st in first st; ch 1, work beginning sc decrease, [skip next sc, (sc, tr, sc) in next sc pushing tr to **right** side] 9 times, ★ skip next sc, work double sc decrease, [skip next sc, (sc, tr, sc) in next sc pushing tr to **right** side] 9 times; repeat from ★ across to last 3 sc, skip next sc, sc decrease; finish off: 225 sts.
Row 5: With **right** side facing, join Pink with slip st in first sc; ch 1, work beginning sc decrease, skip next tr, 2 sc in next sc, sc in next sc, (skip next tr, sc in next 2 sc) 3 times, 3 sc in next tr, ★ (sc in next 2 sc, skip next tr) 4 times, sc in next sc, pull up a loop in sc just worked into, skip next sc, pull up a loop in next sc, YO and draw through all 3 loops on hook, sc in sc just worked into, (skip next tr, sc in next 2 sc) 4 times, 3 sc in next tr; repeat from ★ across to last 14 sts, (sc in next 2 sc, skip next tr) 3 times, sc in next sc, 2 sc in next sc, skip next tr, sc decrease: 177 sts.

Row 6: Ch 1, turn; work beginning sc decrease, ★ † ch 2, skip next sc, (sc in next sc, ch 2, skip next sc) 4 times, (sc, ch 2) twice in next sc, skip next sc, (sc in next sc, ch 2, skip next sc) 4 times †, work double sc decrease; repeat from ★ 6 times **more**, then repeat from † to † once, sc decrease: 89 sc and 88 ch-2 sps.

Row 7: Ch 2, turn; 2 dc in each of next 5 ch-2 sps, ★ † (dc, ch 1, dc) in next ch-2 sp, 2 dc in each of next 4 ch-2 sps, dc in next ch-2 sp, YO, insert hook in ch-2 sp just worked into, YO and pull up a loop, YO and draw through 2 loops on hook †, YO, insert hook in next ch-2 sp, YO and pull up a loop, YO and draw through 2 loops on hook, YO and draw through all 3 loops on hook, dc in ch-2 sp just worked into, 2 dc in each of next 4 ch-2 sps; repeat from ★ 6 times **more**, then repeat from † to † once, YO, insert hook in last sc, YO and pull up a loop, YO and draw through 2 loops on hook, YO and draw through all 3 loops on hook; finish off: 169 sts and 8 ch-1 sps.

Row 8: With **right** side facing, join White with slip st in first dc; ch 2, dc in next 10 dc, (dc, ch 1, dc) in next ch-1 sp, dc in next 9 dc, ★ work double dc decrease, dc in next 9 dc, (dc, ch 1, dc) in next ch-1 sp, dc in next 9 dc; repeat from ★ across to last 2 sts, dc decrease.

Row 9: Ch 1, turn; work beginning sc decrease, ★ † ch 2, skip next dc, (sc in next dc, ch 2, skip next dc) 4 times, (sc, ch 2) twice in next ch-1 sp, skip next dc, (sc in next dc, ch 2, skip next dc) 4 times †, work double sc decrease; repeat from ★ 6 times **more**, then repeat from † to † once, sc decrease: 89 sc and 88 ch-2 sps.

Row 10: Ch 1, turn; work beginning sc decrease, sc in ch-2 sp just worked into, ★ † 2 sc in each of next 4 ch-2 sps, 3 sc in next ch-2 sp, 2 sc in next 4 ch-2 sps, sc in next ch-2 sp †, pull up a loop in ch-2 sp just worked into **and** in next ch-2 sp, YO and draw through all 3 loops on hook, sc in ch-2 sp just worked into; repeat from ★ 6 times **more**, then repeat from † to † once, pull up a loop in ch-2 sp just worked into **and** in last sc, YO and draw through all 3 loops on hook; finish off: 177 sts.

Row 11: With **wrong** side facing, join Pink with slip st in first st; ch 1, work beginning sc decrease, [skip next sc, (sc, tr, sc) in next sc pushing tr to **right** side] 9 times, ★ skip next sc, work double sc decrease, [skip next sc, (sc, tr, sc) in next sc pushing tr to **right** side] 9 times; repeat from ★ across to last 3 sc, skip next sc, sc decrease; finish off: 225 sts.

Row 12: With White, repeat Row 5: 177 sts.

Row 13: Ch 1, turn; work beginning sc decrease, ★ † ch 2, skip next sc, (sc in next sc, ch 2, skip next sc) 4 times, (sc, ch 2) twice in next sc, skip next sc, (sc in next sc, ch 2, skip next sc) 4 times †, work double sc decrease; repeat from ★ 6 times **more**, then repeat from † to † once, sc decrease: 89 sc and 88 ch-2 sps.

Row 14: Ch 2, turn; 2 dc in each of next 5 ch-2 sps, ★ † (dc, ch 1, dc) in next ch-2 sp, 2 dc in each of next 4 ch-2 sps, dc in next ch-2 sp, YO, insert hook in ch-2 sp just worked into, YO and pull up a loop, YO and draw through 2 loops on hook †, YO, insert hook in next ch-2 sp, YO and pull up a loop, YO and draw through 2 loops on hook, YO and draw through all 3 loops on hook, dc in ch-2 sp just worked into, 2 dc in each of next 4 ch-2 sps; repeat from ★ 6 times **more**, then repeat from † to † once, YO, insert hook in last sc, YO and pull up a loop, YO and draw through 2 loops on hook, YO and draw through all 3 loops on hook; finish off: 169 sts and 8 ch-1 sps.

Row 15: With **right** side facing, join Pink with slip st in first dc; ch 2, dc in next 10 dc, (dc, ch 1, dc) in next ch-1 sp, dc in next 9 dc, ★ work double dc decrease, dc in next 9 dc, (dc, ch 1, dc) in next ch-1 sp, dc in next 9 dc; repeat from ★ across to last 2 sts, dc decrease.

Rows 16-147: Repeat Rows 2-15, 9 times; then repeat Rows 2-7 once **more**; at end of Row 147, do **not** finish off.

EDGING
FIRST SIDE

Ch 1, do **not** turn; with **right** side facing, sc evenly across long edge of Afghan Body working hdc in end of Row 4 and Row 11 when necessary to keep edge even; finish off.

SECOND SIDE

With **right** side facing, join Pink with slip st in end of Row 1; ch 1, sc evenly across long edge of Afghan Body working hdc in end of Row 4 and Row 11 when necessary to keep edge even; finish off.

FLORAL FANTASY

*Spring into the season with every flower lover's fantasy — a vibrant floral afghan.
Three-dimensional popcorn stitches infuse this brilliant garden with stunning style.*

Finished Size: 46" x 63" (117 cm x 160 cm)

MATERIALS
Worsted Weight Yarn:
  Aran - 14$^{1}/_{2}$ ounces, 820 yards
    (410 grams, 750 meters)
  Green - 7$^{1}/_{2}$ ounces, 425 yards
    (210 grams, 388.5 meters)
  Purple and Lt Purple - 5$^{1}/_{2}$ ounces, 310 yards
    (160 grams, 283.5 meters) **each**
  Lt Blue, Lt Pink, Pink, and Blue - 5 ounces,
    285 yards (140 grams, 260.5 meters) **each**
  Yellow - 3 ounces, 170 yards
    (90 grams, 155.5 meters)
Crochet hook, size G (4 mm) **or** size needed
  for gauge

GAUGE SWATCH: Each Motif from
point to point = 6" (15.25 cm)
Work same as Motif.

STITCH GUIDE

CLUSTER (uses next 2 ch-3 sps)
★ YO, insert hook in **next** ch-3 sp, YO and pull
up a loop, YO and draw through 2 loops on
hook; repeat from ★ once **more**, YO and draw
through all 3 loops on hook *(Figs. 11a & b,
page 139)*.
TR POPCORN
4 tr in dc indicated, drop loop from hook, insert
hook in first tr of 4-tr group, hook dropped loop
and draw through st *(Fig. 13, page 139)*.
DC POPCORN
4 dc in dc indicated, drop loop from hook, insert
hook in first dc of 4-dc group, hook dropped
loop and draw through st *(Fig. 13, page 139)*.

MOTIF (Make 98)
Rnd 1 (Right side): With Yellow, ch 2, 6 sc in second
ch from hook; join with slip st to first sc.
Rnd 2: Ch 5, (slip st in next sc, ch 5) around; join
with slip st to joining slip st, finish off: 6 ch-5 sps.
Note: For Rnds 3 and 4, make the number of Motifs
with the color indicated on the Key.
Rnd 3: With **right** side facing, join color indicated
with slip st in center ch of any ch-5; ch 3 **(counts as**

first dc), (dc, tr) in same st, ch 2, ★ (tr, 3 dc, tr) in
center ch of next ch-5, ch 2; repeat from ★ around,
(tr, dc) in same st as first dc; join with slip st to first
dc: 30 sts and 6 ch-2 sps.
Rnd 4: Ch 4, 3 tr in same st, drop loop from hook,
insert hook in top of beginning ch-4, hook dropped
loop and draw through st **(beginning tr Popcorn
made)**, ch 3, work dc Popcorn in next dc, ch 3, slip st
in next ch-2 sp, ch 3, skip next tr, work dc Popcorn
in next dc, ch 3, ★ work tr Popcorn in next dc, ch 3,
work dc Popcorn in next dc, ch 3, slip st in next
ch-2 sp, ch 3, skip next tr, work dc Popcorn in next
dc, ch 3; repeat from ★ around; join with slip st to
top of beginning tr Popcorn, finish off: 24 sts and
24 ch-3 sps.
Rnd 5: With **right** side facing, join Green with sc in
first ch-3 sp *(see Joining With Sc, page 140)*; ch 4,
work Cluster, ch 4, sc in next ch-3 sp, ch 5, ★ sc in
next ch-3 sp, ch 4, work Cluster, ch 4, sc in next
ch-3 sp, ch 5; repeat from ★ around; join with slip st
to first sc, finish off: 18 sts, 12 ch-4 sps, and
6 ch-5 sps.
Rnd 6: With **right** side facing, join Aran with sc in
any ch-5 sp; ch 3, sc in same sp, ch 3, sc in next
ch-4 sp, ch 3, sc in next Cluster, ch 3, sc in next
ch-4 sp, ch 3, ★ (sc, ch 3) twice in next ch-5 sp, sc in
next ch-4 sp, ch 3, sc in next Cluster, ch 3, sc in next
ch-4 sp, ch 3; repeat from ★ around; join with slip st
to first sc, finish off: 30 ch-3 sps.

ASSEMBLY
Using Placement Diagram as a guide, join Motifs to
form 7 horizontal strips with 8 Motifs each and
6 horizontal strips with 7 Motifs each.

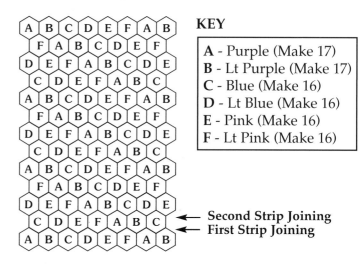

KEY

A - Purple (Make 17)
B - Lt Purple (Make 17)
C - Blue (Make 16)
D - Lt Blue (Make 16)
E - Pink (Make 16)
F - Lt Pink (Make 16)

← Second Strip Joining
← First Strip Joining

Motif Joining: Place two Motifs with **wrong** sides together; join Aran with sc in first corner ch-3 sp on **front Motif**; ch 1, sc in corresponding corner ch-3 sp on **back Motif**, ★ ch 1, sc in next ch-3 sp on **front Motif**, ch 1, sc in next ch-3 sp on **back Motif**; repeat from ★ across working last sc in next corner ch-3 sp on **back Motif**, finish off.

Join remaining Motifs in same manner.

First Strip Joining: Place two strips with **wrong** sides together, join Aran with sc in first corner ch-3 sp on **back strip**; ch 1, sc in corresponding corner ch-3 sp on **front strip**, ★ † ch 1, (sc in next ch-3 sp on **back strip**, ch 1, sc in next ch-3 sp on **front strip**, ch 1) 4 times, sc in next corner ch-3 sp on **back strip**, ch 1, sc in next joining sc on **front strip**, ch 1, sc in same sp on **back strip**, ch 1, (sc in next ch-3 sp on **front strip**, ch 1, sc in next ch-3 sp on **back strip**, ch 1) 4 times, sc in next corner ch-3 sp on **front strip**, ch 1 †, sc in next joining sc on **back strip**, ch 1, sc in same sp on **front strip**; repeat from ★ 5 times **more**; then repeat from † to † once, sc in next ch-3 sp on **back strip**; finish off.

Second Strip Joining: Place two strips with **wrong** sides together, join Aran with sc in first corner ch-3 sp on **front strip**; ch 1, sc in corresponding corner ch-3 sp on **back strip**, ★ † ch 1, (sc in next ch-3 sp on **front strip**, ch 1, sc in next ch-3 sp on **back strip**, ch 1) 4 times, sc in next corner ch-3 sp on **front strip**, ch 1, sc in next joining sc on **back strip**, ch 1, sc in same sp on **front strip**, ch 1, (sc in next ch-3 sp on **back strip**, ch 1, sc in next ch-3 sp on **front strip**, ch 1) 4 times, sc in next corner ch-3 sp on **back strip**, ch 1 †, sc in next joining sc on **front strip**, ch 1, sc in same sp on **back strip**; repeat from ★ 5 times **more**; then repeat from † to † once, sc in next ch-3 sp on **front strip**; finish off.

Join remaining strips by alternating First and Second Strip Joining.

WINDMILL REVERIE

Drift away to a fantasyland of whimsy and dreams with our delicate windmill throw. Three shades of lavender make this reverie a dainty vision.

Finished Size: 45" x 63" (114.5 cm x 160 cm)

MATERIALS
Worsted Weight Yarn:
 Lt Purple - 20 ounces, 1,130 yards
  (570 grams, 1,033.5 meters)
 Purple - 12 ounces, 680 yards
  (340 grams, 622 meters)
 Dk Purple - 12 ounces, 680 yards
  (340 grams, 622 meters)
 Soft White - 4 ounces, 225 yards
  (110 grams, 205.5 meters)
 Crochet hook, size G (4 mm) **or** size needed
  for gauge
 Yarn needle

GAUGE: Each Square = 9" (22.75 cm)

Gauge Swatch: 2^1/$_2$" (6.25 cm)
Work same as Square through Rnd 2.

STITCH GUIDE

BLOCK
Ch 5 **loosely**, dc in back ridge of fourth ch from hook and in last ch (*Fig. 2b, page 137*).

SQUARE (Make 35)
Rnd 1 (Right side): With Lt Purple, ch 3, 11 hdc in third ch from hook; join with slip st to top of beginning ch, finish off: 12 sts.
Note: Loop a short piece of yarn around any stitch on Rnd 1 to mark **right** side.
Rnd 2: With **right** side facing, join Purple with slip st in same st as joining; ch 3, place marker in last ch made for st placement, (dc, ch 3, slip st) in same st, ch 2, skip next 2 hdc, ★ (slip st, ch 3, dc, ch 3, slip st) in next hdc, ch 2, skip next 2 hdc; repeat from ★ 2 times **more**; join with slip st to joining slip st, finish off.
Rnd 3: With **right** side facing, join Soft White with slip st in marked ch; ch 3, remove marker and place in last ch made for st placement, ★ † 3 dc in next dc, ch 3, slip st in next ch, ch 3, slip st in next ch-2 sp, ch 3, skip next slip st and next 2 chs †, slip st in next ch, ch 3; repeat from ★ 2 times **more**, then repeat from † to † once; join with slip st to joining slip st, finish off.

Continued on page 34.

Rnd 4: With **right** side facing, join Lt Purple with slip st in marked ch; ch 3, remove marker and place in last ch made for st placement, ★ † dc in next dc, 3 dc in next dc, dc in next dc, ch 3, slip st in next ch, ch 3, skip next 2 chs and next slip st, slip st in next ch, skip next 2 chs, dc in next slip st, skip next 2 chs, slip st in next ch, ch 3, skip next slip st and next 2 chs †, slip st in next ch, ch 3; repeat from ★ 2 times **more**, then repeat from † to † once; join with slip st to joining slip st, finish off.

Rnd 5: With **right** side facing, join Purple with slip st in marked ch; ch 3, remove marker and place in last ch made for st placement, ★ † dc in next 2 dc, 3 dc in next dc, dc in next 2 dc, ch 3, slip st in next ch, ch 3, skip next 2 chs and next slip st, slip st in next ch, 3 dc in next dc †, (skip next slip st and next 2 chs, slip st in next ch, ch 3) twice; repeat from ★ 2 times **more**, then repeat from † to † once, skip next slip st and next 2 chs, slip st in next ch, ch 3; join with slip st to joining slip st, finish off.

Rnd 6: With **right** side facing, join Dk Purple with slip st in marked ch; ch 3, remove marker and place in last ch made for st placement, ★ † dc in next 3 dc, 3 tr in next dc, dc in next 3 dc, ch 3, slip st in next ch, ch 3, skip next 2 chs and next slip st, slip st in next ch, dc in next dc, 3 dc in next dc, dc in next dc †, (skip next slip st and next 2 chs, slip st in next ch, ch 3) twice; repeat from ★ 2 times **more**, then repeat from † to † once, skip next slip st and next 2 chs, slip st in next ch, ch 3; join with slip st to joining slip st, finish off.

Rnd 7: With **right** side facing, join Lt Purple with sc in marked ch *(see Joining With Sc, page 140)*; ★ † sc in next 3 dc, hdc in next tr, 5 hdc in next tr, hdc in next tr, sc in next 3 dc and in next ch, ch 3, skip next 2 chs and next slip st, slip st in next ch, 2 dc in next dc, dc in next 3 dc, 2 dc in next dc, skip next slip st and next 2 chs, slip st in next ch, ch 3, skip next slip st and in next 2 chs †, sc in next ch; repeat from ★ 2 times **more**, then repeat from † to † once; join with slip st to first sc, finish off.

Rnd 8: With **right** side facing, join Soft White with sc in center hdc of any corner 5-hdc group; (hdc, sc) in same st, ★ † sc in next 7 sts and in next ch, dc in next 7 dc, skip next slip st and next 2 chs, sc in next ch and in next 7 sts †, (sc, hdc, sc) in next hdc; repeat from ★ 2 times **more**, then repeat from † to † once; join with slip st to first sc, finish off: 104 sts.

Rnd 9: With **right** side facing, join Purple with slip st in center hdc of any 3-st corner group; ★ † work Block, skip next st, slip st in **both** loops of next st, slip st in Back Loops Only of next 3 sts, slip st in **both** loops of next st †; repeat from † to † 3 times **more**, (work Block, skip next sc, slip st in **both** loops of next st) twice, slip st in Back Loops Only of next 3 sc, slip st in **both** loops of next sc, repeat from † to † 3 times; repeat from ★ 2 times **more**, work Block; join with slip st to **both** loops of joining slip st, finish off: 20 Blocks.

Rnd 10: With **right** side facing, join Dk Purple with sc in third ch of beginning ch-5 on first Block; sc in next 2 chs, ★ † skip next 2 dc and next slip st, tr in Back Loops Only of next 3 slip sts, skip next slip st and next 2 chs, sc in next 3 chs †; repeat from † to † 3 times **more**, ch 4, tr in **both** loops of next 2 dc, skip next slip st and next 2 chs, sc in next 3 chs; repeat from ★ 2 times **more**, then repeat from † to † 4 times, ch 4, tr in **both** loops of last 2 dc; join with slip st to first sc, finish off: 60 sc, 56 tr, and 16 chs.

ASSEMBLY

With Dk Purple and working through both loops, whipstitch Squares together forming 5 vertical strips of 7 Squares each *(Fig. 21b , page 142)*, beginning in first ch of corner ch-4 on first Square and last ch of corner ch-4 on second Square and ending in last ch of next corner ch-4 on first Square and first ch of next corner ch-4 on second Square.
Whipstitch strips together in same manner.

EDGING

With **right** side facing, join Dk Purple with slip st in any st; ch 1, working from **left** to **right**, work reverse sc *(Figs. 14a-d, page 140)* in each st and in each ch around; join with slip st to first st, finish off.

LI'L FISHERMAN

Extra-wide stripes are sure to delight your "little boy blue." Make this youngster's throw on-the-go by crocheting strips separately then whipstitching them together.

Finished Size: 35" x 46" (89 cm x 117 cm)

MATERIALS
Worsted Weight Yarn:
    Blue - 24 ounces, 1,355 yards
      (680 grams, 1,239 meters)
    Off-White - 8 ounces, 450 yards
      (230 grams, 411.5 meters)
  Crochet hook, size H (5 mm) **or** size needed
    for gauge
  Yarn needle

GAUGE: Each Strip = 5" (12.75 cm) wide

Gauge Swatch: 4$^{1}/_{4}$"w x 3"h (11 cm x 7.5 cm)
Work same as Strip Center for 8 rows.

STITCH GUIDE

FRONT POST SINGLE CROCHET
    (abbreviated FPsc)
Insert hook from **front** to **back** around post of st indicated *(Fig. 9, page 139)*, YO and pull up a loop, YO and draw through both loops on hook.

FRONT POST DOUBLE CROCHET
    (abbreviated FPdc)
YO, insert hook from **front** to **back** around post of st indicated *(Fig. 9, page 139)*, YO and pull up a loop even with loop on hook (3 loops on hook), (YO and draw through 2 loops on hook) twice.

FRONT POST CLUSTER
    (abbreviated FP Cluster)
★ YO, insert hook from **front** to **back** around post of dc indicated *(Fig. 9, page 139)*, YO and pull up a loop even with loop on hook, YO and draw through 2 loops on hook; repeat from ★ once **more**, YO and draw through all 3 loops on hook.

STRIP (Make 7)
CENTER
With Blue, ch 15.
Row 1: Sc in second ch from hook and in each ch across: 14 sc.
Row 2 (Right side): Ch 3 **(counts as first dc, now and throughout)**, turn; dc in next sc and in each sc across.
Note: Loop a short piece of yarn around any stitch to mark Row 2 as **right** side and bottom edge.
Row 3: Ch 1, turn; sc in each dc across.
Row 4: Ch 3, turn; dc in next sc, work FPdc around dc one row **below** next sc, skip next sc behind FPdc, dc in next 2 sc, skip next 3 dc on Row 2 from last FPdc made, work FP Cluster around next dc, skip next sc behind FP Cluster, dc in next 2 sc, work FP Cluster around next dc on Row 2, skip next sc behind FP Cluster, dc in next 2 sc, work FPdc around dc one row **below** next sc, skip next sc behind FPdc, dc in last 2 sc.
Row 5: Ch 1, turn; sc in each st across.
Row 6: Ch 3, turn; dc in next sc, work FPdc around FPdc one row **below** next sc, skip next sc behind FPdc, dc in next 2 sc, skip next FP Cluster one row **below**, work FP Cluster around next dc, skip next sc behind FP Cluster just made, dc in next 2 sc, work FP Cluster around next dc one row **below**, skip next sc behind FP Cluster just made, dc in next 2 sc, work FPdc around FPdc one row **below** next sc, skip next sc behind FPdc, dc in last 2 sc.
Rows 7-119: Repeat Rows 5 and 6, 56 times; then repeat Row 5 once **more**; finish off.

BORDER
With **right** side facing, join Off-White with dc in first sc on Row 119 of Center *(see Joining With Dc, page 140)*; 4 dc in same st, dc in next 2 sc, tr in next 2 sc, dtr in next 4 sc, tr in next 2 sc, dc in next 2 sc, 5 dc in last sc, ch 1; skip first sc row, working around post of dc at end of each dc row, (2 dc in next dc row, ch 1) across; working in free loops of beginning ch *(Fig. 17b, page 141)*, 5 dc in ch at base of first sc, dc in next 2 chs, tr in next 2 chs, dtr in next 4 chs, tr in next 2 chs, dc in next 2 chs, 5 dc in last ch, ch 1; skip first sc row, working around post of dc at end of each dc row, (2 dc in next dc row, ch 1) across; join with slip st to first dc, finish off: 280 sts and 120 ch-1 sps.

ASSEMBLY

Hold two Strips with **wrong** sides together and bottom edges at same end. With Off-White and working through inside loops only, whipstitch Strips together *(Fig. 21a, page 142)*, beginning in first ch-1 **after** corner 5-dc group and ending in last ch-1 **before** next corner 5-dc group.

Join remaining Strips in same manner.

EDGING

With **right** side facing and beginning in top right corner of Afghan, join Off-White with sc in first dc of corner 5-dc group *(see Joining With Sc, page 140)*; † work FPsc around next st, (sc in next st, work FPsc around next st) 10 times, ★ skip next joining, sc in first dc of next 5-dc group on next Strip, work FPsc around next st, (sc in next st, work FPsc around next st) 10 times; repeat from ★ 5 times **more**, sc in next ch-1 sp, (work FPsc around next 2 dc, sc in next ch-1 sp) across to next 5-dc group †, sc in next dc, repeat from † to † once; join with slip st to first sc, finish off.

SUMMER

When summer finally arrives, time seems to slow to a crawl. Take a vacation from your daily cares and spend some time relaxing on the porch with a glass of ice-cold lemonade and a new afghan crocheted in brilliant summer colors. From flower patches and pool parties to Americana, you'll find plenty of sunny themes sure to delight and inspire.

RELAXATION

Summer's here! Set aside some time for rest and relaxation, lounging with our cozy comforter. Post stitches accent the handsome edging.

Finished Size: 51" x 67" (129.5 cm x 170 cm)

MATERIALS
Worsted Weight Yarn:
    61 ounces, 3,450 yards
      (1,730 grams, 3,154.5 meters)
Crochet hook, size H (5 mm) **or** size needed
    for gauge
Yarn needle

GAUGE: Each Square = 8" (20.25 cm)

Gauge Swatch: 7"w x 2"h (17.75 cm x 5 cm)
Work same as Square through Row 3.

STITCH GUIDE

FRONT POST TREBLE CROCHET
    (abbreviated FPtr)
YO twice, insert hook from **front** to **back** around post of st indicated *(Fig. 9, page 139)*, YO and pull up a loop (4 loops on hook), (YO and draw through 2 loops on hook) 3 times. Skip st behind FPtr unless otherwise specified.
BACK POST TREBLE CROCHET
    (abbreviated BPtr)
YO twice, insert hook from **back** to **front** around post of st indicated *(Fig. 9, page 139)*, YO and pull up a loop (4 loops on hook), (YO and draw through 2 loops on hook) 3 times. Skip st in front of BPtr.

SQUARE (Make 48)
CENTER
Ch 26 **loosely**, place marker in third ch from hook for st placement.
Row 1 (Right side): Dc in fourth ch from hook **(3 skipped chs count as first dc)** and in next ch, ★ (skip next ch, dc in next ch, working **around** last dc made, dc in skipped ch) twice, dc in next 3 chs; repeat from ★ 2 times **more**: 24 dc.
Note: Loop a short piece of yarn around any stitch to mark Row 1 as **right** side and bottom edge.

Row 2: Ch 3 **(counts as first dc, now and throughout)**, turn; work BPtr around next dc, dc in next dc, ★ (skip next dc, dc in next dc, working **around** last dc made, dc in skipped dc) twice, dc in next dc, work BPtr around next dc, dc in next dc; repeat from ★ 2 times **more**: 4 BPtr and 20 dc.
Row 3: Ch 3, turn; work FPtr around next BPtr, dc in next dc, ★ (skip next dc, dc in next dc, working **around** last dc made, dc in skipped dc) twice, dc in next dc, work FPtr around next BPtr, dc in next dc; repeat from ★ 2 times **more**: 4 FPtr and 20 dc.
Row 4: Ch 3, turn; work BPtr around next FPtr, dc in next dc, ★ (skip next dc, dc in next dc, working **around** last dc made, dc in skipped dc) twice, dc in next dc, work BPtr around next FPtr, dc in next dc; repeat from ★ 2 times **more**: 4 BPtr and 20 dc.
Rows 5-11: Repeat Rows 3 and 4, 3 times; then repeat Row 3 once **more**; do **not** finish off.

BORDER
Rnd 1: Ch 1, do **not** turn; 2 sc in end of each row across; working in free loops of beginning ch *(Fig. 17b, page 141)*, 3 sc in first ch, sc in next ch and in each ch across to marked ch, 3 sc in marked ch; 2 sc in end of each row across; working in sts across Row 11, 3 sc in first dc, sc in next 22 sts, 3 sc in last dc; join with slip st to first sc: 100 sc.
Rnd 2: Ch 1, sc in each sc around working 3 sc in center sc of each corner 3-sc group; join with slip st to first sc, finish off: 108 sc.

ASSEMBLY
Using photo as a guide, alternating bottom of Squares, and working through both loops, whipstitch Squares together forming 6 vertical strips of 8 Squares each *(Fig. 21b, page 142)*, beginning in center sc of first corner 3-sc group and ending in center sc of next corner 3-sc group; then whipstitch strips together in same manner.

EDGING

Rnd 1: With **right** side facing, join yarn with slip st in center sc of any corner 3-sc group; ch 3, 2 dc in same st, ★ † 2 dc in next sc, dc in next 25 sc, dc in same st as joining on same Square and in same st as joining on next Square, (dc in next 26 sc, dc in same st as joining on same Square and in same st as joining on next Square) across to last Square, dc in next 25 sc, 2 dc in next sc †, 3 dc in next sc; repeat from ★ 2 times **more**, then repeat from † to † once; join with slip st to first dc: 796 dc.

Rnd 2: Ch 3, dc in same st, ★ † dc in next dc, work FPtr around same st, dc in same st, 2 dc in next dc, dc in next 3 dc, work FPtr around next dc, (dc in next 6 dc, work FPtr around next dc) across to within 3 dc of next corner 3-dc group, dc in next 3 dc †, 2 dc in next dc; repeat from ★ 2 times **more**, then repeat from † to † once; join with slip st to first dc.

Rnd 3: Ch 1, sc in same st and in next 2 dc, 3 sc in next FPtr, ★ sc in next dc and in each st across to next corner FPtr, 3 sc in corner FPtr; repeat from ★ 2 times **more**, sc in next dc and in each st across; join with slip st to first sc, finish off.

41

FREEDOM STRIPES

You'll show your true colors when you crochet this patriotic pleaser. The Q-hook beauty is quick to stitch, leaving you plenty of time to enjoy your favorite summer activities.

Finished Size: 47" x 62" (119.5 cm x 157.5 cm)

MATERIALS

Worsted Weight Yarn:
 Off-White - 38½ ounces, 2,180 yards
  (1,090 grams, 1,993.5 meters)
 Blue - 14 ounces, 795 yards
  (400 grams, 727 meters)
 Red - 11¾ ounces, 665 yards
  (330 grams, 608 meters)
Crochet hook, size Q (15 mm)
Yarn needle

Note: Afghan is worked holding three strands of yarn together.

GAUGE: Each Strip = 6¾" (17.25 cm) wide
  2 rows = 3½" (9 cm)

Gauge Swatch: 4½"w x 7"h (11.5 cm x 17.75 cm)
Work same as Center through Row 2.

STRIP A (Make 4)
CENTER

With Off-White, ch 7 **loosely**, place marker in third ch from hook for st placement.
Foundation Row (Right side): (3 Dc, ch 2, 3 dc) in fifth ch from hook, ch 3, skip next ch, slip st in last ch: 6 dc.
Note: Loop a short piece of yarn around any stitch to mark Foundation Row as **right** side and bottom edge.
Row 1: Ch 3 **(counts as first dc, now and throughout)**, do **not** turn; working in free loops of beginning ch **(Fig. 17b, page 141)**, skip next ch, (3 dc, ch 2, 3 dc) in next ch (at base of 6-dc group), dc in marked ch: 8 dc and one ch-2 sp.
Rows 2-31: Ch 3, **turn**; (3 dc, ch 2, 3 dc) in next ch-2 sp, skip next 3 dc, dc in last dc.
Finish off.

EDGING

With **right** side facing, join Blue with slip st in ch-2 sp on Row 31; ch 3, (2 dc, ch 2, 3 dc) in same sp, † dc in next 3 dc; working across end of rows, 2 dc in first row, place marker in last dc made for joining placement, dc in same row, 3 dc in each row across to last row, 2 dc in last row, place marker in last dc made for joining placement, dc in same row; dc in next 3 dc †, (3 dc, ch 2, 3 dc) in next ch-2 sp, repeat from † to † once; join with slip st to first dc, finish off.

STRIP B (Make 3)
CENTER

Work same as Strip A.

EDGING

With Red, work same as Strip A.

ASSEMBLY

With Red, having bottom edges at same end, and working through both loops, whipstitch long edge of Strips together *(Fig. 21b, page 142)*, beginning in first marked dc and ending in last marked dc in the following order: Strip A, (Strip B, Strip A) 3 times.

AMERICANA

Reminiscent of an old-fashioned county fair, this delightful afghan is a true piece of Americana. Bold circles-in-a-square look lovely next to a simple striped border.

Finished Size: 40" x 61" (101.5 cm x 155 cm)

MATERIALS
Worsted Weight Yarn:
Blue - 22 ounces, 1,245 yards
(620 grams, 1,138.5 meters)
Red - 10 ounces, 565 yards
(280 grams, 516.5 meters)
Tan - 10 ounces, 565 yards
(280 grams, 516.5 meters)
Crochet hook, size G (4 mm) **or** size needed
for gauge
Yarn needle

GAUGE: Each Square = 7" (17.75 cm)

Gauge Swatch: 4" (10 cm) diameter
Work same as Square through Rnd 3.

SQUARE (Make 40)
With Red, ch 6; join with slip st to form a ring.
Rnd 1 (Right side): Ch 3 **(counts as first dc, now and throughout)**, 15 dc in ring; join with slip st to first dc: 16 dc.
Note: Loop a short piece of yarn around any stitch to mark Rnd 1 as **right** side.
Rnd 2: Slip st in sp **before** next dc, ch 5, (dc in sp **before** next dc, ch 2) around; join with slip st to third ch of beginning ch-5: 16 ch-2 sps.
Rnd 3: Slip st in first ch-2 sp, ch 3, 2 dc in same sp, ch 1, (3 dc in next ch-2 sp, ch 1) around; join with slip st to first dc, finish off: 48 dc and 16 ch-1 sps.
Rnd 4: With **right** side facing, join Tan with sc in any ch-1 sp *(see Joining With Sc, page 140)*; (ch 3, sc in next ch-1 sp) 3 times, ch 5, ★ sc in next ch-1 sp, (ch 3, sc in next ch-1 sp) 3 times, ch 5; repeat from ★ 2 times **more**; join with slip st to first sc: 16 sc and 16 sps.
Rnd 5: Slip st in first ch-3 sp, ch 3, 2 dc in same sp, 3 dc in each of next 2 ch-3 sps, (3 dc, ch 3, 3 dc) in next ch-5 sp, ★ 3 dc in each of next 3 ch-3 sps, (3 dc, ch 3, 3 dc) in next ch-5 sp; repeat from ★ 2 times **more**; join with slip st to first dc, finish off: 60 dc and 4 ch-3 sps.

Rnd 6: With **right** side facing, join Blue with slip st in any corner ch-3 sp; ch 3, (dc, ch 2, 2 dc) in same sp, ★ dc in each dc across to next corner ch-3 sp, (2 dc, ch 2, 2 dc) in corner ch-3 sp; repeat from ★ 2 times **more**, dc in each dc across; join with slip st to first dc: 76 dc and 4 ch-2 sps.
Rnd 7: Ch 3, dc in next dc, (2 dc, ch 3, 2 dc) in next corner ch-2 sp, ★ dc in each dc across to next corner ch-2 sp, (2 dc, ch 3, 2 dc) in corner ch-2 sp; repeat from ★ 2 times **more**, dc in each dc across; join with slip st to first dc, finish off: 92 dc and 4 ch-3 sps.

ASSEMBLY
With Blue and working through inside loops, whipstitch Squares together forming 5 vertical strips of 8 Squares each *(Fig. 21a, page 142)*, beginning in center ch of first corner ch-3 and ending in center ch of next corner ch-3; then whipstitch strips together in same manner.

EDGING
Rnd 1: With **right** side facing, join Blue with slip st in any corner ch-3 sp; ch 3, (2 dc, ch 2, 3 dc) in same sp, ★ † dc in next 23 dc, (2 dc in next sp, dc in next joining, 2 dc in next sp, dc in next 23 dc) across to next corner ch-3 sp †, (3 dc, ch 2, 3 dc) in corner ch-3 sp; repeat from ★ 2 times **more**, then repeat from † to † once; join with slip st to first dc, finish off: 732 dc and 4 ch-2 sps.
Rnd 2: With **right** side facing, join Red with slip st in any corner ch-2 sp; ch 5, dc in same sp, ch 1, ★ skip next dc, (dc in next dc, ch 1, skip next dc) across to next corner ch-2 sp, (dc, ch 2, dc) in corner ch-2 sp, ch 1; repeat from ★ 2 times **more**, skip next dc, (dc in next dc, ch 1, skip next dc) across; join with slip st to third ch of beginning ch-5, finish off: 372 sps.
Rnd 3: With **right** side facing, join Tan with slip st in any corner ch-2 sp; ch 3, (dc, ch 2, 2 dc) in same sp, ★ 2 dc in each ch-1 sp across to next corner ch-2 sp, (2 dc, ch 2, 2 dc) in corner ch-2 sp; repeat from ★ 2 times **more**, 2 dc in each ch-1 sp across; join with slip st to first dc, finish off: 752 dc and 4 ch-2 sps.

Rnd 4: With **right** side facing, join Blue with slip st in any corner ch-2 sp; ch 3, (dc, ch 2, 2 dc) in same sp, ★ dc in each dc across to next corner ch-2 sp, (2 dc, ch 2, 2 dc) in corner ch-2 sp; repeat from ★ 2 times **more**, dc in each dc across; join with slip st to first dc, do **not** finish off: 768 dc and 4 ch-2 sps.

Rnd 5: Ch 3, dc in next dc, (2 dc, ch 2, 2 dc) in next corner ch-2 sp, ★ dc in each dc across to next corner ch-2 sp, (2 dc, ch 2, 2 dc) in corner ch-2 sp; repeat from ★ 2 times **more**, dc in each dc across; join with slip st to first dc, finish off.

FLOWER PATCH

The lively style of this flower patch throw will keep you smiling all summer long.
Eight of your prettiest yarn scraps make this crocheted garden burst with color.

Finished Size: 51" x 69" (129.5 cm x 175.5 cm)

MATERIALS

Worsted Weight Yarn:
  MC (White) - 45 ounces, 2,960 yards
    (1,280 grams, 2,706.5 meters)
  Color A (Lt Yellow) - 3³/₄ ounces, 250 yards
    (110 grams, 228.5 meters)
  Color B (Green) - 9 ounces, 595 yards
    (260 grams, 544 meters)
  Color C (Lt Pink) - 1¹/₂ ounces, 100 yards
    (40 grams, 91.5 meters)
  Color D (Pink) - 1³/₄ ounces, 120 yards
    (50 grams, 109.5 meters)
  Color E (Lt Blue) - 2¹/₄ ounces, 150 yards
    (60 grams, 137 meters)
  Color F (Blue) - 2³/₄ ounces, 180 yards
    (80 grams, 164.5 meters)
  Color G (Lt Lavender) - 3¹/₄ ounces, 215 yards
    (90 grams, 196.5 meters)
  Color H (Lavender) - 3³/₄ ounces, 250 yards
    (110 grams, 228.5 meters)
Crochet hook, size J (6 mm) **or** size needed
    for gauge
Yarn needle

GAUGE SWATCH: 4" (10 cm) square
Work same as Square.

STITCH GUIDE

BACK POPCORN
4 Sc in st indicated, drop loop from hook, insert hook from **back** to **front** in first sc of 4-sc group, hook dropped loop and draw through, ch 1 to close.
PICOT
(Sc, ch 3, slip st in third ch from hook, sc) in st indicated.
BEGINNING POPCORN
Ch 3, 2 dc in same st, drop loop from hook, insert hook in top of beginning ch-3, hook dropped loop and draw through.
POPCORN
3 Dc in st indicated, drop loop from hook, insert hook in first dc of 3-dc group, hook dropped loop and draw through.

SQUARE

Make 221 Squares in the following Color Sequences:

Make	Rnd 1	Rnd 2	Rnd 3	Rnd 4	Rnd 5	Rnd 6
21	A	C	C	B	MC	MC
24	A	D	D	B	MC	MC
32	A	E	E	B	MC	MC
40	A	F	F	B	MC	MC
48	A	G	G	B	MC	MC
56	A	H	H	B	MC	MC

Rnd 1 (Right side): With Color A ch 2, 8 sc in second ch from hook; join with slip st to first sc, finish off. *Note:* Loop a short piece of yarn around any stitch to mark Rnd 1 as **right** side.
Rnd 2: With **wrong** side facing, join new color with slip st in any sc; ch 1, 2 sc in same st and in each sc around; join with slip st to first sc: 16 sc.
Rnd 3: Ch 1, work Back Popcorn in same st, slip st in next sc, ★ work Back Popcorn in next sc, slip st in next sc; repeat from ★ around; join with slip st to first Back Popcorn, finish off: 8 Back Popcorns.
Rnd 4: With **right** side facing, join Color B with slip st in any slip st on Rnd 3; ch 1, work Picot in same st as joining, slip st in next Back Popcorn, ★ work Picot in next slip st, slip st in next Back Popcorn; repeat from ★ around; join with slip st to first sc: 8 Picots.
Rnd 5: With **right** side facing, join Color B with slip st in center ch of any Picot; ch 1, sc in same st, skip next sc, 4 dc in next slip st, ★ sc in center ch of next Picot, skip next sc, 4 dc in next slip st; repeat from ★ around; join with slip st to first sc: 40 sts.
Rnd 6: Work Beginning Popcorn, ch 3, work Popcorn, ch 1, dc in next dc, hdc in next 2 dc, sc in next 3 sts, hdc in next 2 dc, dc in next dc, ★ work Popcorn, ch 3, Popcorn) in next sc, ch 1, dc in next dc, hdc in next 2 dc, sc in next 3 sts, hdc in next 2 dc, dc in next dc; repeat from ★ around; join with slip st to Beginning Popcorn, finish off.

Continued on page 48.

ASSEMBLY

Afghan is assembled by joining 17 Squares into 13 vertical strips and then by joining strips.

Lay out Squares referring to Placement Diagram. Join two Squares as follows:

With **wrong** sides together and working through inside loops only, join MC with slip st in center ch of any corner ch-3 sp; slip st in each st across to center ch of next corner ch-3 sp; finish off.

Join remaining Squares and strips in same manner.

EDGING

Rnd 1: With **right** side facing and working across top edge, join MC with slip st in first corner ch-3 sp; 3 sc in same sp; † sc in Back loop Only of next 13 sts *(Fig. 15, page 140)*, hdc in joining, (sc in Back Loop Only of next 14 sts, hdc in next joining) 11 times, sc in Back loop Only of next 13 sts, 3 sc in next corner ch-3 sp, sc in Back loop Only of next 13 sts, hdc in joining, (sc in Back Loop Only of next 14 sts, hdc in next joining) 15 times, sc in Back loop Only of next 13 sts †, 3 sc in next corner ch-3 sp, repeat from † to † once; join with slip st to first sc: 900 sts.

Rnd 2: Working in both loops, slip st in next sc, work beginning Popcorn, (ch 3, work Popcorn) twice, in same st, skip next 2 sc, [work (Popcorn, ch 3, Popcorn) in next sc, skip next 3 sc] across to center sc of next corner, ★ work [Popcorn, (ch 3, work Popcorn) twice] in center sc, skip next 2 sc, [work (Popcorn, ch 3, Popcorn) in next sc, skip next 3 sc] across to center sc of next corner; repeat from ★ around; join with slip st to beginning Popcorn: 456 Popcorns.

Rnd 3: Ch 1, 3 sc in first ch-3 sp, slip st in next Popcorn, (3 sc in nextch-3 sp, slip st in next 2 Popcorns) across to first ch-3 sp of next corner, ★ 3 sc in ch-3 sp, slip st in next Popcorn, (3 sc in nextch-3 sp, slip st in next 2 Popcorns) across to first ch-3 sp of next corner; repeat from ★ around; join with slip st to beginning Popcorn, finish off.

PLACEMENT DIAGRAM

H	H	H	H	H	H	H	H	H	H	H	H	H
H	G	G	G	G	G	G	G	G	G	G	G	H
H	G	F	F	F	F	F	F	F	F	F	G	H
H	G	F	E	E	E	E	E	E	E	F	G	H
H	G	F	E	D	D	D	D	D	E	F	G	H
H	G	F	E	D	C	C	C	D	E	F	G	H
H	G	F	E	D	C	C	C	D	E	F	G	H
H	G	F	E	D	C	C	C	D	E	F	G	H
H	G	F	E	D	C	C	C	D	E	F	G	H
H	G	F	E	D	C	C	C	D	E	F	G	H
H	G	F	E	D	C	C	C	D	E	F	G	H
H	G	F	E	D	C	C	C	D	E	F	G	H
H	G	F	E	D	D	D	D	D	E	F	G	H
H	G	F	E	E	E	E	E	E	E	F	G	H
H	G	F	F	F	F	F	F	F	F	F	G	H
H	G	G	G	G	G	G	G	G	G	G	G	H
H	H	H	H	H	H	H	H	H	H	H	H	H

IN BABY'S HONOR

Perfect for a "birth-day," shower, or christening, this charming afghan made in Baby's honor is sure to be a treasured gift. Cluster and picot stitches create a delicate lace edging.

Finished Size: 35" x 46" (89 cm x 117 cm)

MATERIALS
Sport Weight Yarn:
16 ounces, 1,360 yards
(450 grams, 1,243.5 meters)
Crochet hook, size G (4 mm) **or** size needed for gauge

GAUGE: In pattern, 20 sts and 9 rows = 4" (10 cm)

Gauge Swatch: $4^1/4$"w x 4"h (10.75 cm x 10 cm)
Ch 24.
Work same as Afghan Body for 9 rows.
Finish off.

STITCH GUIDE

BEGINNING CLUSTER (uses one ch-1 sp)
Ch 2, ★ YO, insert hook in ch-1 sp indicated, YO and pull up a loop, YO and draw through 2 loops on hook; repeat from ★ once **more**, YO and draw through all 3 loops on hook (*Figs. 10a & b, page 139*).
CLUSTER (uses one ch-1 sp)
★ YO, insert hook in ch-1 sp indicated, YO and pull up a loop, YO and draw through 2 loops on hook; repeat from ★ 2 times **more**, YO and draw through all 4 loops on hook (*Figs. 10a & b, page 139*).
PICOT
Ch 3, slip st in top of last sc made.

AFGHAN BODY

Ch 144, place marker in third ch from hook for st placement.
Row 1 (Right side): Dc in fourth ch from hook **(3 skipped chs count as first dc)** and in next 2 chs, ★ ch 2, skip next 2 chs, dc in next 4 chs; repeat from ★ across: 96 dc and 23 ch-2 sps.
Row 2: Ch 5 **(counts as first dc plus ch 2)**, turn; skip next 2 dc, dc in next dc, ★ 2 dc in next ch-2 sp, dc in next dc, ch 2, skip next 2 dc, dc in next dc; repeat from ★ across: 94 dc and 24 ch-2 sps.
Row 3: Ch 3 **(counts as first dc, now and throughout)**, turn; 2 dc in first ch-2 sp, dc in next dc, ★ ch 2, skip next 2 dc, dc in next dc, 2 dc in next ch-2 sp, dc in next dc; repeat from ★ across: 96 dc and 23 ch-2 sps.
Rows 4-89: Repeat Rows 2 and 3, 43 times; at end of Row 89, do **not** finish off.

EDGING

Rnd 1: Ch 1, do **not** turn; 2 sc in last dc made on Row 89; work 206 sc evenly spaced across end of rows; working in free loops of beginning ch (*Fig. 17b, page 141*), 3 sc in first ch, work 131 sc evenly spaced across to marked ch, 3 sc in marked ch; work 206 sc evenly spaced across end of rows; 3 sc in first dc on Row 89, work 131 sc evenly spaced across, sc in same dc as first sc; join with slip st to first sc: 686 sc.
Rnd 2: Ch 1, (sc, ch 6) twice in same st, skip next 3 sc, (sc in next 2 sc, ch 6, skip next 3 sc) across to center sc of next corner 3-sc group, ★ (sc, ch 6) twice in corner sc, skip next 3 sc, (sc in next 2 sc, ch 6, skip next 3 sc) across to center sc of next corner 3-sc group; repeat from ★ 2 times **more**; join with slip st to first sc: 142 ch-6 sps.

Rnds 3 and 4: Slip st in first 2 chs, ch 1, ★ (sc, ch 6) twice in corner ch-6 sp, (sc in next ch-6 sp, ch 6) across to next corner ch-6 sp; repeat from ★ around; join with slip st to first sc: 150 ch-6 sps.
Rnd 5: (Slip st, ch 3, 9 dc) in first corner ch-6 sp, sc in next ch-6 sp, ch 5, sc in next ch-6 sp, (8 dc in next ch-6 sp, sc in next ch-6 sp, ch 5, sc in next ch-6 sp) across to next corner ch-6 sp, ★ 10 dc in corner ch-6 sp, sc in next ch-6 sp, ch 5, sc in next ch-6 sp, (8 dc in next ch-6 sp, sc in next ch-6 sp, ch 5, sc in next ch-6 sp) across to next corner ch-6 sp; repeat from ★ 2 times **more**; join with slip st to first dc: 408 dc and 50 ch-5 sps.
Rnd 6: Slip st in next dc, ch 4 **(counts as first dc plus ch 1)**, dc in next dc, (ch 1, dc in next dc) 6 times, ch 3, sc in next ch-5 sp, ch 3, † skip next 2 sts, dc in next dc, (ch 1, dc in next dc) 5 times, ch 3, sc in next ch-5 sp, ch 3 †; repeat from † to † across to next corner 10-dc group, ★ skip next 2 sts, dc in next dc, (ch 1, dc in next dc) 7 times, ch 3, sc in next ch-5 sp, ch 3, repeat from † to † across to next corner 10-dc group; repeat from ★ 2 times **more**; join with slip st to first dc: 358 sps.
Rnd 7: (Slip st, work Beginning Cluster) in first ch-1 sp, ♥ (ch 3, work Cluster in next ch-1 sp) 6 times, ch 1, skip next 2 ch-3 sps, † work Cluster in next ch-1 sp, (ch 3, work Cluster in next ch-1 sp) 4 times, ch 1, skip next 2 ch-3 sps †; repeat from † to † 13 times **more**, work Cluster in next ch-1 sp, (ch 3, work Cluster in next ch-1 sp) 6 times, ch 1, skip next 2 ch-3 sps, repeat from † to † 9 times ♥, work Cluster in next ch-1 sp; repeat from ♥ to ♥ once; join with slip st to top of Beginning Cluster: 258 Clusters and 258 sps.
Rnd 8: Slip st in first ch-3 sp, ch 1, (3 sc, work Picot, 2 sc) in same sp and in next 5 ch-3 sps, † sc in next ch-1 sp, [(3 sc, work Picot, 2 sc) in next 4 ch-1 sps, sc in next ch-1 sp] 14 times, (3 sc, work Picot, 2 sc) in next 6 ch-1 sps, sc in next ch-1 sp, [(3 sc, work Picot, 2 sc) in next 4 ch-1 sps, sc in next ch-1 sp] 9 times †, (3 sc, work Picot, 2 sc) in next 6 ch-1 sps, repeat from † to † once; join with slip st to first sc, finish off.

CONTENTMENT

Find contentment as you while away the hours with this pretty pastel coverlet.
Because it's made in squares, it's a great take-along project for ball games or picnics.

Finished Size: 47^1/$_2$" x 63^1/$_2$" (120.5 cm x 161.5 cm)

MATERIALS
Worsted Weight Yarn:
Ecru - 25^1/$_2$ ounces, 1,675 yards
(720 grams, 1,531.5 meters)
Lavender - 7^1/$_2$ ounces, 490 yards
(210 grams, 448 meters)
Green - 5^1/$_2$ ounces, 360 yards
(160 grams, 329 meters)
Blue - 3^1/$_2$ ounces, 230 yards
(100 grams, 210.5 meters)
14" Double-ended hook, size K (6.5 mm) **or**
size needed for gauge
Standard crochet hook, size K (6.5 mm)
Yarn needle

GAUGE SWATCH: 5^1/$_4$" (13.25 cm) square
Work same as Square.

SQUARE (Make 108)

With double-ended hook, Ecru, and leaving an 8"
(20.5 cm) end for sewing, ch 8.
Row 1 (Right side): YO 3 times, working in top loop
of each ch *(Fig. 1)*, insert hook in second ch from
hook, YO and pull up a loop, insert hook in next ch,
YO and pull up a loop, ★ YO 3 times, (insert hook in
next ch, YO and pull up a loop) twice; repeat from ★
once **more**, YO 3 times, insert hook in last ch, YO
and pull up a loop, slide loops to opposite end of
hook: 20 loops.

Fig. 1

Note: Loop a short piece of yarn around any stitch
to mark Row 1 as **right** side.
Row 2: Turn; with Blue, make a slip knot on hook,

draw loop through first loop on hook *(Fig. 2a)*, ★ YO
and draw through 2 loops on hook (one loop of each
color) *(Fig. 2b)*; repeat from ★ across until one loop
remains on hook: 19 horizontal bars.

Fig. 2a

Fig. 2b

Row 3: Ch 1, do **not** turn; [insert hook in top loop of
first horizontal bar *(Fig. 3a)*, YO and pull up a loop
(Fig. 3b)], YO, insert hook in next horizontal bar, YO
and pull up a loop, ★ YO, (insert hook in next
horizontal bar, YO and pull up a loop) 4 times, YO,
insert hook in next horizontal bar, YO and pull up a
loop; repeat from ★ 2 times **more**, YO, (insert hook
in next horizontal bar, YO and pull up a loop) twice,
slide loops to opposite end of hook; cut Blue:
28 loops.

Fig. 3a

Fig. 3b

Carry Ecru **loosely** along edge of Square.
Row 4: Turn; with Ecru, YO and draw through first
loop on hook, (YO and draw through 2 loops on
hook) across until one loop remains on hook:
27 horizontal bars.

Continued on page 52.

Row 5: Ch 1, do **not** turn; insert hook in first horizontal bar, YO and pull up a loop, insert hook in next horizontal bar, YO and pull up a loop, YO, insert hook in next horizontal bar, YO and pull up a loop, ★ YO, (insert hook in next horizontal bar, YO and pull up a loop) 6 times, YO, insert hook in next horizontal bar, YO and pull up a loop; repeat from ★ 2 times **more**, YO, (insert hook in next horizontal bar, YO and pull up a loop) 3 times, slide loops to opposite end of hook: 36 loops.

Row 6: Turn; with Green, make a slip knot on hook, draw loop through first loop on hook, (YO and draw through 2 loops on hook) across until one loop remains on hook: 35 horizontal bars.

Row 7: Ch 1, do **not** turn; insert hook in first horizontal bar, YO and pull up a loop, (insert hook in next horizontal bar, YO and pull up a loop) twice, YO, insert hook in next horizontal bar, YO and pull up a loop, ★ YO, (insert hook in next horizontal bar, YO and pull up a loop) 8 times, YO, insert hook in next horizontal bar, YO and pull up a loop; repeat from ★ 2 times **more**, YO, (insert hook in next horizontal bar, YO and pull up a loop) 4 times, slide loops to opposite end of hook; cut Green: 44 loops.

Row 8: Repeat Row 4: 43 horizontal bars.

Row 9: Ch 1, do **not** turn; insert hook in first horizontal bar, YO and pull up a loop, (insert hook in next horizontal bar, YO and pull up a loop) 3 times, YO, insert hook in next horizontal bar, YO and pull up a loop, ★ YO, (insert hook in next horizontal bar, YO and pull up a loop) 10 times, YO, insert hook in next horizontal bar, YO and pull up a loop; repeat from ★ 2 times **more**, YO, (insert hook in next horizontal bar, YO and pull up a loop) 5 times, slide loops to opposite end of hook: 52 loops.

Row 10: With Lavender, repeat Row 6: 51 horizontal bars.

Row 11: Ch 1, do **not** turn; insert hook in first horizontal bar, YO and pull up a loop, (insert hook in next horizontal bar, YO and pull up a loop) 4 times, YO, insert hook in next horizontal bar, YO and pull up a loop, ★ YO, (insert hook in next horizontal bar, YO and pull up a loop) 12 times, YO, insert hook in next horizontal bar, YO and pull up a loop; repeat from ★ 2 times **more**, YO, (insert hook in next horizontal bar, YO and pull up a loop) 6 times, slide loops to opposite end of hook; cut Lavender: 60 loops.

Row 12: Repeat Row 4: 59 horizontal bars. Change to standard crochet hook.

Row 13: Ch 1, do **not** turn; 2 sc in first horizontal bar, sc in next 5 horizontal bars, ch 1, sc in next horizontal bar, ch 1, ★ sc in next 14 horizontal bars, ch 1, sc in next horizontal bar, ch 1; repeat from ★ 2 times **more**, sc in last 7 horizontal bars; finish off leaving a long end for sewing: 60 sc and 8 chs. Thread yarn needle with long end and sew end of rows together to form Square; secure end. Thread yarn needle with 8" (20.5 cm) end at beginning, weave through beginning chs to close center; secure end.

ASSEMBLY

With Ecru, whipstitch Squares together forming 9 vertical strips of 12 Squares each; then whipstitch strips together in same manner.

Whipstitch Squares together as follows: Holding two Squares with **wrong** sides together, working through **both** loops of each stitch on **both** pieces, and beginning in center sc of first corner, sew through both pieces once to secure the beginning of the seam, leaving an ample yarn end to weave in later. Insert the needle from **front** to **back** through first stitch and pull yarn through (*Fig. 21b, page 142*), ★ insert the needle from **front** to **back** through next stitch and pull yarn through; repeat from ★ across, ending in center sc of next corner.

EDGING

With **right** side facing, standard crochet hook, and working in Back Loops Only (*Fig. 15, page 140*), join Ecru with sc in any corner sc (*see Joining With Sc, page 140*); 2 sc in same st, ★ † sc in next ch and in next 14 sc, (hdc in next ch and in same st as joining on same Square, dc in next joining, hdc in same st as joining on next Square and in next ch, sc in next 14 sc) across to ch **before** next corner sc, sc in next ch †, 3 sc in corner sc; repeat from ★ 2 times **more**, then repeat from † to † once; join with slip st to first sc, finish off.

REMINISCENCE

An afternoon spent reminiscing warms the heart and gives the soul a fresh perspective. With dainty picot edging, this gorgeous comforter is an elegant gift that looks delightful in any décor.

Finished Size: 46" x 60" (117 cm x 152.5 cm)

MATERIALS
Worsted Weight Yarn:
  43 ounces, 2,820 yards
    (1,220 grams, 2578.5 meters)
Crochet hook, size H (5 mm) **or** size needed
  for gauge

GAUGE: In pattern,
  4 repeats = 3" (7.5 cm); 8 rows = 4" (10 cm)

Gauge Swatch: $3^1/2$"w x 4"h (9 cm x 10 cm)
Ch 20 **loosely**.
Work same as Afghan Body for 8 rows.
Finish off.

STITCH GUIDE

PICOT
Ch 3, sc in third ch from hook.

AFGHAN BODY
Ch 196 **loosely**, place markers in third and fourth chs from hook.
Row 1 (Right side): Dc in sixth ch and in seventh ch from hook **(3 skipped chs count as first dc)**, ch 1, working in **front** of dc just made *(Fig. 18, page 141)*, dc in second marked ch, remove marker, ★ skip next 2 chs, dc in next 2 chs, ch 1, working in **front** of dc just made, dc in first skipped ch; repeat from ★ across to last ch, dc in last ch: 48 3-dc groups.
Row 2: Ch 3 **(counts as first dc)**, turn; ★ skip next dc and next ch-1 sp, dc in next 2 dc, ch 1, working in **front** of dc just made, dc in skipped dc; repeat from ★ across to last dc, dc in last dc.
Repeat Row 2 for pattern until Afghan Body measures approximately 50" (127 cm) from beginning ch, ending by working a **wrong** side row; do **not** finish off.

EDGING
Rnd 1: Ch 1, turn; 3 sc in first dc, work 186 sc evenly spaced across to last dc, 3 sc in last dc; work 270 sc evenly spaced across end of rows; working in free loops of beginning ch *(Fig. 17b, page 141)*, 3 sc in first ch, work 186 sc evenly spaced across to marked ch, 3 sc in marked ch; work 270 sc evenly spaced across end of rows; join with slip st to first sc: 924 sc.
Rnd 2: Do **not** turn; slip st in next sc, ch 5 **(counts as first dc plus ch 2, now and throughout)**, skip next 2 sc, ★ (dc in next sc, ch 2, skip next 2 sc) across to next corner sc, (dc, ch 2) twice in corner sc, skip next 2 sc; repeat from ★ 2 times **more**, (dc in next sc, ch 2, skip next 2 sc) across, dc in same st as first dc, ch 1, sc in first dc to form last ch-2 sp: 312 ch-2 sps.
Rnd 3: Ch 5, dc in last ch-2 sp made, ch 2, skip next ch-2 sp, (dc, work Picot, dc, ch 2) twice in next ch-2 sp, skip next ch-2 sp, † (dc, ch 2) twice in next ch-2 sp, skip next ch-2 sp, (dc, work Picot, dc, ch 2) twice in next ch-2 sp, skip next ch-2 sp †; repeat from † to † across to next corner ch-2 sp, ★ (dc, ch 2) 4 times in corner ch-2 sp, skip next ch-2 sp, (dc, work Picot, dc, ch 2) twice in next ch-2 sp, skip next ch-2 sp, repeat from † to † across to next corner ch-2 sp; repeat from ★ 2 times **more**, (dc, ch 2, dc) in same sp as first dc, ch 1, sc in first dc to form last ch-2 sp.
Rnd 4: Ch 5, (dc, work Picot, dc) in next ch-2 sp, ch 2, skip next ch-2 sp and next Picot, (dc, ch 2) twice in next ch-2 sp, skip next Picot and next ch-2 sp, † (dc, work Picot, dc, ch 2) twice in next ch-2 sp, skip next ch-2 sp and next Picot, (dc, ch 2) twice in next ch-2 sp, skip next Picot and next ch-2 sp †; repeat from † to † across to next corner group, ★ [(dc, work Picot, dc) in next ch-2 sp, ch 2] 3 times, skip next ch-2 sp and next Picot, (dc, ch 2) twice in next ch-2 sp, skip next Picot and next ch-2 sp, repeat from † to † across to next corner group; repeat from ★ 2 times **more**, (dc, work Picot, dc) in next ch-2 sp, ch 2, dc in same sp as first dc, work Picot; join with slip st to first dc.

Rnd 5: (Slip st, ch 5, dc) in first ch-2 sp, ch 2, skip next Picot and next ch-2 sp, (dc, work Picot, dc, ch 2) twice in next ch-2 sp, skip next ch-2 sp and next Picot, † (dc, ch 2) twice in next ch-2 sp, skip next Picot and next ch-2 sp, (dc, work Picot, dc, ch 2) twice in next ch-2 sp, skip next ch-2 sp and next Picot †; repeat from † to † across to within one ch-2 sp of next corner Picot, ★ (dc, ch 2) 4 times in next ch-2 sp, skip corner Picot, (dc, ch 2) 4 times in next ch-2 sp, skip next Picot and next ch-2 sp, (dc, work Picot, dc, ch 2) twice in next ch-2 sp, skip next ch-2 sp and next Picot, repeat from † to † across to within one ch-2 sp of next corner Picot; repeat from ★ 2 times **more**, (dc, ch 2) 4 times in next ch-2 sp, skip corner Picot, (dc, ch 2, dc) in same sp as first dc, ch 1, sc in first dc to form last ch-2 sp.

Continued on page 56.

Rnd 6: Ch 5, (dc, work Picot, dc) in last ch-2 sp made, ch 2, skip next 2 ch-2 sps and next Picot, (dc, ch 2) twice in next ch-2 sp, † skip next Picot and next ch-2 sp, (dc, work Picot, dc, ch 2) twice in next ch-2 sp, skip next ch-2 sp and next Picot, (dc, ch 2) twice in next ch-2 sp †; repeat from † to † across to within 4 ch-2 sps of next corner ch-2 sp, ★ ♥ skip next Picot and next 2 ch-2 sps, (dc, work Picot, dc, ch 2) twice in next ch-2 sp, skip next ch-2 sp, (dc, ch 2) twice in corner ch-2 sp, skip next ch-2 sp ♥, (dc, work Picot, dc, ch 2) twice in next ch-2 sp, skip next 2 ch-2 sps and next Picot, (dc, ch 2) twice in next ch-2 sp, repeat from † to † across to within 4 ch-2 sps of next corner ch-2 sp; repeat from ★ 2 times **more**, then repeat from ♥ to ♥ once, dc in same sp as first dc, work Picot; join with slip st to first dc.

Rnd 7: Slip st in first ch-2 sp, ch 5, skip next Picot and next ch-2 sp, (dc, work Picot, dc, ch 2) twice in next ch-2 sp, skip next ch-2 sp and next Picot, ★ (dc, ch 2) twice in next ch-2 sp, skip next Picot and next ch-2 sp, (dc, work Picot, dc, ch 2) twice in next ch-2 sp, skip next ch-2 sp and next Picot; repeat from ★ around, dc in same sp as first dc, ch 1, sc in first dc to form last ch-2 sp.

Rnd 8: Slip st in last ch-2 sp made, ch 9, skip next ch-2 sp and next Picot, slip st in next ch-2 sp, ch 9, skip next Picot and next ch-2 sp, ★ slip st in next ch-2 sp, ch 9, skip next ch-2 sp and next Picot, slip st in next ch-2 sp, ch 9, skip next Picot and next ch-2 sp; repeat from ★ around; join with slip st to first slip st.

Rnds 9 and 10: Ch 11, (slip st in next slip st, ch 11) around; join with slip st to first slip st.
Finish off.

IVY COTTAGE

A tiny woodland cottage covered in ivy is a veritable wonderland for the imagination.
Leaf and popcorn stitches give these climbing vines a charming dimensional texture.

Finished Size: 46" x 70" (117 cm x 178 cm)

MATERIALS
Worsted Weight Yarn:
  Green - 43 ounces, 2,430 yards
    (1,220 grams, 2,222 meters)
  Off-White - 7 ounces, 395 yards
    (200 grams, 361 meters)
Crochet hook, size J (6 mm) **or** size needed
  for gauge
Split ring markers (optional)

GAUGE: 9 dc and 5 rows = 3" (7.5 cm)
    Each Vine Panel = 5⅝" (14.25 cm) wide
    Each Berry Panel = 6⅜" (16.25 cm) wide

Gauge Swatch: 5⅝"w x 3"h (14.25 cm x 7.5 cm)
Work same as Vine Panel through Row 5.

STITCH GUIDE

Note: See Stitch Guide for Post sts, page 18.
LEAF
YO 7 times, working in **front** of previous rows, insert hook in marked st indicated, YO and pull up a loop, remove marker, (YO and draw through 2 loops on hook) 6 times (3 loops on hook), YO 5 times, insert hook in **side** two legs of Leaf *(Fig. 16, page 141)*, YO and pull up a loop, (YO and draw through 2 loops on hook) 5 times (4 loops on hook), YO 5 times, insert hook in same st, YO and pull up a loop, (YO and draw through 2 loops on hook) 9 times.
BACK POPCORN
5 Dc in st indicated, drop loop from hook, insert hook from **back** to **front** in first dc of 5-dc group, hook dropped loop and draw through st *(Fig. 13, page 139)*.
FRONT POPCORN
5 Dc in st indicated, drop loop from hook, insert hook from **front** to **back** in first dc of 5-dc group, hook dropped loop and draw through st *(Fig. 13, page 139)*.

VINE PANEL (Make 4)

With Green, ch 19 **loosely**.

Row 1 (Right side): Dc in back ridge of fourth ch from hook (*Fig. 2b, page 137*) and each ch across **(3 skipped chs count as first dc, now and throughout)**: 17 dc.

Row 2: Ch 3 **(counts as first dc, now and throughout)**, turn; dc in next 8 dc, skip next dc, work BPtr around next dc, place marker in BPtr just made for Leaf placement (*see Markers, page 140*), dc in dc just worked around and in last 6 dc: 16 dc and one BPtr.

Row 3: Ch 3, turn; dc in next 6 dc, ch 1, work FPtr around next BPtr, skip BPtr just worked around and next dc, dc in last 8 dc: 15 dc, one FPtr, and one ch-1 sp.

Row 4: Ch 3, turn; dc in next 6 sts, skip next dc, work BPtr around next FPtr, dc in FPtr just worked around, dc in next ch-1 sp and in last 7 dc: 16 dc and one BPtr.

Row 5: Ch 3, turn; dc in next 8 dc, work FPtr around next BPtr, skip BPtr just worked around, dc in last 7 dc: 16 dc and one FPtr.

Row 6: Ch 3, turn; dc in next 6 dc, work BPtr around next FPtr, place marker in BPtr just made for Leaf placement, skip FPtr just worked around, dc in last 9 dc.

Row 7: Ch 3, turn; dc in next 3 dc, work Leaf in marked BPtr 5 rows **below**, skip next dc from last dc made, dc in next 3 dc, skip next dc, work FPtr around next BPtr, ch 1, skip BPtr just worked around, dc in last 7 dc: 14 dc, one FPtr, one Leaf, and one ch-1 sp.

Row 8: Ch 3, turn; dc in next 6 dc, dc in next ch-1 sp and in next FPtr, work BPtr around FPtr just worked into, skip next dc, dc in last 7 sts: 16 dc and one BPtr.

Row 9: Ch 3, turn; dc in next 5 dc, skip next dc, work FPtr around next BPtr, dc in BPtr just worked around and in last 9 dc.

Row 10: Ch 3, turn; dc in next 8 dc, skip next dc, work BPtr around next FPtr, place marker in BPtr just made for Leaf placement, dc in FPtr just worked around and in last 6 dc.

Row 11: Ch 3, turn; dc in next 6 dc, ch 1, work FPtr around next BPtr, skip BPtr just worked around and next dc, dc in next 3 dc, work Leaf in marked BPtr 5 rows **below**, skip next dc from last dc made, dc in last 4 dc: 14 dc, one FPtr, one Leaf, and one ch-1 sp.

Rows 12-110: Repeat Rows 4-11, 12 times; then repeat Rows 4-6 once **more**: 16 dc and one BPtr.

Row 111: Ch 3, turn; dc in next 3 dc, work Leaf in marked BPtr 5 rows **below**, skip next dc from last dc made, dc in next 4 dc, ch 1, skip next BPtr, dc in last 7 dc: 15 dc, one Leaf, and one ch-1 sp.

Row 112: Ch 3, turn; dc in next 6 dc, dc in next ch-1 sp and in each st across.

Rows 113 and 114: Ch 3, turn; dc in next dc and in each dc across.

Row 115: Ch 3, turn; dc in next 11 dc, work Leaf in marked BPtr 5 rows **below**, skip next dc from last dc made, dc in last 4 dc.

Rows 116 and 117: Ch 3, turn; dc in next dc and in each st across.

Finish off.

BERRY PANEL (Make 3)

With Green, ch 21 **loosely**.

Row 1: Dc in back ridge of fourth ch from hook and each ch across: 19 dc.

Row 2 (Right side): Ch 3, turn; dc in next dc and in each dc across.

Row 3: Ch 3, turn; dc in next 9 dc, skip next dc, work BPtr around next dc, dc in dc just worked around and in last 7 dc: 18 dc and one BPtr.

Row 4: Ch 3, turn; dc in next 5 dc, skip next dc, work FPtr around next dc, dc in dc just worked around and in next BPtr, work FPtr around BPtr just worked into, skip next dc, dc in last 9 dc: 17 dc and 2 FPtr.

Row 5: Ch 3, turn; dc in next 7 dc, skip next dc, work BPtr around next FPtr, dc in FPtr just worked around, place marker in last dc made for Leaf placement, dc in next dc, work Back Popcorn in next dc, work BPtr around next FPtr, skip FPtr just worked around, work Back Popcorn in next dc, dc in last 5 dc: 15 dc, 2 BPtr, and 2 Back Popcorns.

Row 6: Ch 3, turn; dc in next 4 dc, work Front Popcorn in next Back Popcorn, dc in next 3 sts, ch 1, skip next dc, work FPtr around next BPtr, skip BPtr just worked around, dc in last 8 dc: 16 dc, one FPtr, one Front Popcorn, and one ch-1 sp.

Row 7: Ch 3, turn; dc in next 7 sts, work BPtr around next FPtr, skip FPtr just worked around, dc in next ch-1 sp and in last 9 sts.

Row 8: Ch 3, turn; dc in next 8 dc, skip next dc, work FPtr around next BPtr, dc in BPtr just worked around and in next dc, work FPtr around dc just worked into, skip next dc, dc in last 6 dc: 17 dc and 2 FPtr.

Row 9: Ch 3, turn; dc in next 3 dc, work Back Popcorn in next dc, skip next dc, work BPtr around next FPtr, work Back Popcorn in FPtr just worked around, dc in next 3 sts, place marker in last dc made for Leaf placement, work BPtr around FPtr just worked into, skip next dc, dc in last 8 dc: 15 dc, 2 BPtr, and 2 Back Popcorns.

Row 10: Ch 3, turn; dc in next 3 dc, work Leaf in marked dc 5 rows **below**, skip next dc from last dc made, dc in next 2 dc, skip next dc, work FPtr around next BPtr, dc in BPtr just worked around, ch 1, skip next dc, dc in next 3 sts, work Front Popcorn in next BPtr, dc in last 5 sts: 15 dc, one FPtr, one Leaf, one Front Popcorn, and one ch-1 sp.

Row 11: Ch 3, turn; dc in next 8 sts and in next ch-1 sp, skip next dc, work BPtr around next FPtr, dc in FPtr just worked around and in last 7 sts.

Rows 12 and 13: Repeat Rows 4 and 5: 15 dc, 2 BPtr, and 2 Back Popcorns.

Row 14: Ch 3, turn; dc in next 4 dc, work Front Popcorn in next Back Popcorn, dc in next 3 sts, ch 1, skip next dc, work FPtr around next BPtr, skip BPtr just worked around, dc in next 3 dc, work Leaf in marked dc 5 rows **below**, skip next dc from last dc made, dc in last 4 dc: 15 dc, one FPtr, one Leaf, one Front Popcorn, and one ch-1 sp.

Rows 15-110: Repeat Rows 7-14, 12 times: 15 dc, one FPtr, one Leaf, one Front Popcorn, and one ch-1 sp.

Row 111: Ch 3, turn; dc in next 6 sts, skip next dc, work BPtr around next FPtr, dc in FPtr just worked around, dc in next ch-1 sp and in last 9 sts: 18 dc and one BPtr.

Row 112: Ch 3, turn; dc in next 11 sts, work FPtr around BPtr just worked into, skip next dc, dc in last 6 dc: 18 dc and one FPtr.

Row 113: Ch 3, turn; dc in next 3 dc, work Back Popcorn in next dc, skip next dc, work BPtr around next FPtr, work Back Popcorn in FPtr just worked around, dc in last 12 dc: 16 dc, one BPtr, and 2 Back Popcorns.

Row 114: Ch 3, turn; dc in next 3 dc, work Leaf in marked dc 5 rows **below**, skip next dc from last dc made, dc in next 8 sts, work Front Popcorn in next BPtr, dc in last 5 sts: 17 dc, one Leaf, and one Front Popcorn.

Rows 115-117: Ch 3, turn; dc in next dc and in each st across.
Finish off.

FINISHING
RIGHT SIDE TRIM
With **right** side facing and working around post of dc at end of rows along right side, join Off-White with slip st in last row of any Panel; ch 1, working from **left** to **right**, work reverse sc in same row *(Figs. 14a-d, page 140)*, work 2 reverse sc in next row, work (reverse sc in next row, 2 reverse sc in next row) across to last row, (work reverse sc, slip st) in last row; finish off.
Repeat for each Panel.

LEFT SIDE TRIM AND JOINING
Alternating Panels and beginning and ending with a Vine Panel, join Panels as follows:
Row 1: With **right** side facing and working around post of dc at end of rows along left side, join Off-White with slip st in first row of Panel; ch 1, working from **left** to **right**, work reverse sc in same row, work 2 reverse sc in next row, work (reverse sc in next row, 2 reverse sc in next row) across to last row, (work reverse sc, slip st) in last row; do **not** finish off.
Row 2: Ch 5, do **not** turn; working in end of rows **around** reverse sc, skip next row, slip st in next row, ★ ch 5, skip next row, slip st in next row; repeat from ★ across.
Row 3 (Joining row): Ch 2, hold **previous Panel** and **new Panel** with **right** sides facing you and bottom edges together; working in end of rows **around** reverse sc of **new Panel**, slip st in Row 1, ch 2, ★ slip st in next ch-5 sp on **previous Panel**, ch 2, skip next row on **new Panel**, slip st in next row, ch 2; repeat from ★ across, slip st in end of Row 117 on **previous Panel**; finish off.
Join remaining Panels in same manner.

LAST PANEL LEFT SIDE TRIM
Row 1: With **right** side facing and working around post of dc at end of rows along left side of last joined Panel, join Off-White with slip st in first row; ch 1, working from **left** to **right**, work reverse sc in same row, work 2 reverse sc in next row, work (reverse sc in next row, 2 reverse sc in next row) across to last row, (work reverse sc, slip st) in last row; finish off.

EDGING
With **right** side facing, join Off-White with slip st in any corner st; ch 1, working from **left** to **right**, work reverse sc evenly around; join with slip st to first st, finish off.

POOL PARTY

A festive pool party is a refreshing diversion on a balmy summer afternoon.
Bright variegated yarn gives this cool cover-up a touch of spunk.

Finished Size: 47" x 62" (119.5 cm x 157.5 cm)

MATERIALS
Worsted Weight Yarn:
Blue - 31 ounces, 1,870 yards
(880 grams, 1,710 meters)
Variegated - 14^1/$_2$ ounces, 875 yards
(410 grams, 800 meters)
Green - 14 ounces, 845 yards
(400 grams, 772.5 meters)
Crochet hook, size I (5.5 mm) **or** size needed
for gauge

GAUGE: In pattern, 16 sc and 12 rows = 4" (10 cm)

Gauge Swatch: 4^1/$_4$"w x 4"h (10.75 cm x 10 cm)
With Blue, ch 18 **loosely**.
Work same as Afghan for 12 rows.

Note: Each row is worked across length of Afghan.
When joining yarn and finishing off, leave a 9"
(23 cm) end to be worked into fringe.

STITCH GUIDE

CLUSTER (uses next 3 dc)
★ YO, insert hook in **next** dc, YO and pull up a
loop, YO and draw through 2 loops on hook;
repeat from ★ 2 times **more**, YO and draw
through all 4 loops on hook (*Figs. 11a & b,
page 139*).

AFGHAN
With Blue, ch 249 **loosely**.
Row 1 (Wrong side): Sc in back ridge of second ch
from hook (*Fig. 2b, page 137*) and in each ch across:
248 sc.
Note: Loop a short piece of yarn around the **back** of
any stitch on Row 1 to mark **right** side.

Rows 2-4: Ch 1, turn; sc in each sc across; at end of
Row 4, finish off.
Row 5: With **wrong** side facing, join Variegated with
dc in first sc (*see Joining With Dc, page 140*); skip
next sc, 3 dc in next sc, (skip next 2 sc, 3 dc in next
sc) across to last 2 sc, skip next sc, dc in last sc:
82 3-dc groups.
Row 6: Ch 4 (**counts as first dc plus ch 1, now and
throughout**), turn; work Cluster, (ch 2, work
Cluster) across to last dc, ch 1, dc in last dc;
finish off: 82 Clusters and 83 sps.
Row 7: With **wrong** side facing, join Blue with sc in
first dc (*see Joining With Sc, page 140*); sc in next
ch-1 sp and in next Cluster, (2 sc in next ch-2 sp, sc
in next Cluster) across to last ch-1 sp, sc in last
ch-1 sp and in last dc: 248 sc.
Rows 8-10: Ch 1, turn; sc in each sc across; at end of
Row 10, finish off.
Row 11: With **wrong** side facing, join Green with dc
in first sc; skip next sc, 3 dc in next sc, (skip next
2 sc, 3 dc in next sc) across to last 2 sc, skip next sc,
dc in last sc: 82 3-dc groups.
Row 12: Ch 4, turn; work Cluster, (ch 2, work
Cluster) across to last dc, ch 1, dc in last dc;
finish off: 82 Clusters and 83 sps.
Row 13: With **wrong** side facing, join Blue with sc in
first dc; sc in next ch-1 sp and in next Cluster, (2 sc
in next ch-2 sp, sc in next Cluster) across to last
ch-1 sp, sc in last ch-1 sp and in last dc: 248 sc.
Repeat Rows 2-13 for pattern, until Afghan
measures approximately 47" (119.5 cm) from
beginning ch, ending by working Row 10.

INDEPENDENCE DAY

Like the first flag, lovingly created by Betsy Ross, this crocheted comforter symbolizes the spirit of this great country. The all-American throw is just right for displaying with pride.

Finished Size: 33¹/₂" x 58" (85 cm x 147.5 cm)

MATERIALS
Worsted Weight Yarn:
Red - 11 ounces, 625 yards
(310 grams, 571.5 meters)
Ecru - 10 ounces, 565 yards
(280 grams, 516.5 meters)
Blue - 5 ounces, 285 yards
(140 grams, 260.5 meters)
Crochet hooks, sizes F (3.75 mm) **and** I (5.5 mm)
or sizes needed for gauge
Yarn needle

GAUGE: With larger size hook, in pattern,
4 dc-groups = 4" (10 cm);
7 rows = 4¹/₂" (11.5 cm)

Gauge Swatch: 4¹/₂" (11.5 cm) square
With Red and larger size hook, ch 16.
Work same as Stripes for 7 rows.
Finish off.

Note: Each row is worked across length of Afghan.

STRIPES
With Red and larger size hook, ch 175.
Row 1 (Right side): Working in back ridges of beginning ch *(Fig. 2b, page 137)*, 3 dc in fifth ch from hook, (skip next 2 chs, 3 dc in next ch) across to last 2 chs, skip next ch, dc in last ch: 57 dc-groups.
Note: Loop a short piece of yarn around any stitch to mark Row 1 as **right** side.
Row 2: Ch 3 **(counts as first dc, now and throughout)**, turn; 2 dc in same st, (skip next 2 dc, 3 dc in next dc) across to last 3 dc, skip next 2 dc, 2 dc in last dc, dc in next ch: 58 dc-groups.
Row 3: Ch 3, turn; skip next dc, 3 dc in next dc, (skip next 2 dc, 3 dc in next dc) across to last 3 dc, skip next 2 dc, dc in last dc: 57 dc-groups.
Row 4: Ch 3, turn; 2 dc in same st, (skip next 2 dc, 3 dc in next dc) across to last 4 dc, skip next 2 dc, 2 dc in last dc, dc in next dc; finish off: 58 dc-groups.
Row 5: With **right** side facing, join Ecru with dc in first dc *(see Joining With Dc, page 140)*; skip next dc, 3 dc in next dc, (skip next 2 dc, 3 dc in next dc) across to last 3 dc, skip next 2 dc, dc in last dc: 57 dc-groups.

Rows 6-8: Repeat Rows 2-4.
Row 9: With Red, repeat Row 5.
Rows 10-24: Repeat Rows 2-9 once, then repeat Rows 2-8 once **more**.
Row 25: With **right** side facing, join Red with dc in first dc; skip next dc, (3 dc in next dc, skip next 2 dc) 35 times, dc in next dc, leave remaining 22 dc-groups unworked: 35 dc-groups.
Row 26: Ch 3, turn; 2 dc in same st, (skip next 2 dc, 3 dc in next dc) across to last 4 dc, skip next 2 dc, 2 dc in next dc, dc in last dc: 36 dc-groups.
Row 27: Ch 3, turn; skip next dc, 3 dc in next dc, (skip next 2 dc, 3 dc in next dc) across to last 3 dc, skip next 2 dc, dc in last dc: 35 dc-groups.
Row 28: Ch 3, turn; 2 dc in same st, (skip next 2 dc, 3 dc in next dc) across to last 4 dc, skip next 2 dc, 2 dc in next dc, dc in last dc; finish off: 36 dc-groups.
Row 29: With **right** side facing, join Ecru with dc in first dc; skip next dc, 3 dc in next dc, (skip next 2 dc, 3 dc in next dc) across to last 3 dc, skip next 2 dc, dc in last dc: 35 dc-groups.
Rows 30-32: Repeat Rows 26-28.
Row 33: With Red, repeat Row 29.
Rows 34-52: Repeat Rows 26-33 twice, then repeat Rows 26-28 once **more**.

BLUE FIELD
Row 1: With **right** side facing and larger size hook, join Blue with slip st in top of last dc on Row 25 of Stripes; 2 dc in same dc on Row 24 as last dc, (skip next 2 dc, 3 dc in next dc) across to last 3 dc, skip next 2 dc, dc in last dc: 22 dc-groups.
Row 2: Ch 3, turn; 2 dc in same st, skip next 2 dc, (3 dc in next dc, skip next 2 dc) across, slip st in top of first dc on next row of Stripes.
Row 3: Ch 2, slip st in top of last dc on next row of Stripes, turn; dc in slip st at base of beginning ch-2, (skip next 2 dc, 3 dc in next dc) across to last 3 dc, skip next 2 dc, dc in last dc.
Rows 4-28: Repeat Rows 2 and 3, 12 times; then repeat Row 2 once **more**.
Finish off.

STAR (Make 13)
Rnd 1 (Right side): With Ecru and smaller size hook, ch 2, 5 sc in second ch from hook; join with slip st to first sc.

Rnd 2: Ch 1, 3 sc in same st and in each sc around; join with slip st to first sc: 15 sc.

Rnd 3: Ch 1, sc in same st, ch 6 **loosely**, working in back ridge of chs, slip st in second ch from hook, sc in next ch, hdc in next ch, dc in next ch, tr in last ch, skip next 2 sc, ★ sc in next sc, ch 6 **loosely**, slip st in second ch from hook, sc in next ch, hdc in next ch, dc in next ch, tr in last ch, skip next 2 sc; repeat from ★ 3 times **more**; join with slip st to first sc, finish off leaving a long end for sewing.

Using photo as a guide for placement, sew Stars on Blue Field.

SETTING SAIL

Sail off to the high seas with this nautical afghan featuring granny-square ships with jaunty red sails. Rings of golden stitches make delightful suns.

Finished Size: 51" x 66" (129.5 cm x 167.5 cm)

MATERIALS
Worsted Weight Yarn:
White - 16 ounces, 1,050 yards
(450 grams, 960 meters)
Lt Blue - 13^1/$_2$ ounces, 885 yards
(380 grams, 809 meters)
Red - 8^1/$_2$ ounces, 555 yards
(240 grams, 507.5 meters)
Blue - 6^1/$_2$ ounces, 425 yards
(180 grams, 388.5 meters)
Gold - 20 yards (18.5 meters)
Crochet hook, size I (5.5 mm) **or** size needed
for gauge
Yarn needle

GAUGE SWATCH: 3" (7.5 cm) square
Work same as Square A.

Referring to the Key, page 66, make the number of Squares specified in the colors indicated.

SQUARE A
With color indicated, ch 4; join with slip st to form a ring.
Rnd 1 (Right side): Ch 3 **(counts as first dc, now and throughout)**, 2 dc in ring, (ch 2, 3 dc in ring) 3 times, hdc in first dc to form last ch-2 sp: 12 dc and 4 ch-2 sps.
Note: Loop a short piece of yarn around any stitch to mark Rnd 1 as **right** side.
Rnd 2: Ch 3, (2 dc, ch 2, 3 dc) in last ch-2 sp made, ch 1, ★ (3 dc, ch 2, 3 dc) in next ch-2 sp, ch 1; repeat from ★ 2 times **more**; join with slip st to first dc, finish off: 24 dc and 8 sps.

SQUARE B
With first color indicated, ch 4; join with slip st to form a ring.
Rnd 1 (Right side): Ch 5 **(counts as first dc plus ch 2)**, 3 dc in ring, cut first color, with second color indicated, YO and draw through, ch 1, (3 dc, ch 2, 3 dc) in ring, cut second color, with first color, YO and draw through, ch 1, 2 dc in ring; join with slip st to first dc: 12 dc and 4 ch-2 sps.
Note: Mark Rnd 1 as **right** side.

Rnd 2: Slip st in first ch-2 sp, ch 3, (2 dc, ch 2, 3 dc) in same sp, ch 1, 3 dc in next ch-2 sp, cut first color, with second color, YO and draw through, ch 1, 3 dc in same sp, ch 1, (3 dc, ch 2, 3 dc) in next ch-2 sp, ch 1, 3 dc in next ch-2 sp, cut second color, with first color, YO and draw through, ch 1, 3 dc in same sp, ch 1; join with slip st to first dc, finish off: 24 dc and 8 sps.

SQUARE C
With Gold, ch 4; join with slip st to form a ring.
Rnd 1 (Right side): Ch 1, 12 sc in ring; join with slip st to first sc, finish off.
Note: Mark Rnd 1 as **right** side.
Rnd 2: With **right** side facing, join White with slip st in any sc; ch 2, hdc in next sc, 2 hdc in next sc, (hdc in next 2 sc, 2 hdc in next sc) around; join with slip st to top of beginning ch-2: 16 sts.
Rnd 3: Ch 3, 2 dc in same st, ch 2, 3 dc in next hdc, ch 1, skip next 2 hdc, ★ 3 dc in next hdc, ch 2, 3 dc in next hdc, ch 1, skip next 2 hdc; repeat from ★ 2 times **more**; join with slip st to first dc, finish off: 24 dc and 8 sps.

ASSEMBLY
With matching color, using Placement Diagram as a guide and working through inside loops only, whipstitch Squares together forming 16 vertical strips of 21 Squares each *(Fig. 21a, page 142)*; then whipstitch strips together in same manner.

EDGING
Rnd 1: With **right** side facing, join Red with sc in any corner ch-2 sp *(see Joining With Sc, page 140)*; sc in same sp, sc evenly around entire Afghan working 3 sc in each corner ch-2 sp, sc in same sp as first sc; join with slip st to first sc.
Rnd 2: Ch 1, 2 sc in same st, sc in each sc across to center sc of next corner 3-sc group, ★ 3 sc in center sc, sc in each sc across to center sc of next corner 3-sc group; repeat from ★ 2 times **more**, sc in same st as first sc; join with slip st to first sc, finish off.

Rnd 3: With **right** side facing, join White with sc in same st as joining; sc in same st and in each sc across to center sc of next corner 3-sc group, ★ 3 sc in center sc, sc in each sc across to center sc of next corner 3-sc group; repeat from ★ 2 times **more**, sc in same st as first sc; join with slip st to first sc.

Rnd 4: Ch 1, 2 sc in same st, sc in each sc across to center sc of next corner 3-sc group, ★ 3 sc in center sc, sc in each sc across to center sc of next corner 3-sc group; repeat from ★ 2 times **more**, sc in same st as first sc; join with slip st to first sc, finish off.

Rnds 5 and 6: With Blue, repeat Rnds 3 and 4.

KEY

Square A
- ☐ - Lt Blue (Make 124)
- ☐ - White (Make 60)
- ■ - Blue (Make 24)
- ■ - Red (Make 20)

Square B
- ◿ - White & Red (Make 72)
- ◿ - White & Blue (Make 24)

Square C
- ⊙ - Gold & White (Make 12)

PLACEMENT DIAGRAM

SEASIDE TREASURE

With an inviting style and a memorable design, this appealing afghan is truly a seaside treasure. The striking squares are joined as you go for no-sew convenience.

Finished Size: 45" x 60" (114.5 cm x 152.5 cm)

MATERIALS
Worsted Weight Yarn:
  31¹/₂ ounces, 1,780 yards
    (890 grams, 1,627.5 meters)
  Crochet hook, size J (6 mm) **or** size needed
    for gauge

GAUGE: Each Square = 7¹/₂" (19 cm)

Gauge Swatch: 3" (7.5 cm) diameter
Work same as Square through Rnd 2.

STITCH GUIDE

2-DC CLUSTER (uses one st or sp)
★ YO, insert hook in st or sp indicated, YO and pull up a loop, YO and draw through 2 loops on hook; repeat from ★ once **more**, YO and draw through all 3 loops on hook (*Figs. 10a & b, page 139*).

3-DC CLUSTER (uses one ch-2 sp)
★ YO, insert hook in ch-2 sp indicated, YO and pull up a loop, YO and draw through 2 loops on hook; repeat from ★ 2 times **more**, YO and draw through all 4 loops on hook (*Figs. 10a & b, page 139*).

FIRST SQUARE

Ch 5; join with slip st to form a ring.

Rnd 1 (Right side): Ch 1, 12 sc in ring; join with slip st to first sc.

Note: Loop a short piece of yarn around any stitch to mark Rnd 1 as **right** side.

Rnd 2: Ch 2, dc in same st, (ch 3, work 2-dc Cluster in next sc) around, ch 1, hdc in first dc to form last ch-3 sp: 12 ch-3 sps.

Rnd 3: Ch 1, sc in last ch-3 sp made, (ch 4, sc in next ch-3 sp) around, ch 2, hdc in first sc to form last ch-4 sp.

Rnd 4: Ch 1, 2 sc in last ch-4 sp made, (2 sc, ch 2, 2 sc) in next ch-4 sp and in each ch-4 sp around, 2 sc in same sp as first sc, hdc in first sc to form last ch-2 sp.

Rnd 5: Ch 2, work 2-dc Cluster in last ch-2 sp made, ch 4, (sc in next ch-2 sp, ch 4) twice, ★ work (3-dc Cluster, ch 5, 3-dc Cluster) in next ch-2 sp, ch 4, (sc in next ch-2 sp, ch 4) twice; repeat from ★ 2 times **more**, work 3-dc Cluster in same sp as first 2-dc Cluster, ch 2, dc in top of 2-dc Cluster to form last ch-5 sp: 16 sps.

Rnd 6: Ch 4 **(counts as first tr)**, 3 dc in last ch-5 sp made, 4 dc in each of next 3 ch-4 sps, ★ (3 dc, tr, ch 3, tr, 3 dc) in next ch-5 sp, 4 dc in each of next 3 ch-4 sps; repeat from ★ 2 times **more**, (3 dc, tr) in same sp as first tr, ch 1, hdc in first tr to form last ch-3 sp: 80 sts and 4 ch-3 sps.

Rnd 7: Ch 1, sc in last ch-3 sp made, ch 5, skip next 2 sts, (sc in next dc, ch 5, skip next 2 sts) 6 times, ★ (sc, ch 5) twice in next corner ch-3 sp, skip next 2 sts, (sc in next dc, ch 5, skip next 2 sts) 6 times; repeat from ★ 2 times **more**, sc in same sp as first sc, ch 5; join with slip st to first sc, finish off: 32 ch-5 sps.

ADDITIONAL SQUARES

The method used to connect the Squares is a no-sew joining also know as "join-as-you-go." After the First Square is made, each remaining Square is worked through Rnd 6, then crocheted together as Rnd 7 is worked across the last side(s), working One Side or Two Side Joining. Holding Squares with **wrong** sides together, work slip st into spaces as indicated.

Work same as First Square through Rnd 6: 80 sts and 4 ch-3 sps.

Rnd 7 (Joining rnd): Work One or Two Side Joining, forming 6 rows of 8 Squares each.

Continued on page 68.

ONE SIDE JOINING

Rnd 7 (Joining rnd): Ch 1, sc in last ch-3 sp made, ch 5, skip next 2 sts, (sc in next dc, ch 5, skip next 2 sts) 6 times, [(sc, ch 5) twice in next corner ch-3 sp, skip next 2 sts, (sc in next dc, ch 5, skip next 2 sts) 6 times] twice, sc in next corner ch-3 sp, ch 2; holding Squares with **wrong** sides together, slip st in center ch of corresponding corner ch-5 on **previous Square**, ch 2, sc in same sp as last sc made on **new Square**, ch 2, slip st in center ch of next ch-5 on **previous Square**, ch 2, skip next 2 sts on **new Square**, ★ sc in next dc, ch 2, slip st in center ch of next ch-5 on **previous Square**, ch 2, skip next 2 sts on **new Square**; repeat from ★ across, sc in same sp as first sc, ch 2, slip st in center ch of next corner ch-5 on **previous Square**, ch 2; join with slip st to first sc on **new Square**, finish off.

Note: When working into a corner ch that has been previously joined, work into the same ch.

TWO SIDE JOINING

Rnd 7 (Joining rnd): Ch 1, sc in last ch-3 sp made, ch 5, skip next 2 sts, (sc in next dc, ch 5, skip next 2 sts) 6 times, (sc, ch 5) twice in next corner ch-3 sp, skip next 2 sts, (sc in next dc, ch 5, skip next 2 sts) 6 times, sc in next corner ch-3 sp, ch 2; holding Squares with **wrong** sides together, slip st in center ch of corresponding corner ch-5 on **previous Square**, † ch 2, sc in same sp as last sc made on **new Square**, ch 2, slip st in center ch of next ch-5 on **previous Square**, ch 2, skip next 2 sts on **new Square**, ★ sc in next dc, ch 2, slip st in center ch of next ch-5 on **previous Square**, ch 2, skip next 2 sts on **new Square**; repeat from ★ across to next corner ch-5 sp †, sc in corner ch-5 sp, ch 2, slip st in center ch of next corner ch-5 on **previous Square**, repeat from † to † once, sc in same sp as first sc, ch 2, slip st in center ch of next corner ch-5 on **previous Square**, ch 2; join with slip st to first sc on **new Square**, finish off.

OCEAN VIEW

A deep blue afghan with a foamy white border inspires daydreams of an ocean view. This classic color scheme will get along swimmingly with many décors.

Finished Size: 49" x 63$\frac{1}{2}$" (124.5 cm x 161.5 cm)

MATERIALS

Worsted Weight Yarn:
    Blue - 37 ounces, 2,090 yards
        (1,050 grams, 1,911 meters)
    White - 8 ounces, 450 yards
        (230 grams, 411.5 meters)
    Crochet hook, size H (5 mm) **or** size needed
        for gauge

GAUGE: In pattern, 12 sts and 8 rows = 4" (10 cm)

Gauge Swatch: 4$\frac{1}{4}$"w x 3$\frac{1}{2}$"h (10.75 cm x 9 cm)
With Blue, ch 16.
Row 1: Dc in fourth ch from hook **(3 skipped chs count as first dc)**, skip next 2 chs, (3 dc in next ch, skip next 2 chs) 3 times, 2 dc in last ch: 13 dc.
Row 2: Ch 3 **(counts as first dc, now and throughout)**, turn; skip next dc, 3 dc in sp **before** next dc **(Fig. 20, page 141)**, (skip next 3 dc, 3 dc in sp **before** next dc) 3 times, skip next dc, dc in last dc: 14 dc.
Row 3: Ch 3, turn; dc in same st, skip next 3 dc, (3 dc in sp **before** next dc, skip next 3 dc) 3 times, 2 dc in last dc: 13 dc.

Rows 4-6: Repeat Rows 2 and 3 once, then repeat Row 2 once **more**.
Finish off.

AFGHAN BODY

With Blue, ch 133.
Row 1 (Right side): Dc in fourth ch from hook **(3 skipped chs count as first dc)**, (skip next 2 chs, 3 dc in next ch) across to last 3 chs, skip next 2 chs, 2 dc in last ch: 130 dc.
Note: Loop a short piece of yarn around any stitch to mark Row 1 as **right** side.
Row 2: Ch 3 **(counts as first dc, now and throughout)**, turn; skip next dc, 3 dc in sp **before** next dc **(Fig. 20, page 141)**, (skip next 3 dc, 3 dc in sp **before** next dc) across to last 2 dc, skip next dc, dc in last dc: 131 dc.
Row 3: Ch 3, turn; dc in same st, (skip next 3 dc, 3 dc in sp **before** next dc) 5 times, ch 1, ★ (skip next 3 dc, 3 dc in sp **before** next dc) 8 times, ch 1; repeat from ★ 3 times **more**, skip next 3 dc, (3 dc in sp **before** next dc, skip next 3 dc) 5 times, 2 dc in last dc: 130 dc and 5 ch-1 sps.

Continued on page 70.

68

Row 4: Ch 3, turn; skip next dc, 3 dc in sp **before** next dc, (skip next 3 dc, 3 dc in sp **before** next dc) 4 times, ch 3, dc in next ch-1 sp, ch 3, ★ (skip next 3 dc, 3 dc in sp **before** next dc) 7 times, ch 3, dc in next ch-1 sp, ch 3; repeat from ★ 3 times **more**, (skip next 3 dc, 3 dc in sp **before** next dc) 5 times, skip next dc, dc in last dc: 121 dc and 10 ch-3 sps.

Row 5: Ch 3, turn; dc in same st, (skip next 3 dc, 3 dc in sp **before** next dc) 4 times, ch 3, sc in next ch-3 sp, sc in next dc and in next ch-3 sp, ch 3, ★ (skip next 3 dc, 3 dc in sp **before** next dc) 6 times, ch 3, sc in next ch-3 sp, sc in next dc and in next ch-3 sp, ch 3; repeat from ★ 3 times **more**, skip next 3 dc, (3 dc in sp **before** next dc, skip next 3 dc) 4 times, 2 dc in last dc: 115 sts and 10 ch-3 sps.

Row 6: Ch 3, turn; skip next dc, 3 dc in sp **before** next dc, (skip next 3 dc, 3 dc in sp **before** next dc) 3 times, ch 3, sc in next ch-3 sp, sc in next 3 sc and in next ch-3 sp, ch 3, ★ (skip next 3 dc, 3 dc in sp **before** next dc) 5 times, ch 3, sc in next ch-3 sp, sc in next 3 sc and in next ch-3 sp, ch 3; repeat from ★ 3 times **more**, (skip next 3 dc, 3 dc in sp **before** next dc) 4 times, skip next dc, dc in last dc: 111 sts and 10 ch-3 sps.

Row 7: Ch 3, turn; dc in same st, (skip next 3 dc, 3 dc in sp **before** next dc) 3 times, ★ † ch 1, 3 dc in next ch-3 sp, ch 3, skip next sc, sc in next 3 sc, ch 3, 3 dc in next ch-3 sp, ch 1 †, (skip next 3 dc, 3 dc in sp **before** next dc) 4 times; repeat from ★ 3 times **more**, then repeat from † to † once, skip next 3 dc, (3 dc in sp **before** next dc, skip next 3 dc) 3 times, 2 dc in last dc: 115 sts and 20 sps.

Row 8: Ch 3, turn; skip next dc, 3 dc in sp **before** next dc, (skip next 3 dc, 3 dc in sp **before** next dc) twice, ★ ch 3, dc in next ch-1 sp, ch 3, 3 dc in next ch-3 sp, ch 3, skip next sc, dc in next sc, ch 3, 3 dc in next ch-3 sp, ch 3, dc in next ch-1 sp, ch 3, (skip next 3 dc, 3 dc in sp **before** next dc) 3 times; repeat from ★ across to last 2 dc, skip next dc, dc in last dc: 101 sts and 30 ch-3 sps.

Row 9: Ch 3, turn; dc in same st, (skip next 3 dc, 3 dc in sp **before** next dc) twice, ★ ch 3, sc in next ch-3 sp, sc in next dc and in next ch-3 sp, ch 3, 3 dc in next ch-3 sp, ch 1, 3 dc in next ch-3 sp, ch 3, sc in next ch-3 sp, sc in next dc and in next ch-3 sp, ch 3, (skip next 3 dc, 3 dc in sp **before** next dc) twice; repeat from ★ across to last 4 dc, skip next 3 dc, 2 dc in last dc: 100 sts and 25 sps.

Row 10: Ch 3, turn; skip next dc, 3 dc in sp **before** next dc, skip next 3 dc, 3 dc in sp **before** next dc, ★ † ch 3, sc in next ch-3 sp, sc in next 3 sc and in next ch-3 sp, ch 3, 3 dc in next ch-1 sp, ch 3, sc in next ch-3 sp, sc in next 3 sc and in next ch-3 sp, ch 3 †, skip next 3 dc, 3 dc in sp **before** next dc;

repeat from ★ 3 times **more**, then repeat from † to † once, (skip next 3 dc, 3 dc in sp **before** next dc) twice, skip next dc, dc in last dc: 91 sts and 20 ch-3 sps.

Row 11: Ch 3, turn; dc in same st, skip next 3 dc, 3 dc in sp **before** next dc and in next ch-3 sp, ★ † ch 3, skip next sc, sc in next 3 sc, ch 3, 3 dc in next ch-3 sp, ch 1, 3 dc in next ch-3 sp, ch 3, skip next sc, sc in next 3 sc, ch 3 †, 3 dc in each of next 2 ch-3 sps; repeat from ★ 3 times **more**, then repeat from † to † once, 3 dc in next ch-3 sp, skip next 3 dc, 3 dc in sp **before** next dc, skip next 3 dc, 2 dc in last dc: 100 sts and 25 sps.

Row 12: Ch 3, turn; skip next dc, 3 dc in sp **before** next dc, skip next 3 dc, 3 dc in sp **before** next dc, ★ † 3 dc in next ch-3 sp, ch 3, skip next sc, dc in next sc, ch 3, 3 dc in next ch-3 sp, ch 3, dc in next ch-1 sp, ch 3, 3 dc in next ch-3 sp, ch 3, skip next sc, dc in next sc, ch 3, 3 dc in next ch-3 sp †, skip next 3 dc, 3 dc in sp **before** next dc; repeat from ★ 3 times **more**, then repeat from † to † once, (skip next 3 dc, 3 dc in sp **before** next dc) twice, skip next dc, dc in last dc: 101 dc and 30 ch-3 sps.

Row 13: Ch 3, turn; dc in same st, (skip next 3 dc, 3 dc in sp **before** next dc) twice, ★ 3 dc in next ch-3 sp, ch 1, 3 dc in next ch-3 sp, ch 3, sc in next ch-3 sp, sc in next dc and in next ch-3 sp, ch 3, 3 dc in next ch-3 sp, ch 1, 3 dc in next ch-3 sp, (skip next 3 dc, 3 dc in sp **before** next dc) twice; repeat from ★ across to last 4 dc, skip next 3 dc, 2 dc in last dc: 115 sts and 20 sps.

Row 14: Ch 3, turn; skip next dc, 3 dc in sp **before** next dc, (skip next 3 dc, 3 dc in sp **before** next dc) twice, ★ 3 dc in next ch-1 sp, ch 3, sc in next ch-3 sp, sc in next 3 sc and in next ch-3 sp, ch 3, 3 dc in next ch-1 sp, (skip next 3 dc, 3 dc in sp **before** next dc) 3 times; repeat from ★ across to last 2 dc, skip next dc, dc in last dc: 111 sts and 10 ch-3 sps.

Row 15: Ch 3, turn; dc in same st, (skip next 3 dc, 3 dc in sp **before** next dc) 3 times, 3 dc in next ch-3 sp, ch 3, skip next sc, sc in next 3 sc, ch 3, 3 dc in next ch-3 sp, ★ (skip next 3 dc, 3 dc in sp **before** next dc) 4 times, 3 dc in next ch-3 sp, ch 3, skip next sc, sc in next 3 sc, ch 3, 3 dc in next ch-3 sp; repeat from ★ 3 times **more**, skip next 3 dc, (3 dc in sp **before** next dc, skip next 3 dc) 3 times, 2 dc in last dc: 115 sts and 10 ch-3 sps.

Row 16: Ch 3, turn; skip next dc, 3 dc in sp **before** next dc, (skip next 3 dc, 3 dc in sp **before** next dc) 3 times, 3 dc in next ch-3 sp, ch 3, skip next sc, dc in next sc, ch 3, 3 dc in next ch-3 sp, ★ (skip next 3 dc, 3 dc in sp **before** next dc) 5 times, 3 dc in next ch-3 sp, ch 3, skip next sc, dc in next sc, ch 3, 3 dc in next ch-3 sp; repeat from ★ 3 times **more**, (skip next

3 dc, 3 dc in sp **before** next dc) 4 times, skip next dc, dc in last dc: 121 dc and 10 ch-3 sps.

Row 17: Ch 3, turn; dc in same st, (skip next 3 dc, 3 dc in sp **before** next dc) 4 times, 3 dc in next ch-3 sp, ch 1, 3 dc in next ch-3 sp, ★ (skip next 3 dc, 3 dc in sp **before** next dc) 6 times, 3 dc in next ch-3 sp, ch 1, 3 dc in next ch-3 sp; repeat from ★ 3 times **more**, skip next 3 dc, (3 dc in sp **before** next dc, skip next 3 dc) 4 times, 2 dc in last dc: 130 dc and 5 ch-1 sps.

Row 18: Ch 3, turn; skip next dc, 3 dc in sp **before** next dc, (skip next 3 dc, 3 dc in sp **before** next dc) 4 times, 3 dc in next ch-1 sp, ★ (skip next 3 dc, 3 dc in sp **before** next dc) 7 times, 3 dc in next ch-1 sp; repeat from ★ 3 times **more**, (skip next 3 dc, 3 dc in sp **before** next dc) 5 times, skip next dc, dc in last dc: 131 dc.

Row 19: Ch 3, turn; dc in same st, (skip next 3 dc, 3 dc in sp **before** next dc) 5 times, ch 1, ★ (skip next 3 dc, 3 dc in sp **before** next dc) 8 times, ch 1; repeat from ★ 3 times **more**, skip next 3 dc, (3 dc in sp **before** next dc, skip next 3 dc) 5 times, 2 dc in last dc: 130 dc and 5 ch-1 sps.

Row 20: Ch 3, turn; skip next dc, 3 dc in sp **before** next dc, (skip next 3 dc, 3 dc in sp **before** next dc) 4 times, ch 3, dc in next ch-1 sp, ch 3, ★ (skip next 3 dc, 3 dc in sp **before** next dc) 7 times, ch 3, dc in next ch-1 sp, ch 3; repeat from ★ 3 times **more**, (skip next 3 dc, 3 dc in sp **before** next dc) 5 times, skip next 3 dc, dc in last dc: 121 dc and 10 ch-3 sps.

Row 21: Ch 3, turn; dc in same st, (skip next 3 dc, 3 dc in sp **before** next dc) 4 times, ch 3, sc in next ch-3 sp, sc in next dc and in next ch-3 sp, ch 3, ★ (skip next 3 dc, 3 dc in sp **before** next dc) 6 times, ch 3, sc in next ch-3 sp, sc in next dc and in next ch-3 sp, ch 3; repeat from ★ 3 times **more**, skip next 3 dc, (3 dc in sp **before** next dc, skip next 3 dc) 4 times, 2 dc in last dc: 115 sts and 10 ch-3 sps.

Row 22: Ch 3, turn; skip next dc, 3 dc in sp **before** next dc, (skip next 3 dc, 3 dc in sp **before** next dc) 3 times, ch 3, sc in next ch-3 sp, sc in next 3 sc and in next ch-3 sp, ch 3, ★ (skip next 3 dc, 3 dc in sp **before** next dc) 5 times, ch 3, sc in next ch-3 sp, sc in next 3 sc and in next ch-3 sp, ch 3; repeat from ★ 3 times **more**, (skip next 3 dc, 3 dc in sp **before** next dc) 4 times, skip next dc, dc in last dc: 111 sts and 10 ch-3 sps.

Row 23: Ch 3, turn; dc in same st, (skip next 3 dc, 3 dc in sp **before** next dc) 3 times, ★ † ch 1, 3 dc in next ch-3 sp, ch 3, skip next sc, sc in next 3 sc, ch 3, 3 dc in next ch-3 sp, ch 1 †, (skip next 3 dc, 3 dc in sp **before** next dc) 4 times; repeat from ★ 3 times **more**, then repeat from † to † once, skip next 3 dc, (3 dc in sp **before** next dc, skip next 3 dc) 3 times, 2 dc in last dc: 115 sts and 20 sps.

Row 24: Ch 3, turn; skip next dc, 3 dc in sp **before** next dc, (skip next 3 dc, 3 dc in sp **before** next dc) twice, ★ ch 3, dc in next ch-1 sp, ch 3, 3 dc in next ch-3 sp, ch 3, skip next sc, dc in next sc, ch 3, 3 dc in next ch-3 sp, ch 3, dc in next ch-1 sp, ch 3, (skip next 3 dc, 3 dc in sp **before** next dc) 3 times; repeat from ★ across to last 2 dc, skip next dc, dc in last dc: 101 sts and 30 ch-3 sps.

Rows 25-114: Repeat Rows 9-24, 5 times; then repeat Rows 9-18 once **more**.

Row 115: Ch 3, turn; dc in same st, (skip next 3 dc, 3 dc in sp **before** next dc) across to last 4 dc, skip next 3 dc, 2 dc in last dc; finish off.

EDGING

Rnd 1: With **right** side facing and beginning in top right corner, join White with dc in end of Row 115 *(see Joining With Dc, page 140)*; 2 dc in end of same row; working across Row 115, skip next dc, 3 dc in sp **before** next dc, (skip next 3 dc, 3 dc in sp **before** next dc) across to last 2 dc, skip last 2 dc; working in end of rows, (3 dc, ch 3, 3 dc) in first row, (skip next row, 3 dc in next row) across to last 2 rows, skip next row, (3 dc, ch 3, 3 dc) in last row; working in sps across beginning ch, 3 dc in each sp across; working in end of rows, (3 dc, ch 3, 3 dc) in first row, skip next row, (3 dc in next row, skip next row) across, 3 dc in same row as first dc, ch 1, hdc in first dc to form last ch-3 sp: 618 dc (206 3-dc groups) and 4 ch-3 sps.

Rnds 2-4: Ch 3, turn; 2 dc in last ch-3 sp made, skip next 3 dc, (3 dc in sp **before** next dc, skip next 3 dc) across to next corner ch-3 sp, ★ (3 dc, ch 3, 3 dc) in corner ch-3 sp, skip next 3 dc, (3 dc in sp **before** next dc, skip next 3 dc) across to next corner ch-3 sp; repeat from ★ 2 times **more**, 3 dc in same sp as first dc, ch 1, hdc in first dc to form last ch-3 sp: 654 dc (218 3-dc groups) and 4 ch-3 sps.

Rnd 5: Ch 3, turn; 2 dc in last ch-3 sp made, skip next 3 dc, (3 dc in sp **before** next dc, skip next 3 dc) across to next corner ch-3 sp, ★ (3 dc, ch 3, 3 dc) in corner ch-3 sp, skip next 3 dc, (3 dc in sp **before** next dc, skip next 3 dc) across to next corner ch-3 sp; repeat from ★ 2 times **more**, 3 dc in same sp as first dc, ch 3; join with slip st to first dc, finish off: 666 dc (222 3-dc groups) and 4 ch-3 sps.

Rnd 6: With **right** side facing, join Blue with dc in any corner ch-3 sp; (2 dc, ch 3, 3 dc) in same sp, ★ skip next 3 dc, (3 dc in sp **before** next dc, skip next 3 dc) across to next corner ch-3 sp, (3 dc, ch 3, 3 dc) in corner ch-3 sp; repeat from ★ 2 times **more**, skip next 3 dc, (3 dc in sp **before** next dc, skip next 3 dc) across; join with slip st to first dc, finish off.

AUTUMN

Autumn breezes in with glorious colors, crackling leaves, and a crisp feeling of excitement in the air. As the weather begins to turn cooler and families gather for football games and holiday feasts, it's good to have comforting afghans on hand. The following pages will give you plenty of choices in muted fall colors that will complement any décor.

CINNAMON TOAST

On a chilly autumn morning, nothing is more comforting than a warm slice of Mom's cinnamon toast. Worked in shades of brown, this cozy coverlet will provide that same sense of harmony.

Finished Size: 49" x 68" (124.5 cm x 172.5 cm)

MATERIALS
Worsted Weight Yarn:
Ecru - 17^1/$_4$ ounces, 1,185 yards
    (490 grams, 1,083.5 meters)
Brown - 13^1/$_4$ ounces, 910 yards
    (380 grams, 832 meters)
Lt Brown - 13^1/$_4$ ounces, 910 yards
    (380 grams, 832 meters)
Crochet hook, size H (5 mm) **or** size needed
    for gauge

GAUGE: In pattern, 3 repeats = 4^3/$_4$" (12 cm);
        8 rows = 3^1/$_2$" (9 cm)

Gauge Swatch: 5^1/$_4$"w x 3^1/$_2$"h (13.25 cm x 9 cm)
With Brown, ch 17 **loosely**.
Work same as Afghan Body for 8 rows.

AFGHAN BODY
With Brown, ch 147 **loosely**.

Row 1: Sc in second ch from hook and in next ch, ch 3, ★ skip next 2 chs, sc in next 3 chs, ch 3; repeat from ★ across to last 4 chs, skip next 2 chs, sc in last 2 chs: 88 sc and 29 ch-3 sps.

Row 2 (Right side): Ch 1, turn; sc in first sc, ★ 5 dc in next ch-3 sp, skip next sc, sc in next sc; repeat from ★ across; finish off: 145 dc and 30 sc.

Note: Loop a short piece of yarn around any stitch to mark Row 2 as **right** side.

Row 3: With **wrong** side facing, join Lt Brown with slip st in first sc; ch 4 **(counts as first dc plus ch 1)**, skip next dc, sc in next 3 dc, ★ ch 3, skip next 3 sts, sc in next 3 dc; repeat from ★ across to last 2 sts, ch 1, skip next dc, dc in last sc; do **not** finish off: 87 sc and 28 ch-3 sps.

Row 4: Ch 3 **(counts as first dc)**, turn; 2 dc in same st, skip next sc, sc in next sc, ★ 5 dc in next ch-3 sp, skip next sc, sc in next sc; repeat from ★ across to last 2 sts, skip next sc, 3 dc in last dc; finish off: 146 dc and 29 sc.

Row 5: With **wrong** side facing, join Ecru with sc in first dc *(see Joining With Sc, page 140)*; sc in next dc, ch 3, ★ skip next 3 sts, sc in next 3 dc, ch 3; repeat from ★ across to last 5 sts, skip next 3 sts, sc in last 2 dc; do **not** finish off: 88 sc and 29 ch-3 sps.

Row 6: Ch 1, turn; sc in first sc, ★ 5 dc in next ch-3 sp, skip next sc, sc in next sc; repeat from ★ across; finish off: 145 dc and 30 sc.

Rows 7 and 8: With Brown, repeat Rows 3 and 4.

Rows 9 and 10: With Lt Brown, repeat Rows 5 and 6.

Rows 11 and 12: With Ecru, repeat Rows 3 and 4.

Rows 13 and 14: With Brown, repeat Rows 5 and 6.

Rows 15-148: Repeat Rows 3-14, 11 times; then repeat Rows 3 and 4 once **more**.

EDGING
Rnd 1: With **right** side facing, join Ecru with sc in first dc on Row 148; sc in same st and in next dc, ch 3, (skip next 3 sts, sc in next 3 dc, ch 3) across to last 5 sts, skip next 3 sts, sc in next dc, 3 sc in last dc; working in end of rows, 2 sc in first row, sc in next 3 rows, 2 sc in each of next 2 rows, (sc in next 2 rows, 2 sc in each of next 2 rows) across to last 6 rows, sc in next 3 rows, 2 sc in next row, sc in next row, skip last row; working in sps and in free loops of beginning ch *(Fig. 17b, page 141)*, 3 sc in ch at base of first sc, skip next ch, 3 sc in next sp, (sc in next 3 chs, 3 sc in next sp) across to last 2 chs, skip next ch, 3 sc in last ch; working in end of rows, skip first row, sc in next row, 2 sc in next row, sc in next 3 rows, 2 sc in each of next 2 rows, (sc in next 2 rows, 2 sc in each of next 2 rows) across to last 4 rows, sc in next 3 rows, 2 sc in last row; sc in same st as first sc; join with slip st to first sc: 707 sc.

Rnd 2: Ch 1, sc in same st, 5 dc in next ch-3 sp, (skip next sc, sc in next sc, 5 dc in next ch-3 sp) across to within one sc of next corner 3-sc group, skip next 2 sc, ★ sc in next sc, skip next 2 sc, 5 dc in next sc, skip next 2 sc; repeat from ★ around; join with slip st to first sc: 132 5-dc groups.

Rnd 3: Slip st in next dc, ch 1, sc in same st, ch 2, skip next dc, (sc, ch 3, sc) in next dc, ch 2, skip next dc, sc in next dc, ch 1, skip next sc, ★ sc in next dc, ch 2, skip next dc, (sc, ch 3, sc) in next dc, ch 2, skip next dc, sc in next dc, ch 1, skip next st; repeat from ★ around; join with slip st to first sc, finish off.

EVERGREEN VISTA

An early snowfall transforms an evergreen forest into an enchanting snow-covered vista. Finish this natural wonder with a lush fringe.

Finished Size: 46¹/₂" x 58¹/₂" (118 cm x 148.5 cm)

MATERIALS
Worsted Weight Yarn:
Green - 31 ounces, 2,125 yards
(880 grams, 1,943 meters)
Ecru - 23¹/₂ ounces, 1,610 yards
(670 grams, 1,472 meters)
Crochet hook, size J (6 mm) **or** size needed
for gauge
Yarn needle

GAUGE: Each Strip = 3¹/₄" (8.25 cm) wide
In pattern, (sc, ch 1)
7 times = 4" (10 cm)

Gauge Swatch: 4"w x 1³/₄"h (10 cm x 4.5 cm)
Ch 14 **loosely**.
Work same as Strip First Half.

STITCH GUIDE

> **TREBLE CROCHET** *(abbreviated tr)*
> YO twice, insert hook in sc indicated, YO and
> pull up a loop (4 loops on hook), (YO and draw
> through 2 loops on hook) 3 times.
> **DOUBLE TREBLE CROCHET**
>   *(abbreviated dtr)*
> YO 3 times, insert hook in sc indicated, YO and
> pull up a loop (5 loops on hook), (YO and draw
> through 2 loops on hook) 4 times.

STRIP (Make 14)
FIRST HALF
With Green, ch 206 **loosely**.
Row 1: Sc in second ch from hook, ★ ch 1, skip next ch, sc in next ch; repeat from ★ across: 103 sc and 102 ch-1 sps.
Row 2 (Right side): Ch 1, turn; sc in first sc, (sc in next ch-1 sp, ch 1) across to last ch-1 sp, sc in last ch-1 sp and in last sc: 104 sc and 101 ch-1 sps.
Note: Loop a short piece of yarn around any stitch to mark Row 2 as **right** side.
Row 3: Ch 1, turn; sc in first sc, ch 1, (sc in next ch-1 sp, ch 1) across to last 2 sc, skip next sc, sc in last sc: 103 sc and 102 ch-1 sps.

Row 4: Ch 1, turn; sc in first sc, (sc in next ch-1 sp, ch 1) across to last ch-1 sp, sc in last ch-1 sp and in last sc: 104 sc and 101 ch-1 sps.
Row 5: Ch 1, turn; sc in first sc, ch 1, (sc in next ch-1 sp, ch 1) across to last 2 sc, skip next sc, sc in last sc; finish off: 103 sc and 102 ch-1 sps.
Row 6: With **right** side facing, join Ecru with sc in first sc *(see Joining With Sc, page 140)*; ★ working in **front** of next ch-1 *(Fig. 18, page 141)*, dc in sc one row **below** ch-1, working in **front** of next sc, tr in sc 2 rows **below** sc, working in **front** of next ch-1, dtr in sc 3 rows **below** ch-1, working in **front** of next sc, tr in sc 2 rows **below** sc, working in **front** of next ch-1, dc in sc one row **below** ch-1, skip 2 sc from last sc made, sc in next sc; repeat from ★ across; finish off.

SECOND HALF
Row 1: With **right** side facing, working in sps and in free loops *(Fig. 17b, page 141)* across beginning ch, join Green with sc in ch at base of first sc; (sc in next sp, ch 1) across to last sp, sc in last sp and in last ch: 104 sc and 101 ch-1 sps.
Row 2-5: Work same as Rows 3-6 of first half.

ASSEMBLY
With Ecru and working through both loops, whipstitch long edge of Strips together beginning in first sc and ending in last sc *(Fig. 21b, page 142)*.

TRIM
FIRST SIDE
Row 1: With **wrong** side facing and working across long edge, join Ecru with sc in first sc; sc in next dc, ch 1, ★ skip next st, sc in next st, ch 1; repeat from ★ across to last 3 sts, skip next tr, sc in last 2 sts.
Row 2: Ch 1, turn; slip st in first sc, ch 1, (slip st in next ch-1 sp, ch 1) across to last 2 sc, skip next sc, slip st in last sc; finish off.

SECOND SIDE
Work same as First Side.

Holding 10 strands of corresponding color yarn together, each 17" (43 cm) long, add fringe evenly spaced across short edges of Afghan *(Figs. 22b & d, page 142)*.

MAGNIFICENT RIPPLES

*Worked in rich, vibrant jewel tones, this magnificent rippled wrap is fit for
a king! The striking color palette is sure to draw plenty of compliments.*

Finished Size: 49¹/₂" x 68" (125.5 cm x 172.5 cm)

MATERIALS
Worsted Weight Yarn:
  Black - 13¹/₂ ounces, 885 yards
    (380 grams, 809 meters)
  Green - 7¹/₂ ounces, 490 yards
    (210 grams, 448 meters)
  Burgundy - 7 ounces, 460 yards
    (200 grams, 420.5 meters)
  Gold - 7 ounces, 460 yards
    (200 grams, 420.5 meters)
  Purple - 7 ounces, 460 yards
    (200 grams, 420.5 meters)
Crochet hook, size H (5 mm) **or** size needed
  for gauge

GAUGE: In pattern, one repeat
      from point to point = 4¹/₂" (11.5 cm);
      6 rows = 4" (10 cm)

Gauge Swatch: 9"w x 6"h (22.75 cm x 15.25 cm)
Ch 44 **loosely**.
Work same as Afghan for 6 rows.

STITCH GUIDE

RIGHT DECREASE
YO, insert hook in same st or sp as last dc made,
YO and pull up a loop, YO and draw through
2 loops on hook, YO, skip next ch-2 sp, insert
hook in next st, YO and pull up a loop, YO and
draw through 2 loops on hook, YO and draw
through all 3 loops on hook.

LEFT DECREASE
YO, insert hook in next st, YO and pull up a
loop, YO and draw through 2 loops on hook,
YO, skip next dc, insert hook in sp **before** next
dc (*Fig. 20, page 141*), YO and pull up a loop,
YO and draw through 2 loops on hook, YO and
draw through all 3 loops on hook.

ENDING DECREASE (uses last 2 dc)
★ YO, insert hook in **next** dc, YO and pull up a
loop, YO and draw through 2 loops on hook;
repeat from ★ once **more**, YO and draw through
all 3 loops on hook (**counts as one dc**).

AFGHAN
With Green, ch 242 **loosely**.

Row 1 (Right side): Working in back ridges of
beginning ch (*Fig. 2b, page 137*), dc in fourth ch from
hook, skip next ch, [(dc, ch 2, dc) in next ch, skip
next 2 chs] twice, dc in next ch, (ch 1, dc in same ch)
3 times, ★ skip next 2 chs, (dc, ch 2, dc) in next ch,
skip next 2 chs, dc in next ch, ch 2, YO, insert hook
in same ch as last dc made, YO and pull up a loop,
YO and draw through 2 loops on hook, YO, skip
next 2 chs, insert hook in next ch, YO and pull up a
loop, YO and draw through 2 loops on hook, YO
and draw through all 3 loops on hook, YO, skip next
3 chs, insert hook in next ch, YO and pull up a loop,
YO and draw through 2 loops on hook, YO, skip
next 2 chs, insert hook in next ch, YO and pull up a
loop, YO and draw through 2 loops on hook, YO
and draw through all 3 loops on hook, ch 2, dc in
same ch as second leg of st just made, skip next
2 chs, (dc, ch 2, dc) in next ch, skip next 2 chs, dc in
next ch, (ch 1, dc in same ch) 3 times; repeat from ★
9 times **more**, [skip next 2 chs, (dc, ch 2, dc) in next
ch] twice, (YO, skip next ch, insert hook in next ch,
YO and pull up a loop, YO and draw through
2 loops on hook) twice, YO and draw through all
3 loops on hook: 134 sts and 77 sps.

Note: Loop a short piece of yarn around any stitch
to mark Row 1 as **right** side.

Rows 2 and 3: Ch 2, turn; skip first st, dc in next dc,
skip next dc, (dc, ch 2, dc) in sp **before** next dc
(*Fig. 20, page 141*), skip next 2 dc, (dc, ch 2, dc) in sp
before next dc, skip next ch-1 sp, dc in next ch-1 sp,
(ch 1, dc in same sp) 3 times, ★ skip next 2 dc, (dc,
ch 2, dc) in sp **before** next dc, skip next 2 dc, dc in
sp **before** next dc, ch 2, work right decrease, work
left decrease, ch 2, dc in same sp as last leg of
left decrease just made, skip next 2 dc, (dc, ch 2, dc)
in sp **before** next dc, skip next ch-1 sp, dc in next
ch-1 sp, (ch 1, dc in same sp) 3 times; repeat from ★
9 times **more**, [skip next 2 dc, (dc, ch 2, dc) in sp
before next dc] twice, skip next ch-2 sp, work
ending decrease.
Finish off.

Row 4: With **wrong** side facing, join Black with slip st in first dc; ch 2, dc in next dc, skip next dc, (dc, ch 2, dc) in sp **before** next dc, skip next 2 dc, (dc, ch 2, dc) in sp **before** next dc, skip next ch-1 sp, dc in next ch-1 sp, (ch 1, dc in same sp) 3 times, ★ skip next 2 dc, (dc, ch 2, dc) in sp **before** next dc, skip next 2 dc, dc in sp **before** next dc, ch 2, work right decrease, work left decrease, ch 2, dc in same sp as last leg of left decrease just made, skip next 2 dc, (dc, ch 2, dc) in sp **before** next dc, skip next ch-1 sp, dc in next ch-1 sp, (ch 1, dc in same sp) 3 times; repeat from ★ 9 times **more**, [skip next 2 dc, (dc, ch 2, dc) in sp **before** next dc] twice, skip next ch-2 sp, work ending decrease; finish off.

Row 5: With **right** side facing, join Purple with slip st in first dc; ch 2, dc in next dc, skip next dc, (dc, ch 2, dc) in sp **before** next dc, skip next 2 dc, (dc, ch 2, dc) in sp **before** next dc, skip next ch-1 sp, dc in next ch-1 sp, (ch 1, dc in same sp) 3 times, ★ skip next 2 dc, (dc, ch 2, dc) in sp **before** next dc, skip next 2 dc, dc in sp **before** next dc, ch 2, work right decrease, work left decrease, ch 2, dc in same sp as last leg of left decrease just made, skip next 2 dc, (dc, ch 2, dc) in sp **before** next dc, skip next ch-1 sp, dc in next ch-1 sp, (ch 1, dc in same sp) 3 times; repeat from ★ 9 times **more**, [skip next 2 dc, (dc, ch 2, dc) in sp **before** next dc] twice, skip next ch-2 sp, work ending decrease; finish off.
Row 6: Repeat Row 4.

Continued on page 80.

Row 7: With **right** side facing, join Burgundy with slip st in first dc; ch 2, dc in next dc, skip next dc, (dc, ch 2, dc) in sp **before** next dc, skip next 2 dc, (dc, ch 2, dc) in sp **before** next dc, skip next ch-1 sp, dc in next ch-1 sp, (ch 1, dc in same sp) 3 times, ★ skip next 2 dc, (dc, ch 2, dc) in sp **before** next dc, skip next 2 dc, dc in sp **before** next dc, ch 2, work right decrease, work left decrease, ch 2, dc in same sp as last leg of left decrease just made, skip next 2 dc, (dc, ch 2, dc) in sp **before** next dc, skip next ch-1 sp, dc in next ch-1 sp, (ch 1, dc in same sp) 3 times; repeat from ★ 9 times **more**, [skip next 2 dc, (dc, ch 2, dc) in sp **before** next dc] twice, skip next ch-2 sp, work ending decrease, do **not** finish off.
Rows 8-10: Repeat Rows 2-4.

Row 11: With Gold, repeat Row 5.
Row 12: Repeat Row 4.
Row 13: With Purple, repeat Row 7.
Rows 14-16: Repeat Rows 2-4.
Row 17: With Green, repeat Row 5.
Row 18: Repeat Row 4.
Row 19: With Gold, repeat Row 7.
Rows 20-22: Repeat Rows 2-4.
Row 23: With Burgundy, repeat Row 5.
Row 24: Repeat Row 4.
Row 25: With Green, repeat Row 7.
Rows 26-99: Repeat Rows 2-25, 3 times; then repeat Rows 2 and 3 once **more**.
Finish off.

FIRST FROST

A visit from Jack Frost turns the colorful autumn landscape into a sparkling icy-blue wonderland. Subtly scalloped edges add to the appearance of falling flurries.

Finished Size: 46" x 64" (117 cm x 162.5 cm)

MATERIALS
Worsted Weight Yarn:
    42 ounces, 2,880 yards
      (1,190 grams, 2,633.5 meters)
Crochet hook, size H (5 mm) **or** size needed
    for gauge
Yarn needle

GAUGE: Each Motif = 4³/₄" (12 cm)
        (straight edge to straight edge)

Gauge Swatch: 2³/₄" (7 cm) diameter
Work same as Motif through Rnd 2.

STITCH GUIDE

CLUSTER (uses one dc)
★ YO twice, insert hook in dc indicated, YO and pull up a loop, (YO and draw through 2 loops on hook) twice; repeat from ★ 3 times **more**, YO and draw through all 5 loops on hook *(Figs. 10a & b, page 139)*. Push Cluster to **right** side.
DECREASE (uses next 2 sps)
★ YO, insert hook in **next** sp, YO and pull up a loop, YO and draw through 2 loops on hook; repeat from ★ once **more**, YO and draw through all 3 loops on hook **(counts as one dc)**.

DOUBLE DECREASE (uses next 3 dc)
★ YO, insert hook in **next** dc, YO and pull up a loop, YO and draw through 2 loops on hook; repeat from ★ 2 times **more**, YO and draw through all 4 loops on hook **(counts as one dc)**.

MOTIF (Make 128)
Rnd 1 (Right side): Ch 7, dc in seventh ch from hook **(6 skipped chs count as first dc plus ch 3)**, ch 3, (dc in same ch, ch 3) 4 times; join with slip st to first dc: 6 ch-3 sps.
Note: Loop a short piece of yarn around any stitch to mark Rnd 1 as **right** side.
Rnd 2: Slip st in first ch-3 sp, ch 1, turn; sc in same sp, ch 1, work Cluster in next dc, ch 1, ★ (sc, ch 3, sc) in next ch-3 sp, ch 1, work Cluster in next dc, ch 1; repeat from ★ around, sc in same sp as first sc, ch 3; join with slip st to first sc, do **not** finish off: 6 Clusters and 6 ch-3 sps.
Rnd 3: Turn; slip st in first ch-3 sp, ch 6, dc in same sp, ch 1, tr in next Cluster, ch 1, ★ (dc, ch 3, dc) in next ch-3 sp, ch 1, tr in next Cluster, ch 1; repeat from ★ around; join with slip st to third ch of beginning ch-6: 18 sts and 18 sps.
Rnd 4: Ch 3 **(counts as first dc)**, do **not** turn; (dc, ch 3, dc) in next ch-3 sp, ★ dc in next dc, (dc in next ch-1 sp and in next st) twice, (dc, ch 3, dc) in next ch-3 sp; repeat from ★ 4 times **more**, (dc in next st and in next ch-1 sp) twice; join with slip st to first dc, finish off: 42 dc and 6 ch-3 sps.

Continued on page 82.

HALF MOTIF (Make 14)

Ch 5, place marker in second ch from hook for st placement; join with slip st to form a ring.

Row 1 (Right side): Ch 4 **(counts as first dc plus ch 1, now and throughout)**, dc in ring, (ch 3, dc in ring) twice, ch 1, dc in marked ch, remove marker: 5 dc and 4 sps.

Note: Mark Row 1 as **right** side.

Row 2: Ch 4, turn; sc in next ch-1 sp, ch 1, work Cluster in next dc, ch 1, ★ (sc, ch 3, sc) in next ch-3 sp, ch 1, work Cluster in next dc, ch 1; repeat from ★ once **more**, sc in next ch-1 sp, ch 1, dc in last dc: 3 Clusters and 10 sps.

Row 3: Ch 4, turn; dc in next ch-1 sp, ch 1, tr in next Cluster, ch 1, ★ (dc, ch 3, dc) in next ch-3 sp, ch 1, tr in next Cluster, ch 1; repeat from ★ once **more**, skip next ch-1 sp, dc in next ch-1 sp, ch 1, dc in last dc; finish off: 11 sts and 10 sps.

Row 4: With **right** side facing, join yarn with slip st in first dc; ch 4, (dc in next ch-1 sp and in next st) 3 times, (dc, ch 3, dc) in next ch-3 sp, dc in next dc, (dc in next ch-1 sp and in next st) twice, (dc, ch 3, dc) in next ch-3 sp, (dc in next st and in next ch-1 sp) 3 times, ch 1, dc in last dc; finish off: 23 dc and 4 sps.

ASSEMBLY

Using Placement Diagram as a guide, working in both loops whipstitch Motifs together forming 8 horizontal strips of 9 Motifs each and 7 horizontal strips of 8 Motifs and 2 Half Motifs each (*Fig. 21b, page 142*), beginning in center ch of first corner ch-3 and ending in center ch of next corner ch-3; then whipstitch strips together, beginning in first dc on Half Motif and center ch of first ch-3 on Motif and ending in last dc on Half Motif and center ch of last ch-3 on Motif.

PLACEMENT DIAGRAM

82

BORDER

Rnd 1: With **right** side facing and working across top edge, join yarn with slip st in first unworked ch-3 sp of first corner; ch 5 **(counts as first dc plus ch 2)**, † dc in next 7 dc, (ch 2, dc in next ch-3 sp, ch 2, dc in next 7 dc, decrease, dc in next 7 dc) 8 times, (ch 2, dc in next ch-3 sp, ch 2, dc in next 7 dc) twice, ★ ch 1, hdc in next joining; working in end of rows on Half Motif, (sc in next row, ch 1) 4 times, sc in ring, (ch 1, sc in next row) 4 times, hdc in next joining, ch 1, dc in next 7 dc; repeat from ★ 6 times **more**, ch 2 †, dc in next ch-3 sp, ch 2, repeat from † to † once; join with slip st to first dc: 556 sts and 184 sps.

Rnd 2: Ch 4, † dc in next ch-2 sp, ch 1, dc in next dc, ch 1, (skip next dc, dc in next dc, ch 1) 3 times, (dc in next ch-2 sp, ch 1, dc in next dc, ch 1) twice, ★ skip next dc, (dc in next dc, ch 1, skip next dc) twice, double decrease, ch 1, (skip next dc, dc in next dc, ch 1) 3 times, (dc in next ch-2 sp, ch 1, dc in next dc, ch 1) twice; repeat from ★ 7 times **more**, (skip next dc, dc in next dc, ch 1) 3 times, (dc in next ch-2 sp, ch 1, dc in next dc, ch 1) twice, (skip next dc, dc in next dc, ch 1) 3 times, [dc in next hdc, ch 1, (dc in next ch-1 sp, ch 1) 8 times, skip next sc, dc in next hdc, ch 1, dc in next dc, ch 1, (skip next dc, dc in next dc, ch 1) 3 times] 7 times, dc in next ch-2 sp, ch 1 †, dc in next dc, place marker around dc just made for st placement, ch 1, repeat from † to † once; join with slip st to first dc: 398 dc.

Rnd 3: Ch 1, (sc in same st, ch 1) twice, † (sc in next dc, ch 1) 6 times, (sc, ch 1) twice in next dc, ★ (sc in next dc, ch 1) 9 times, (sc, ch 1) twice in next dc; repeat from ★ 7 times **more**, (sc in next dc, ch 1) 6 times, (sc, ch 1) twice in next dc †, (sc in next dc, ch 1) across to marked dc, (sc, ch 1) twice in marked dc, repeat from † to † once, (sc in next dc, ch 1) across; join with slip st to first sc.

Rnd 4: (Slip st in next ch-1 sp, ch 1) around; join with slip st to first slip st, finish off.

PERFECT WELCOME

This pretty pineapple wrap displays the traditional symbol of hospitality and offers a perfect welcome to all your guests. Crochet one for the living room and another for the guest room.

Finished Size: 44 1/2" x 64 1/2" (113 cm x 164 cm)

MATERIALS
Worsted Weight Yarn:
    32 1/2 ounces, 1,980 yards
      (920 grams, 1,810.5 meters)
Crochet hook, size H (5 mm) **or** size needed
    for gauge

GAUGE: 12 dc and 7 rows = 4" (10 cm)

Gauge Swatch: 4" (10 cm) square
Ch 14 **loosely.**
Row 1: Dc in fourth ch from hook **(3 skipped chs count as first dc)** and in each ch across: 12 dc.
Rows 2-7: Ch 3 **(counts as first dc)**, turn; dc in next dc and in each dc across.
Finish off.

STITCH GUIDE

> **CLUSTER** *(uses one ch)*
> Ch 2, hdc in second ch from hook *(Figs. 10a & b, page 139).*
> **TREBLE CROCHET** *(abbreviated tr)*
> YO twice, insert hook in sc indicated, YO and pull up a loop (4 loops on hook), (YO and draw through 2 loops on hook) 3 times.
> **DOUBLE TREBLE CROCHET**
>   *(abbreviated dtr)*
> YO 3 times, insert hook in sc indicated, YO and pull up a loop (5 loops on hook), (YO and draw through 2 loops on hook) 4 times.

AFGHAN BODY

Ch 127 **loosely,** place marker in third ch from hook for st placement.
Row 1: Dc in fourth ch from hook **(3 skipped chs count as first dc)** and in each ch across: 125 dc.
Row 2 (Right side): Ch 3 **(counts as first dc, now and throughout)**, turn; dc in next 6 dc, tr in next dc, (dtr, ch 3, dtr) in next dc, tr in next dc, ★ dc in next 15 dc, tr in next dc, (dtr, ch 3, dtr) in next dc, tr in next dc; repeat from ★ across to last 7 dc, dc in last 7 dc: 132 sts and 7 ch-3 sps.

Row 3: Ch 3, turn; dc in next 4 dc, ★ † ch 2, skip next 3 sts, dc in next dtr, 5 dc in next ch-3 sp, dc in next dtr, ch 2, skip next 3 sts †, dc in next 11 dc; repeat from ★ 5 times **more**, then repeat from † to † once, dc in last 5 dc: 125 dc and 14 ch-2 sps.
Row 4: Ch 3, turn; dc in next 3 dc, ★ † ch 1, skip next dc and next ch-2 sp, (dc in next dc, ch 1) 7 times, skip next ch-2 sp and next dc †, dc in next 9 dc; repeat from ★ 5 times **more**, then repeat from † to † once, dc in last 4 dc: 111 dc and 56 ch-1 sps.
Row 5: Ch 3, turn; dc in next 2 dc, ★ † ch 2, skip next ch-1 sp, slip st in next ch-1 sp, (work Cluster, slip st in next ch-1 sp) 5 times, ch 2, skip next ch-1 sp and next dc †, dc in next 7 dc; repeat from ★ 5 times **more**, then repeat from † to † once, dc in last 3 dc: 48 dc, 35 Clusters, and 14 ch-2 sps.
Row 6: Ch 3, turn; dc in next dc, ★ † ch 3, skip next ch-2 sp, slip st in next Cluster (ch-1 sp at top), (work Cluster, slip st in next Cluster) 4 times, ch 3, skip next dc †, dc in next 5 dc; repeat from ★ 5 times **more**, then repeat from † to † once, dc in last 2 dc: 34 dc, 28 Clusters, and 14 ch-3 sps.
Row 7: Ch 3, turn; dc in next dc, ★ † dc in next ch-3 sp, ch 3, slip st in next Cluster, (work Cluster, slip st in next Cluster) 3 times, ch 3, dc in next ch-3 sp †, dc in next 5 dc; repeat from ★ 5 times **more**, then repeat from † to † once, dc in last 2 dc: 48 dc, 21 Clusters, and 14 ch-3 sps.
Row 8: Ch 3, turn; dc in next 2 dc, ★ † dc in next ch-3 sp, ch 3, slip st in next Cluster, (work Cluster, slip st in next Cluster) twice, ch 3, dc in next ch-3 sp †, dc in next 7 dc; repeat from ★ 5 times **more**, then repeat from † to † once, dc in last 3 dc: 62 dc, 14 Clusters, and 14 ch-3 sps.
Row 9: Ch 3, turn; dc in next 3 dc, ★ † dc in next ch-3 sp, ch 3, slip st in next Cluster, work Cluster, slip st in next Cluster, ch 3, dc in next ch-3 sp †, dc in next 9 dc; repeat from ★ 5 times **more**, then repeat from † to † once, dc in last 4 dc: 76 dc, 7 Clusters, and 14 ch-3 sps.
Row 10: Ch 3, turn; dc in next 4 dc and in next ch-3 sp, ch 3, slip st in next Cluster, ch 3, dc in next ch-3 sp, ★ dc in next 4 dc, tr in next dc, (dtr, ch 3, dtr) in next dc, tr in next dc, dc in next 4 dc and in next ch-3 sp, ch 3, slip st in next Cluster, ch 3, dc in next ch-3 sp; repeat from ★ across to last 5 dc, dc in last 5 dc: 103 sts and 20 ch-3 sps.

Continued on page 84.

Row 11: Ch 3, turn; dc in next 5 dc, 2 dc in next ch-3 sp, ch 1, 2 dc in next ch-3 sp, ★ dc in next 3 dc, ch 2, skip next 3 sts, dc in next dtr, 5 dc in next ch-3 sp, dc in next dtr, ch 2, skip next 3 sts, dc in next 3 dc, 2 dc in next ch-3 sp, ch 1, 2 dc in next ch-3 sp; repeat from ★ across to last 6 dc, dc in last 6 dc: 118 dc and 19 sps.

Row 12: Ch 3, turn; dc in next 7 dc and in next ch-1 sp, ★ dc in next 4 dc, ch 1, skip next dc and next ch-2 sp, (dc in next dc, ch 1) 7 times, skip next ch-2 sp and next dc, dc in next 4 dc and in next ch-1 sp; repeat from ★ across to last 8 dc, dc in last 8 dc: 113 dc and 48 ch-1 sps.

Row 13: Ch 3, turn; dc in next 11 dc, ★ † ch 2, skip next ch-1 sp, slip st in next ch-1 sp, (work Cluster, slip st in next ch-1 sp) 5 times, ch 2, skip next ch-1 sp and next dc †, dc in next 7 dc; repeat from ★ 4 times **more**, then repeat from † to † once, dc in last 12 dc: 59 dc, 30 Clusters, and 12 ch-2 sps.

Row 14: Ch 3, turn; dc in next 10 dc, ★ † ch 3, slip st in next Cluster, (work Cluster, slip st in next Cluster) 4 times, ch 3, skip next dc †, dc in next 5 dc; repeat from ★ 4 times **more**, then repeat from † to † once, dc in last 11 dc: 47 dc, 24 Clusters, and 12 ch-3 sps.

Row 15: Ch 3, turn; dc in next 10 dc, ★ † dc in next ch-3 sp, ch 3, slip st in next Cluster, (work Cluster, slip st in next Cluster) 3 times, ch 3, dc in next ch-3 sp †, dc in next 5 dc; repeat from ★ 4 times **more**, then repeat from † to † once, dc in last 11 dc: 59 dc, 18 Clusters, and 12 ch-3 sps.

Row 16: Ch 3, turn; dc in next 11 dc, ★ † dc in next ch-3 sp, ch 3, slip st in next Cluster, (work Cluster, slip st in next Cluster) twice, ch 3, dc in next ch-3 sp †, dc in next 7 dc; repeat from ★ 4 times **more**, then repeat from † to † once, dc in last 12 dc: 71 dc, 12 Clusters, and 12 ch-3 sps.

Row 17: Ch 3, turn; dc in next 12 dc, ★ † dc in next ch-3 sp, ch 3, slip st in next Cluster, work Cluster, slip st in next Cluster, ch 3, dc in next ch-3 sp †, dc in next 9 dc; repeat from ★ 4 times **more**, then repeat from † to † once, dc in last 13 dc: 83 dc, 6 Clusters, and 12 ch-3 sps.

Row 18: Ch 3, turn; dc in next 6 dc, tr in next dc, (dtr, ch 3, dtr) in next dc, tr in next dc, ★ dc in next 4 dc and in next ch-3 sp, ch 3, slip st in next Cluster, ch 3, dc in next ch-3 sp and in next 4 dc, tr in next dc, (dtr, ch 3, dtr) in next dc, tr in next dc; repeat from ★ across to last 7 dc, dc in last 7 dc: 108 sts and 19 ch-3 sps.

Row 19: Ch 3, turn; dc in next 4 dc, ★ † ch 2, skip next 3 sts, dc in next dtr, 5 dc in next ch-3 sp, dc in next dtr, ch 2, skip next 3 sts †, dc in next 3 dc, 2 dc in next ch-3 sp, ch 1, 2 dc in next ch-3 sp, dc in next 3 dc; repeat from ★ 5 times **more**, then repeat from † to † once, dc in last 5 dc: 119 dc and 20 sps.

Row 20: Ch 3, turn; dc in next 3 dc, ch 1, skip next dc and next ch-2 sp, (dc in next dc, ch 1) 7 times, skip next ch-2 sp and next dc, dc in next 4 dc, ★ dc in next ch-1 sp and in next 4 dc, ch 1, skip next dc and next ch-2 sp, (dc in next dc, ch 1) 7 times, skip next ch-2 sp and next dc, dc in next 4 dc; repeat from ★ across: 111 dc and 56 ch-1 sps.

Rows 21-105: Repeat Rows 5-20, 5 times; then repeat Rows 5-9 once **more**: 76 dc, 7 Clusters, and 14 ch-3 sps.

Row 106: Ch 3, turn; dc in next 4 dc and in next ch-3 sp, ch 3, slip st in next Cluster, ch 3, dc in next ch-3 sp, ★ dc in next 11 dc and in next ch-3 sp, ch 3, slip st in next Cluster, ch 3, dc in next ch-3 sp; repeat from ★ across to last 5 dc, dc in last 5 dc: 90 dc and 14 ch-3 sps.

Row 107: Ch 3, turn; dc in next 5 dc, 2 dc in next ch-3 sp, ch 1, 2 dc in next ch-3 sp, ★ dc in next 13 dc, 2 dc in next ch-3 sp, ch 1, 2 dc in next ch-3 sp; repeat from ★ across to last 6 dc, dc in last 6 dc: 118 dc and 7 ch-1 sps.

Row 108: Ch 3, turn; dc in next dc and in each dc and each ch-1 sp across; do **not** finish off: 125 dc.

EDGING

Rnd 1: Ch 1, do **not** turn; sc in top of last dc on Row 108, ch 1; working in end of rows, (sc in top of next row, ch 1) across to marked ch; working in free loops of beginning ch *(Fig. 17b, page 141)*, (sc, ch 2, sc) in marked ch, ch 1, (skip next ch, sc in next ch, ch 1) across to last 2 chs, skip next ch, (sc, ch 2, sc) in last ch, ch 1; working in end of rows, sc in top of first row, ch 1, (sc in top of next row, ch 1) across to last row; working in dc across Row 108, (sc, ch 2, sc) in first dc, (ch 1, skip next dc, sc in next dc) across, ch 2; join with slip st to first sc: 344 sps.

Rnd 2: Slip st in first ch-1 sp, ch 4, ★ (dc in next ch-1 sp, ch 1) across to next corner ch-2 sp, (dc, ch 3, dc) in corner ch-2 sp, ch 1; repeat from ★ around; join with slip st to third ch of beginning ch-4: 348 sps.

Rnd 3: Ch 4, ★ (dc in next dc, ch 1) across to next corner ch-3 sp, (dc, ch 3, dc) in corner ch-3 sp, ch 1; repeat from ★ around to last dc, dc in last dc, ch 1; join with slip st to third ch of beginning ch-4: 356 sps.

Rnd 4: ★ (Slip st in next ch-1 sp, ch 2) across to next corner ch-3 sp, (slip st, ch 2) twice in corner ch-3 sp; repeat from ★ around to last 2 ch-1 sps, (slip st in next ch-1 sp, ch 2) twice; join with slip st to first slip st, finish off.

FALL REMEMBRANCE

Granny squares in a potpourri of colors offer a lovely fall remembrance. A black background provides a unifying theme for the autumnal scraps.

Finished Size: 48$\frac{1}{2}$" x 67$\frac{1}{2}$" (123 cm x 171.5 cm)

MATERIALS
Worsted Weight Yarn:
Black - 22$\frac{1}{2}$ ounces, 1,475 yards
(640 grams, 1,348.5 meters)
Scraps - 27 ounces, 1,770 yards
(770 grams, 1,618.5 meters) **total**
Note: We used 8 different colors.
Crochet hook, size I (5.5 mm) **or** size needed for gauge
Yarn needle

GAUGE: Each Square = 4$\frac{3}{4}$" (12 cm)

Gauge Swatch: 1$\frac{1}{2}$" (3.75 cm) square
Work same as Square through Rnd 1.

To work **color change**, work last dc to within one step of completion, hook new yarn *(Fig. 19, page 141)* and draw through both loops on hook.

SQUARE (Make 117)
Rnd 1 (Right side)**:** With Scrap color, ch 4; 2 dc in fourth ch from hook **(3 skipped chs count as first dc)**, ch 3, (3 dc in same ch, ch 3) 3 times; join with slip st to first dc, finish off: 12 dc and 4 ch-3 sps.
Note: Loop a short piece of yarn around any stitch to mark Rnd 1 as **right** side.
Rnd 2: With **right** side facing, join next Scrap color with dc in any ch-3 sp *(see Joining With Dc, page 140)*; (2 dc, ch 3, 3 dc) in same sp, ch 1, ★ (3 dc, ch 3, 3 dc) in next ch-3 sp, ch 1; repeat from ★ 2 times **more**; join with slip st to first dc, finish off: 24 dc and 8 sps.
Rnd 3: With **right** side facing, join next Scrap color with dc in any corner ch-3 sp; (2 dc, ch 3, 3 dc) in same sp, ch 1, 3 dc in next ch-1 sp, ch 1, ★ (3 dc, ch 3, 3 dc) in next corner ch-3 sp, ch 1, 3 dc in next ch-1 sp, ch 1; repeat from ★ 2 times **more**; join with slip st to first dc, finish off: 36 dc and 12 sps.
Rnd 4: With **right** side facing, join Black with dc in any corner ch-3 sp; (2 dc, ch 3, 3 dc) in same sp, ch 1, (3 dc in next ch-1 sp, ch 1) twice, ★ (3 dc, ch 3, 3 dc) in next corner ch-3 sp, ch 1, (3 dc in next ch-1 sp, ch 1) twice; repeat from ★ 2 times **more**; join with slip st to first dc, finish off: 48 dc and 16 sps.

ASSEMBLY
With Black and working in both loops, whipstitch Squares together forming 9 vertical strips of 13 Squares each *(Fig. 21b, page 142)*, beginning in center ch of first corner ch-3 and ending in center ch of next corner ch-3; then whipstitch strips together in same manner.

EDGING
Rnd 1: With **right** side facing, join Black with sc in any corner ch-3 sp *(see Joining With Sc, page 140)*; ch 3, sc in same sp, ch 1, skip next dc, sc in next dc, ch 1, (sc in next ch-1 sp, ch 1, skip next dc, sc in next dc, ch 1) 3 times, ★ † (sc in next sp, ch 1) twice, skip next dc, sc in next dc, ch 1, (sc in next ch-1 sp, ch 1, skip next dc, sc in next dc, ch 1) 3 times †; repeat from † to † across to next corner ch-3 sp, (sc, ch 3, sc) in corner ch-3 sp, ch 1, skip next dc, sc in next dc, ch 1, (sc in next ch-1 sp, ch 1, skip next dc, sc in next dc, ch 1) 3 times; repeat from ★ 2 times **more**, then repeat from † to † across; join with slip st to first sc: 396 sps.
Rnd 2: Ch 1, ★ (sc, ch 3, sc) in next corner ch-3 sp, ch 1, (sc in next ch-1 sp, ch 1) across to next corner ch-3 sp; repeat from ★ around; join with slip st to first sc: 400 sps.
Rnd 3: Slip st in next corner ch-3 sp, ch 3 **(counts as first dc)**, (2 dc, ch 3, 3 dc) in same sp, ch 1, skip next ch-1 sp, ★ (3 dc in next ch-1 sp, ch 1, skip next ch-1 sp) across to next corner ch-3 sp, (3 dc, ch 3, 3 dc) in corner ch-3 sp, ch 1, skip next ch-1 sp; repeat from ★ 2 times **more**, (3 dc in next ch-1 sp, ch 1, skip next ch-1 sp) across; join with slip st to first dc, finish off: 204 sps.
Rnds 4-6: With **right** side facing, join any Scrap color with dc in any corner ch-3 sp; 2 dc in same sp, ch 1, ★ (3 dc in next ch-1 sp, ch 1) across to next corner ch-3 sp, 3 dc in corner ch-3 sp changing to next Scrap color in last dc made *(Fig. 19, page 141)*, ch 3, 3 dc in same sp, ch 1; repeat from ★ 2 times **more**, (3 dc in next ch-1 sp, ch 1) across, 3 dc in same sp as first dc, ch 3; join with slip st to first dc, finish off: 216 sps.
Rnd 7: With **right** side facing, join Black with dc in any corner ch-3 sp; (2 dc, ch 3, 3 dc) in same sp, ch 1, ★ (3 dc in next ch-1 sp, ch 1) across to next corner ch-3 sp, (3 dc, ch 3, 3 dc) in corner ch-3 sp, ch 1; repeat from ★ 2 times **more**, (3 dc in next ch-1 sp, ch 1) across; join with slip st to first dc, do **not** finish off.

Rnd 8: (Slip st, ch 1, sc) in next dc, ch 1, (sc, ch 2, sc) in next corner ch-3 sp, ch 1, ★ skip next dc, sc in next dc, ch 1, (sc in next ch-1 sp, ch 1, skip next dc, sc in next dc, ch 1) across to next corner ch-3 sp, (sc, ch 2, sc) in corner ch-3 sp, ch 1; repeat from ★ 2 times **more**, (skip next dc, sc in next dc, ch 1, sc in next ch-1 sp, ch 1) across; join with slip st to first sc.

Rnd 9: Slip st in next ch-1 sp, ch 1, (slip st, ch 2, slip st) in next corner ch-2 sp, ch 1, ★ (slip st in next ch-1 sp, ch 1) across to next corner ch-2 sp, (slip st, ch 2, slip st) in corner ch-2 sp, ch 1; repeat from ★ 2 times **more**, (slip st in next ch-1 sp, ch 1) across; join with slip st to first slip st, finish off.

COUNTRY KALEIDOSCOPE

Muted country colors twirl and dance in this folksy "kaleidoscope" comforter. Nine of your favorite scrap colors give patchwork appeal to this charming cover-up.

Finished Size: 50" x 62" (127 cm x 157.5 cm)

MATERIALS
Worsted Weight Yarn:
  MC (Ecru) - $12^1/_2$ ounces, 820 yards
    (360 grams, 750 meters)
  Color A (Red) - $3^1/_4$ ounces, 215 yards
    (90 grams, 196.5 meters)
  Color B (Grey) - $3^1/_4$ ounces, 215 yards
    (90 grams, 196.5 meters)
  Color C (Yellow) - $3^1/_4$ ounces, 215 yards
    (90 grams, 196.5 meters)
  Color D (Green) - $3^1/_4$ ounces, 215 yards
    (90 grams, 196.5 meters)
  Color E (Lt Blue) - $3^3/_4$ ounces, 250 yards
    (110 grams, 228.5 meters)
  Color F (Blue) - $4^1/_2$ ounces, 295 yards
    (130 grams, 269.5 meters)
  Color G (Lt Brown) - $4^1/_2$ ounces, 295 yards
    (130 grams, 269.5 meters)
  Color H (Brown) - $3^1/_2$ ounces, 230 yards
    (100 grams, 210.5 meters)
  Color I (Black) - $4^1/_4$ ounces, 280 yards
    (120 grams, 256 meters)
Crochet hook, size K (7 mm) **or** size needed
    for gauge
Yarn needle

GAUGE SWATCH: $6^1/_2$" (16.5 cm) square
Work same as Square.

STITCH GUIDE

> **FRONT POST DOUBLE CROCHET**
>   *(abbreivated FPdc)*
> YO, insert hook from **front** to **back** around post of st indicated, YO and pull up a loop even with last st made *(Fig. 9, page 139)*, (YO and draw through 2 loops on hook) twice.
> **V-ST**
> (Dc, ch 1, dc) in st or sp indicated.

SQUARE
Make 8 Squares **each** in the following Color Sequences:

Rnd 1	Rnd 2	Rnd 3	Rnd 4	Rnd 5	Rnd 6	Rnd 7	Rnd 8
A	A	B	A	B	A	B	MC
B	B	A	B	A	B	A	MC
C	C	D	C	D	C	D	MC
D	D	C	D	C	D	C	MC
E	E	F	E	F	E	F	MC
F	F	E	F	E	F	E	MC
G	G	H	G	H	G	H	MC
H	H	G	H	G	H	G	MC
MC	MC	H	G	H	MC	G	MC
E	E	C	F	C	E	F	MC

With first color ch 5; join with slip st to form a ring.
Rnd 1 (Right side): Ch 1, 16 sc in ring; join with slip st to Back Loop Only of first sc *(Fig. 15, page 140)*.
Note: Loop a short piece of yarn around any stitch to mark Rnd 1 as **right** side.
Rnd 2: Ch 1, sc in Back Loop Only of same st, ch 1, skip next sc, ★ sc in Back Loop Only of next sc, ch 1, skip next sc; repeat from ★ around; join with slip st to first sc: 8 sc.
Rnd 3: With **right** side facing, join next color with slip st in any ch-1 sp; ch 1, sc in same sp, dc in free loop of sc one rnd **below** next sc *(Fig. 17a, page 141)*, skip sc behind dc, ★ sc in next ch-1 sp, dc in free loop of sc one rnd **below** next sc, skip sc behind dc; repeat from ★ around; join with slip st to Back Loop Only of first sc, finish off: 16 sts.
Rnd 4: With **right** side facing and working in Back Loops Only, join next color with slip st in same st as joining; ch 1, sc in same st, work (FPdc, ch 1, FPdc) around next dc *(Fig. 9, page 139)*, ★ sc in next sc, work (FPdc, ch 1, FPdc) around next dc; repeat from ★ around; join with slip st to first sc: 8 sc.
Rnd 5: With **right** side facing and working in Back Loops Only, join next color with slip st in same st as joining; ch 1, sc in same st and in next FPdc, ch 1, dc in next ch-1 sp, ch 1, ★ sc in next 3 sts, ch 1, dc in next ch-1 sp, ch 1; repeat from ★ around to last FPdc, sc in last FPdc; join with slip st to first sc, finish off: 24 sc.

88

Continued on page 90.

Rnd 6: With **right** side facing and working in Back Loops Only, join next color with slip st in ch to left of any dc; ch 1, sc in same st and in next sc, dc in free loop of sc one rnd **below** next sc, skip sc behind dc, sc in next sc and next ch, work (FPdc, ch 1, FPdc) around next dc, ★ sc in next ch and in next sc, , dc in free loop of sc one rnd **below** next sc, skip sc behind dc, sc in next sc and next ch, work (FPdc, ch 1, FPdc) around next dc; repeat from ★ around; join with slip st to first sc, finish off: 32 sc.

Rnd 7: With **right** side facing and working in Back Loops Only, join next color with slip st in any ch-1 sp; ch 3, (dc, ch 2, 2 dc) in same sp, ★ † dc in next sc, skip next sc, work (FPdc, ch 1, FPdc) around next dc, skip next sc, hdc in next sc, sc in next ch-1 sp, hdc in next sc, skip next sc, work (FPdc, ch 1, FPdc) around next dc, skip next sc, dc in next sc †, (2 dc, ch 2, 2 dc) in next ch-1 sp; repeat from ★ 2 times **more**, then repeat from † to † once; join with slip st to top of beginning ch-3, finish off: 4 ch-2 sps.

Rnd 8: With **right** side facing, join next color with slip st in any ch-2 sp; ch 4, [dc, (ch 1, dc) twice] in same sp, ★ † skip next dc, work V-St in next dc and in next ch-1 sp, skip next 2 sts, work V-St in next sc and in next ch-1 sp, skip next 2 sts, work V-St in next dc †, work [V-St, ch 1, V-St (corner)] in next ch-2 sp;

repeat from ★ 2 times **more**, then repeat from † to † once; join with slip st to third ch of beginning ch-4, finish off.

ASSEMBLY

Afghan is assembled by joining 10 Squares into 8 vertical strips and then by joining strips. Join two Squares as follows:
With **wrong** sides together and working through **both** thicknesses, join Color I with slip st in corner ch 1; ch 1, sc in same sp, (ch 1, sc in next ch-1 sp) across to next corner ch-1 sp; finish off. Join remaining Squares and strips in same manner.

EDGING

Rnd 1: With **right** side facing, join Color I with slip st in any corner ch-1 sp; ch 1, (sc, ch 1, sc) in same sp, ch 1, (sc in next ch-1 sp, ch 1) across to next corner ch-1 sp, ★ (sc, ch 1, sc) in ch-1 sp, ch 1, (sc in next ch-1 sp, ch 1) across to next corner ch-1 sp; repeat from ★ around; join with slip st to first sc.

Rnd 2: Ch 1, turn; sc in first ch-1 sp, ch 1, ★ (sc in next ch-1 sp, ch 1) across to next corner ch-1 sp, (sc, ch 1, sc) in ch-1 sp, ch 1; repeat from ★ around; join with slip st to first sc, finish off.

AUTUMN BRILLIANCE

Echoing the brilliance of autumn, this richly hued afghan and pillow set is a comfy way to welcome the season. The squares are defined by a distinguished arrangement of colorful "leaves."

Finished Sizes:
Afghan - 49" x 63" (124.5 cm x 160 cm)
Pillow - 14¹/₂" (37 cm) square

MATERIALS
Worsted Weight Yarn:
    Green - 36 ounces, 2,035 yards
        (1,020 grams, 1,861 meters)
    Gold and Red - 12 ounces, 680 yards
        (340 grams, 622 meters) **each**
    Tan - 4 ounces, 225 yards
        (110 grams, 205.5 meters)
Crochet hook, size H (5 mm) **or** size needed for gauge
Pillow finishing materials: 14" (35.5 cm) square purchased pillow form, two 14¹/₂" (37 cm) fabric squares for pillow form cover, sewing machine, sewing needle and thread

GAUGE SWATCH: 6³/₄" (17.25 cm) square
Work same as Square.

STITCH GUIDE

> **LEAF**
> Ch 2, (hdc, ch 2, slip st, ch 3, dc, ch 3, slip st, ch 2, hdc, ch 2, slip st) in st or sp indicated.

SQUARE (Make 63 for Afghan; make 8 for Pillow)

With Medium Sage, ch 6; join with slip st to form a ring.

Rnd 1 (Right side): Ch 3, dc in ring, ch 3, ★ slip st in ring, ch 3, dc in ring, ch 3; repeat from ★ 6 times **more**; join with slip st to joining slip st, finish off: 8 dc.

Note: Loop a short piece of yarn around any stitch on Rnd 1 to mark **right** side.

90

Continued on page 92.

Rnd 2: With **right** side facing, join Gold with slip st in any dc; work Leaf in same st, ch 2, sc in next dc, ch 2, ★ (slip st, work Leaf) in next dc, ch 2, sc in next dc, ch 2; repeat from ★ 2 times **more**; join with slip st to joining slip st, finish off: 4 Leaves and 4 sc.

Rnd 3: With **right** side facing, join Warm Brown with slip st in any dc; work Leaf in same st, ch 3, (dc, ch 3) twice in next sc, ★ (slip st, work Leaf) in next dc, ch 3, (dc, ch 3) twice in next sc; repeat from ★ 2 times **more**; join with slip st to joining slip st, finish off: 4 Leaves and 12 ch-3 sps.

Rnd 4: With **right** side facing, join Cherry Red with slip st in dc at tip of any Leaf; work Leaf in same st, ★ † ch 4, (slip st, work Leaf) in ch-3 sp **between** next 2 dc, ch 4 †, (slip st, work Leaf) in dc at tip of next Leaf; repeat from ★ 2 times **more**, then repeat from † to † once; join with slip st to joining slip st, finish off: 8 Leaves and 8 ch-4 sps.

Rnd 5: With **right** side facing, join Medium Sage with sc in dc at tip of any corner Leaf; 2 sc in same st, ★ † ch 3, (tr, ch 2) twice in next ch-4 sp, sc in next dc, (ch 2, tr) twice in next ch-4 sp, ch 3 †, 3 sc in next dc; repeat from ★ 2 times **more**, then repeat from † to † once; join with slip st to first sc, do **not** finish off: 32 sts and 24 sps.

Rnd 6: Ch 1, sc in same st, ★ † 3 sc in next sc, sc in next sc, 3 sc in next ch-3 sp, (sc in next tr, 2 sc in next ch-2 sp) twice, sc in next sc, (2 sc in next ch-2 sp, sc in next tr) twice, 3 sc in next ch-3 sp †, sc in next sc; repeat from ★ 2 times **more**, then repeat from † to † once; join with slip st to first sc: 96 sc.

Rnd 7: Ch 3 **(counts as first dc)**, dc in next sc and in each sc around working 3 dc in center sc of each corner 3-sc group; join with slip st to first dc, finish off: 104 dc.

AFGHAN FINISHING
ASSEMBLY

Place two Squares with **wrong** sides together. Working through inside loop only, join Gold with slip st in center dc of first corner 3-dc group; (ch 1, slip st in next dc) across working last st in center dc of next corner 3-dc group; finish off. Join remaining Squares in same manner, forming 7 vertical strips of 9 Squares each; then join strips in same manner.

EDGING

Rnd 1: With **right** side facing and working in Back Loops Only *(Fig. 15, page 140)*, join Gold with sc in any dc; sc in each dc around working hdc in each joining dc and 3 sc in center dc of each corner 3-dc group; join with slip st to **both** loops of first sc.

Rnd 2: Ch 1, sc in both loops of same st and each st around working 3 sc in center sc of each corner 3-sc group; join with slip st to first sc, finish off.

PILLOW FINISHING
PILLOW FORM

Matching right sides and raw edges, use a $^1/_4$" (7 mm) seam allowance to sew fabric squares together, leaving bottom edge open. Clip seam allowances at corners. Turn cover right side out, carefully pushing corners outward. Insert pillow form and sew final closure by hand.

FRONT/BACK ASSEMBLY

Place two Squares with **wrong** sides together. Working through inside loop only, join Gold with slip st in center dc of first corner 3-dc group; (ch 1, slip st in next dc) across working last st in center dc of next corner 3-dc group; finish off. Join remaining Squares in same manner, forming 4 vertical strips of 2 Squares each; then join strips in same manner to form one block of 4 Squares for Front and another block of 4 Squares for Back.

EDGING

Back: With **right** side facing and working in Back Loops Only, join Gold with sc in any dc; sc in each dc around working hdc in each joining dc and 3 sc in center dc of each corner 3-dc group; join with slip st to **both** loops of first sc, finish off: 216 sc.

Front: Work same as Back; do **not** finish off.

Joining Rnd: Place Front and Back with **wrong** sides together. With Front facing and working in **both** loops of each st on **both** pieces, slip st in same st, ch 1, (slip st in next st, ch 1) around inserting pillow form before closing; join with slip st to first slip st, finish off.

APPLE ORCHARD

Fill up that bushel basket! A hand-picked apple is a thoughtful gift for Teacher — and another one keeps the doctor away! Scalloped edging adds a sweet, old-fashioned touch to this harvest wrap.

Finished Size: 48" x 60" (122 cm x 152.5 cm)

MATERIALS

Worsted Weight Yarn:
　Green - 15 ounces, 850 yards
　　(430 grams, 777 meters)
　Red - 14 ounces, 790 yards
　　(400 grams, 722.5 meters)
　Tan - 11 ounces, 620 yards
　　(310 grams, 567 meters)
　Brown - small amount
Crochet hooks, sizes F (3.75 mm) **and**
　H (5 mm) **or** sizes needed for gauge
Yarn needle

GAUGE: Each Block = 7$\frac{1}{4}$" (18.5 cm)

Gauge Swatch: 3" (7.5 cm) diameter
Work same as Strip A Block through Rnd 2.

STITCH GUIDE

> **TREBLE CROCHET** *(abbreviated tr)*
> YO twice, insert hook in sc indicated, YO and pull up a loop (4 loops on hook), (YO and draw through 2 loops on hook) 3 times.

STRIP A (Make 3)

BLOCK (Make 7)
Rnd 1 (Right side): With Red and larger size hook, ch 4, 11 dc in fourth ch from hook **(3 skipped chs count as first dc, now and throughout)**; join with slip st to first dc: 12 dc.
Note: Loop a short piece of yarn around any stitch to mark Rnd 1 as **right** side.
Rnd 2: Ch 3 **(counts as first dc, now and throughout)**, dc in same st, 2 dc in next dc and in each dc around; join with slip st to first dc: 24 dc.
Rnd 3: Ch 3, dc in same st and in next dc, (2 dc in next dc, dc in next dc) around; join with slip st to first dc, finish off: 36 dc.
Rnd 4: With **right** side facing, join Tan with dc in same st as joining *(see Joining With Dc, page 140)*; dc in same st, dc in next 2 dc, (2 dc in next dc, dc in next 2 dc) around; join with slip st to first dc: 48 dc.
Rnd 5: Ch 3, dc in same st and in next 3 dc, (2 dc in next dc, dc in next 3 dc) around; join with slip st to first dc: 60 dc.

Rnd 6: Ch 1, sc in same st and in next 3 dc, ★ † ch 1, skip next dc, hdc in next dc, ch 1, skip next dc, dc in next dc, ch 1, skip next dc, (tr, ch 4, tr) in next dc, ch 1, skip next dc, dc in next dc, ch 1, skip next dc, hdc in next dc, ch 1, skip next dc †, sc in next 4 sc; repeat from ★ 2 times **more**, then repeat from † to † once; join with slip st to first sc: 40 sts and 28 sps.
Rnd 7: Ch 1, sc in same st and in each st and ch-1 sp around working 5 sc in each corner ch-4 sp; join with slip st to first sc, finish off: 84 sc.

STEM (Make 7)
With Brown and smaller size hook, ch 6, slip st in second ch from hook and in each ch across; finish off leaving a long end for sewing.
Using photo as a guide for placement, sew Stem to right side of Block.

LEAF (Make 14)
With Green and smaller size hook, ch 7, slip st in second ch from hook, sc in next ch, hdc in next ch, dc in next ch, hdc in next ch, slip st in last ch; finish off leaving a long end for sewing.
Using photo as a guide for placement, sew 2 Leaves to each Block placing one on each side of Stem.

ASSEMBLY
With Tan, using photo as a guide and working in both loops, whipstitch Blocks together forming a Strip *(Fig. 21a, page 142)*, beginning in center sc of first corner 5-sc group and ending in center sc of next corner 5-sc group.

BORDER
With **right** side facing, larger size hook, and working across short edge of strip, join Green with dc in center sc of corner 5-sc group; ch 3, dc in same st, † dc in next 20 sc, (dc, ch 3, dc) in next sc, dc in next 20 sc, ★ dc in same st as joining on same Block, dc in joining and in same st as joining on next Block, dc in next 20 sc, dc in same st as joining on same Block and in next Block, dc in next 20 sc; repeat from ★ 2 times **more** †, (dc, ch 3, dc) in next sc, repeat from † to † once; join with slip st to first dc, finish off: 358 dc and 4 ch-3 sps.

Continued on page 94.

STRIP B (Make 2)
CENTER
With Red and larger size hook, ch 160.

Rnd 1: 4 Dc in fourth ch from hook, place marker around first dc made to mark **right** side and st placement, skip next 2 chs, slip st in next ch, ★ skip next 2 chs, 5 dc in next ch, skip next 2 chs, slip st in next ch; repeat from ★ across to last 3 chs, skip next 2 chs, 9 dc in last ch; working in free loops of beginning ch *(Fig. 17b, page 141)*, skip next 2 chs, slip st in next ch, skip next 2 chs, (5 dc in next ch, skip next 2 chs, slip st in next ch, skip next 2 chs) across, 4 dc in same ch as first dc; join with slip st to first dc, finish off: 268 dc.

Rnd 2: With **right** side facing, join Green with dc in marked dc; dc in same st, † hdc in next dc, sc in next dc, hdc in next dc, working **around** next slip st *(Fig. 18, page 141)*, dc in same ch as next slip st, ★ hdc in next dc, sc in next 3 dc, hdc in next dc, working **around** next slip st, dc in same ch as next slip st; repeat from ★ across to next 9-dc group, hdc in next dc, sc in next dc, hdc in next dc, 3 dc in next dc, dc in next dc †, 3 dc in next dc, repeat from † to † once, dc in same st as first dc; join with slip st to first dc, do **not** finish off: 328 sts.

TRIM
FIRST SIDE
Row 1: Ch 3, dc in next dc and in each st across ending in center dc of next 3-dc group, leave remaining sts unworked: 161 dc.

Row 2: Ch 4 **(counts as first dc, plus ch 1)**, turn; skip next dc, dc in next dc, ★ ch 1, skip next dc, dc in next dc; repeat from ★ across; finish off: 81 dc and 80 ch-1 sps.

Row 3: With **right** side facing, join Red with dc in first dc; dc in each ch-1 sp and in each dc across; finish off: 161 dc.

Row 4: With **wrong** side facing, join Green with dc in first dc; ★ ch 1, skip next dc, dc in next dc; repeat from ★ across; finish off: 81 dc and 80 ch-1 sps.

SECOND SIDE
Row 1: With **right** side facing, skip 3 dc from First Side and join Green with dc in next dc; dc in next dc and in each st across to last 3 dc, leave remaining 3 dc unworked: 161 dc.

Rows 2-4: Repeat Rows 2-4 of First Side: 81 dc and 80 ch-1 sps.

ASSEMBLY
With Green and working through both loops, whipstitch Strips together *(Fig. 21b, page 142)*, beginning in center ch of first corner ch-3 on Strip A and first dc on Strip B, and ending in center ch of next corner ch-3 on Strip A and last dc on Strip B in the following order: Strip A, (Strip B, Strip A) twice.

EDGING
Rnd 1: With **right** side facing, larger size hook, and working across short edge of Afghan, join Green with dc in first corner ch-3 sp on Strip A; † dc in next 11 dc, 2 dc in next dc, dc in next 10 dc, ★ dc in next sp and in next joining, 2 dc in each of next 4 rows on Strip B, dc in same st as dc on Row 1 of Trim, dc in next 3 dc, dc in same st as dc on Row 1 of Trim, 2 dc in each of next 4 rows, dc in next joining and in next sp, dc in next 22 dc; repeat from ★ once **more**, (dc, ch 3, dc) in next corner ch-3 sp; working across long edge of Afghan, dc in each dc across to next corner ch-3 sp †, (dc, ch 3, dc) in corner ch-3 sp, repeat from † to † once, dc in same sp as first dc, dc in first dc to form last ch-3 sp: 556 dc and 4 ch-3 sps.

Rnd 2: Ch 6 **(counts as first dc plus ch 3)**, dc in last ch-3 sp made, ch 1, dc in next dc, ch 1, (skip next dc, dc in next dc, ch 1) across to next corner ch-3 sp, ★ (dc, ch 3, dc) in corner ch-3 sp, ch 1, dc in next dc, ch 1, (skip next dc, dc in next dc, ch 1) across to next corner ch-3 sp; repeat from ★ 2 times **more**; join with slip st to first dc, finish off: 288 dc and 288 sps.

Rnd 3: With **right** side facing, join Red with dc in any corner ch-3 sp; 4 dc in same sp, ★ dc in each dc and in each ch-1 sp across to next corner ch-3 sp, 5 dc in corner ch-3 sp; repeat from ★ 2 times **more**, dc in each dc and in each ch-1 sp across; join with slip st to first dc, finish off: 592 dc.

Rnd 4: With **right** side facing, join Green with dc in center dc of any corner 5-dc group; ★ † ch 1, skip next dc, (dc in next dc, ch 1, skip next dc) across to center dc of next corner 5-dc group †, (dc, ch 3, dc) in center dc; repeat from ★ 2 times **more**, then repeat from † to † once, dc in same st as first dc, ch 2, sc in first dc to form last ch-3 sp: 300 dc and 300 sps.

Rnd 5: Ch 3, dc in each dc and in each ch-1 sp across to next corner ch-3 sp, ★ (dc, ch 3, dc) in corner ch-3 sp, dc in each dc and in each ch-1 sp across to next corner ch-3 sp; repeat from ★ 2 times **more**, dc in same sp as first dc, ch 2, sc in first dc to form last ch-3 sp: 604 dc and 4 ch-3 sps.

Rnd 6: Ch 3, dc in each dc across to next corner ch-3 sp, ★ (dc, ch 3, dc) in corner ch-3 sp, dc in each dc across to next corner ch-3 sp; repeat from ★ 2 times **more**, dc in same sp as first dc, ch 3; join with slip st to first dc, finish off: 612 dc and 4 ch-3 sps.

Rnd 7: With **right** side facing, join Red with dc in any corner ch-3 sp, 4 dc in same sp, ★ † slip st in next dc, (skip next dc, 5 dc in next dc, skip next dc, slip st in next dc) across to next corner ch-3 sp †, 5 dc in corner ch-3 sp; repeat from ★ 2 times **more**, then repeat from † to † once; join with slip st to first dc, finish off.

QUIET REFUGE

Create your own quiet refuge as you curl up in this coverlet and lose yourself in reflection and daydreams. Popcorn and twisted post stitches form a subtle texture on this understated afghan.

Finished Size: 45^{1}/$_{2}$" x 64^{1}/$_{2}$" (115.5 cm x 164 cm)

MATERIALS

Worsted Weight Yarn:
  71 ounces, 4,010 yards
    (2,020 grams, 3,666.5 meters)
Crochet hook, size J (6 mm) **or** size needed
  for gauge

GAUGE: 8 dc and 6 rows = 3" (7.5 cm)

Gauge Swatch: 6" (15.25 cm) square
Ch 18 **loosely**.
Row 1: Dc in fourth ch from hook **(3 skipped chs count as first dc)** and in each ch across: 16 dc.
Rows 2-12: Ch 3 **(counts as first dc)**, turn; dc in next dc and in each dc across.
Finish off.

STITCH GUIDE

> ### FRONT POST DOUBLE CROCHET
> **(abbreviated FPdc)**
> YO, insert hook from **front** to **back** around post of st indicated **(Fig. 9, page 139)**, YO and pull up a loop even with last st made, (YO and draw through 2 loops on hook) twice. Skip st behind FPdc.
>
> ### BACK POST DOUBLE CROCHET
> **(abbreviated BPdc)**
> YO, insert hook from **back** to **front** around post of FPdc indicated **(Fig. 9, page 139)**, YO and pull up a loop even with last st made, (YO and draw through 2 loops on hook) twice. Skip st in front of BPdc.
>
> ### POPCORN
> 4 Dc in dc indicated, drop loop from hook, insert hook in first dc of 4-dc group, hook dropped loop and draw through st **(Fig. 13, page 139)**.
>
> ### TWIST (uses next 4 sts)
> Skip next 2 sts, work FPdc around each of next 2 sts, working in **front** of last 2 FPdc made **(Fig. 18, page 141)**, work FPdc around second skipped st, work FPdc around first skipped st.

AFGHAN BODY

Ch 145 **loosely**, place marker in third ch from hook for st placement.
Row 1 (Wrong side): Dc in fourth ch from hook **(3 skipped chs count as first dc)** and in each ch across: 143 dc.
Note: Loop a short piece of yarn around **back** of any dc on Row 1 to mark **right** side.
Row 2: Ch 3 **(counts as first dc, now and throughout)**, turn; work FPdc around next st, dc in next dc, work Popcorn in next dc, dc in next dc, work FPdc around next st, ★ † dc in next 5 dc, work Twist, dc in next 5 dc, work Popcorn in next dc, dc in next 5 dc, work Twist, dc in next 5 dc, work FPdc around next st †, (dc in next dc, work FPdc around next st) twice; repeat from ★ 2 times **more**, then repeat from † to † once, dc in next dc, work Popcorn in next dc, dc in next dc, work FPdc around next st, dc in last dc.
Row 3: Ch 3, turn; work BPdc around next FPdc, dc in next 3 sts, work BPdc around next FPdc, ★ † dc in next 5 dc, work BPdc around each of next 4 FPdc, dc in next 11 sts, work BPdc around each of next 4 FPdc, dc in next 5 dc, work BPdc around next FPdc †, (dc in next dc, work BPdc around next FPdc) twice; repeat from ★ 2 times **more**, then repeat from † to † once, dc in next 3 sts, work BPdc around next FPdc, dc in last dc.
Row 4: Ch 3, turn; work FPdc around next BPdc, dc in next dc, work Popcorn in next dc, dc in next dc, work FPdc around next BPdc, ★ † dc in next 5 dc, work FPdc around each of next 4 BPdc, dc in next 4 dc, work Popcorn in next dc, dc in next dc, work Popcorn in next dc, dc in next 4 dc, work FPdc around each of next 4 BPdc, dc in next 5 dc, work FPdc around next BPdc †, (dc in next dc, work FPdc around next BPdc) twice; repeat from ★ 2 times **more**, then repeat from † to † once, dc in next dc, work Popcorn in next dc, dc in next dc, work FPdc around next BPdc, dc in last dc.
Row 5: Repeat Row 3.

Continued on page 98.

Row 6: Ch 3, turn; work FPdc around next BPdc, dc in next dc, work Popcorn in next dc, dc in next dc, work FPdc around next BPdc, ★ † dc in next 5 dc, work Twist, dc in next 3 dc, work Popcorn in next dc, (dc in next dc, work Popcorn in next dc) twice, dc in next 3 dc, work Twist, dc in next 5 dc, work FPdc around next BPdc †, (dc in next dc, work FPdc around next BPdc) twice; repeat from ★ 2 times **more**, then repeat from † to † once, dc in next dc, work Popcorn in next dc, dc in next dc, work FPdc around next BPdc, dc in last dc.

Rows 7-9: Repeat Rows 3 and 4 once, then repeat Row 3 once **more**.

Rows 10 and 11: Repeat Rows 2 and 3.

Row 12: Ch 3, turn; work FPdc around next BPdc, dc in next dc, work Popcorn in next dc, dc in next dc, work FPdc around next BPdc, ★ † dc in next 5 dc, work FPdc around each of next 4 BPdc, dc in next 11 dc, work FPdc around each of next 4 BPdc, dc in next 5 dc, work FPdc around next BPdc †, (dc in next dc, work FPdc around next BPdc) twice; repeat from ★ 2 times **more**, then repeat from † to † once, dc in next dc, work Popcorn in next dc, dc in next dc, work FPdc around next BPdc, dc in last dc.

Row 13: Repeat Row 3.

Row 14: Ch 3, turn; work FPdc around next BPdc, dc in next dc, work Popcorn in next dc, dc in next dc, work FPdc around next BPdc, ★ † dc in next 5 dc, work Twist, dc in next 3 dc, skip next 2 dc, work 5 FPdc around next dc, skip next 2 dc, dc in next 3 dc, work Twist, dc in next 5 dc, work FPdc around next BPdc †, (dc in next dc, work FPdc around next BPdc) twice; repeat from ★ 2 times **more**, then repeat from † to † once, dc in next dc, work Popcorn in next dc, dc in next dc, work FPdc around next BPdc, dc in last dc.

Row 15: Ch 3, turn; work BPdc around next FPdc, dc in next 3 sts, work BPdc around next FPdc, ★ † dc in next 5 dc, work BPdc around each of next 4 FPdc, dc in next 3 dc, ch 2, skip next 2 FPdc, sc in next FPdc, ch 2, skip next 2 FPdc, dc in next 3 dc, work BPdc around each of next 4 FPdc, dc in next 5 dc, work BPdc around next FPdc †, (dc in next dc, work BPdc around next FPdc) twice; repeat from ★ 2 times **more**, then repeat from † to † once, dc in next 3 sts, work BPdc around next FPdc, dc in last dc.

Row 16: Ch 3, turn; work FPdc around next BPdc, dc in next dc, work Popcorn in next dc, dc in next dc, work FPdc around next BPdc, ★ † dc in next 5 dc, work FPdc around next each of 4 BPdc, dc in next 11 sts, work FPdc around next each of 4 BPdc, dc in next 5 dc, work FPdc around next BPdc †, (dc in next dc, work FPdc around next BPdc) twice; repeat from ★ 2 times **more**, then repeat from † to † once, dc in next dc, work Popcorn in next dc, dc in next dc, work FPdc around next BPdc, dc in last dc.

Row 17: Repeat Row 3.

Rows 18-139: Repeat Rows 2-17, 7 times; then repeat Rows 2-11 once **more**.

Trim: Ch 1, turn; sc in first dc and in each st across to last dc, 3 sc in last dc; sc evenly across end of rows to beginning ch; working in free loops of beginning ch (*Fig. 17b, page 141*), 3 sc in first ch, sc in each ch across to marked ch, 3 sc in marked ch; sc evenly across end of rows, 2 sc in same st as first sc; join with slip st to first sc, finish off.

Holding 6 strands of yarn together, each 20" (51 cm) long, add fringe in every third stitch across short edges of Afghan (*Figs. 22a & c, page 142*).

WARM & COZY

Get warm and cozy as you nestle near the hearth with our toasty throw.
Popcorn, cable, and shell stitches make this homey comforter snuggly-soft.

Finished Size: 54" x 73" (137 cm x 185.5 cm)

MATERIALS
Worsted Weight Yarn:
  64 ounces, 3,615 yards
    (1,820 grams, 3,305.5 meters)
  Crochet hook, size J (6 mm) **or** size needed
    for gauge

GAUGE: 11 dc and 8 rows = 4" (10 cm)

Gauge Swatch: 4" (10 cm) square
Ch 13 **loosely**.
Row 1: Dc in fourth ch from hook **(3 skipped chs count as first dc)** and in each ch across: 11 dc.
Rows 2-8: Ch 3 **(counts as first dc)**, turn; dc in next dc and in each dc across.
Finish off.

STITCH GUIDE

FRONT POST DOUBLE CROCHET
  (abbreviated FPdc)
YO, insert hook from **front** to **back** around post of st indicated *(Fig. 9, page 139)*, YO and pull up a loop even with loop on hook, (YO and draw through 2 loops on hook) twice.

BACK POST DOUBLE CROCHET
  (abbreviated BPdc)
YO, insert hook from **back** to **front** around post of FPdc indicated *(Fig. 9, page 139)*, YO and pull up a loop even with loop on hook, (YO and draw through 2 loops on hook) twice.

POPCORN
4 Dc in dc indicated, drop loop from hook, insert hook in first dc of 4-dc group, hook dropped loop and draw through *(Fig. 13, page 139)*.

CABLE (uses next 4 sts)
Skip next 2 sts, work FPdc around next 2 sts, work FPdc around second skipped st, work FPdc around first skipped st.

SHELL
2 Dc in st or sp indicated, (ch 1, 2 dc in same st or sp) twice.

AFGHAN BODY

Ch 136 **loosely**, place marker in third ch from hook for Edging placement.
Row 1: Dc in fourth ch from hook **(3 skipped chs count as first dc)** and in each ch across: 134 dc.
Row 2 (Right side): Ch 3 **(counts as first dc, now and throughout)**, turn; ★ † work FPdc around next dc, (dc in next dc, work FPdc around next dc) twice, dc in next 2 dc, work Popcorn in next dc, dc in next 2 dc, work FPdc around next dc, dc in next 2 dc, work Cable, dc in next 2 dc, work FPdc around next dc, dc in next 2 dc, work Popcorn in next dc, dc in next 2 dc †, work FPdc around next dc, (dc in next dc, work FPdc around next dc) twice, dc in next 5 dc, work FPdc around next dc, dc in next dc, skip next 3 dc, work Shell in next dc, skip next 3 dc, dc in next dc, work FPdc around next dc, dc in next 5 dc; repeat from ★ once **more**, then repeat from † to † once, (work FPdc around next dc, dc in next dc) 3 times: 132 sts and 4 ch-1 sps.
Row 3: Ch 3, turn; ★ † work BPdc around next FPdc, (dc in next dc, work BPdc around next FPdc) twice, dc in next 5 sts, work BPdc around next FPdc, dc in next 2 dc, work BPdc around next 4 FPdc, dc in next 2 dc, work BPdc around next FPdc, dc in next 5 sts †, work BPdc around next FPdc, (dc in next dc, work BPdc around next FPdc) twice, dc in next 5 dc, work BPdc around next FPdc, dc in next dc, ch 2, (sc in next ch-1 sp, ch 2) twice, skip next 2 dc, dc in next dc, work BPdc around next FPdc, dc in next 5 dc; repeat from ★ once **more**, then repeat from † to † once, (work BPdc around next FPdc, dc in next dc) 3 times: 124 sts and 6 ch-2 sps.
Row 4: Ch 3, turn; ★ † (work FPdc around next BPdc, dc in next dc) 3 times, (work Popcorn in next dc, dc in next dc) twice, work FPdc around next BPdc, dc in next 2 dc, work FPdc around next 4 BPdc, dc in next 2 dc, work FPdc around next BPdc, (dc in next dc, work Popcorn in next dc) twice, (dc in next dc, work FPdc around next BPdc) 3 times †, dc in next 5 dc, work FPdc around next BPdc, dc in next dc, skip next ch-2 sp, work Shell in next ch-2 sp, skip next ch-2 sp, dc in next dc, work FPdc around next BPdc, dc in next 5 dc; repeat from ★ once **more**, then repeat from † to † once, dc in last dc; off: 132 sts and 4 ch-1 sps.

Continued on page 100.

Row 5: Ch 3, turn; ★ † work BPdc around next FPdc, (dc in next dc, work BPdc around next FPdc) twice, dc in next 5 sts, work BPdc around next FPdc, dc in next 2 dc, work BPdc around next 4 FPdc, dc in next 2 dc, work BPdc around next FPdc, dc in next 5 sts †, work BPdc around next FPdc, (dc in next dc, work BPdc around next FPdc) twice, dc in next 5 dc, work BPdc around next FPdc, dc in next dc, ch 2, (sc in next ch-1 sp, ch 2) twice, skip next 2 dc, dc in next dc, work BPdc around next FPdc, dc in next 5 dc; repeat from ★ once **more**, then repeat from † to † once, (work BPdc around next FPdc, dc in next dc) 3 times: 124 sts and 6 ch-2 sps.

Row 6: Ch 3, turn; ★ † work FPdc around next BPdc, (dc in next dc, work FPdc around next BPdc) twice, dc in next 2 dc, work Popcorn in next dc, dc in next 2 dc, work FPdc around next dc, dc in next 2 dc, work Cable, dc in next 2 dc, work FPdc around next BPdc, dc in next 2 dc, work Popcorn in next dc, dc in next 2 dc †, work FPdc around next BPdc, (dc in next dc, work FPdc around next BPdc) twice, dc in next 5 dc, work FPdc around next BPdc, dc in next dc, skip next ch-2 sp, work Shell in next ch-2 sp, skip next ch-2 sp, dc in next dc, work FPdc around next BPdc, dc in next 5 dc; repeat from ★ once **more**, then repeat from † to † once, (work FPdc around next BPdc, dc in next dc) 3 times: 132 sts and 4 ch-1 sps.

Row 7: Repeat Row 5.

Row 8: Ch 3, turn; ★ † work FPdc around next BPdc, (dc in next dc, work FPdc around next BPdc) twice, dc in next 5 dc, work FPdc around next BPdc, dc in next 2 dc, work FPdc around next 4 BPdc, dc in next 2 dc, work FPdc around next BPdc, dc in next 5 dc †, work FPdc around next BPdc, (dc in next dc, work FPdc around next BPdc) twice, dc in next 5 dc, work FPdc around next BPdc, dc in next dc, skip next ch-2 sp, work Shell in next ch-2 sp, skip next ch-2 sp, dc in next dc, work FPdc around next BPdc, dc in next 5 dc; repeat from ★ once **more**, then repeat from † to † once, (work FPdc around next BPdc, dc in next dc) 3 times: 132 sts and 4 ch-1 sps.

Rows 9 and 10: Repeat Rows 5 and 6.

Repeat Rows 3-10 for pattern until Afghan Body measures approximately 67$\frac{1}{2}$" (171.5 cm) from beginning ch, ending by working Row 7; do **not** finish off.

EDGING

Rnd 1: Ch 3, turn; 4 dc in same st, ★ dc in each st across to next ch-2 sp, 2 dc in next ch-2 sp, dc in next sc, dc in next ch-2 sp and in next sc, 2 dc in next ch-2 sp; repeat from ★ once **more**, dc in each st across to last dc, 5 dc in last dc; work 182 dc evenly spaced across end of rows; working in free loops of beginning ch *(Fig. 17b, page 141)*, 5 dc in marked ch, dc in next ch and in each ch across to last ch, 5 dc in last ch; work 182 dc evenly spaced across end of rows; join with slip st to first dc: 648 dc.

Rnd 2: (Slip st, ch 3, dc) in next dc, (ch 1, 2 dc in same st) twice, skip next dc, work Shell in next dc, ★ (skip next 4 dc, work Shell in next dc) across to center dc of next corner 5-dc group, skip center dc, work Shell in next dc; repeat from ★ 2 times **more**, skip next 4 dc, (work Shell in next dc, skip next 4 dc) across; join with slip st to first dc: 132 Shells.

Rnd 3: Slip st in next dc and in next ch-1 sp, ch 1, sc in same sp, ch 2, sc in next ch-1 sp, ch 4, ★ sc in next ch-1 sp, ch 2, sc in next ch-1 sp, ch 4; repeat from ★ around; join with slip st to first sc: 264 sps.

Rnd 4: Slip st in first ch-2 sp, ch 3, (dc, ch 1, 2 dc) in same sp, sc in next ch-4 sp, (work Shell in next ch-2 sp, sc in next ch-4 sp) around, 2 dc in same sp as first dc, sc in first dc to form last ch-1 sp: 132 sc and 132 Shells.

Rnd 5: Ch 1, sc in last ch-1 sp made, ch 2, sc in next ch-1 sp, † ch 4, skip next 2 dc, sc in next sc, ch 4, (sc in next ch-1 sp, ch 2, sc in next ch-1 sp, ch 4) 28 times, skip next 2 dc, sc in next sc †, (ch 4, sc in next ch-1 sp, ch 2, sc in next ch-1 sp) 38 times, repeat from † to † once, (ch 4, sc in next ch-1 sp, ch 2, sc in next ch-1 sp) across, ch 1, dc in first sc to form last ch-4 sp: 268 sps.

Rnd 6: Ch 1, (sc, ch 3, sc) in last ch-4 sp made and in each sp around; join with slip st to first sc, finish off.

TIMELESS TWEED

Add a touch of sophistication to your living room or home office with this timeless tweed blanket. Crochet with two strands of yarn to achieve the distinct "tweedy" look.

Finished Size: 48" x 67" (122 cm x 170 cm)

MATERIALS
Worsted Weight Yarn:
  Dk Blue - 22¹/₂ ounces, 1,270 yards
    (640 grams, 1,161.5 meters)
  Blue - 20¹/₂ ounces, 1,160 yards
    (580 grams, 1,060.5 meters)
  White - 18 ounces, 1,015 yards
    (510 grams, 928 meters)
  Yellow - 18 ounces, 1,015 yards
    (510 grams, 928 meters)
Crochet hook, size K (6.5 mm) **or** size needed
  for gauge
Safety pins
Yarn needle

Note: Afghan is worked holding two strands of yarn together.

GAUGE SWATCH: 4³/₄" (12 cm) square
Work same as Square.

SQUARE (Make 117)
Holding one strand of White and one strand of Yellow together, ch 6; join with slip st to form a ring.
Rnd 1 (Right side): Ch 3 **(counts as first dc)**, 15 dc in ring; join with slip st to first dc, slip loop from hook onto safety pin to keep piece from unraveling while working next rnd: 16 dc.
Note: Loop a short piece of yarn around any stitch to mark Rnd 1 as **right** side.
Keep dropped yarn and safety pin to **wrong** side, now and throughout.
Rnd 2: With **right** side facing and holding one strand of Blue and one strand of Dk Blue together, join yarn with sc in joining slip st *(see Joining With Sc, page 140)*; ch 1, skip first dc, (sc in next dc, ch 1) around; join with slip st to first sc, slip loop from hook onto safety pin to keep piece from unraveling while working next rnd: 16 sc and 16 ch-1 sps.
Rnd 3: With **wrong** side facing, remove safety pin from Rnd 1 and place loop onto hook; ch 3, sc in ch-1 sp **behind** ch-3, ch 1, (sc in next ch-1 sp, ch 1) around; join with slip st to first sc, finish off.

Rnd 4: With **right** side facing and working **behind** Rnd 3, remove safety pin from Rnd 2 and place loop onto hook; ch 3, sc in sc in **front** of ch-3, ch 1, (dc, ch 3, dc) in next sc, ch 1, sc in next sc, ch 1, slip st in next sc, ch 1, ★ sc in next sc, ch 1, (dc, ch 3, dc) in next sc, ch 1, sc in next sc, ch 1, slip st in next sc, ch 1; repeat from ★ 2 times **more**; join with slip st to first sc, finish off: 20 sps.

ASSEMBLY
With one strand of Dk Blue and working in both loops, whipstitch Squares together *(Fig. 21b, page 141)*, forming 9 vertical strips of 13 Squares each, beginning in center ch of first corner ch-3 and ending in center ch of next corner ch-3; whipstitch strips together in same manner.

EDGING
Rnd 1: With **right** side facing and holding one strand of Blue and one strand of Dk Blue together, join yarn with sc in any corner ch-3 sp; ch 2, sc in same sp, ch 1, ★ (sc in next sp, ch 1) across to next corner ch-3 sp, (sc, ch 2, sc) in corner ch-3 sp, ch 1; repeat from ★ 2 times **more**, (sc in next sp, ch 1) across; join with slip st to first sc: 264 sc and 264 sps.
Rnd 2: Ch 1, turn; ★ (sc in next ch-1 sp, ch 1) across to next corner ch-2 sp, (sc, ch 2, sc) in corner ch-2 sp, ch 1; repeat from ★ around; join with slip st to first sc, slip loop from hook onto safety pin to keep piece from unraveling while working next rnd: 268 sc and 268 sps.
Rnd 3: With **right** side facing and holding one strand of White and one strand of Yellow together, join yarn with sc in any corner ch-2 sp; ch 2, sc in same sp, ch 1, ★ (sc in next ch-1 sp, ch 1) across to next corner ch-2 sp, (sc, ch 2, sc) in corner ch-2 sp, ch 1; repeat from ★ 2 times **more**, (sc in next ch-1 sp, ch 1) across; join with slip st to first sc, slip loop from hook onto safety pin to keep piece from unraveling while working next rnd: 272 sc and 272 sps.
Rnd 4: With **wrong** side facing, remove safety pin from Rnd 2 and place loop onto hook; ch 2, sc in ch-1 sp **behind** ch-2, ch 1, ★ (sc in next ch-1 sp, ch 1) across to next corner ch-2 sp, (sc, ch 2, sc) in corner ch-2 sp, ch 1; repeat from ★ 3 times **more**, sc in last ch-1 sp, ch 1; join with slip st to first sc, slip loop from hook onto safety pin to keep piece from unraveling while working next rnd: 276 sc and 276 sps.

Rnd 5: With **right** side facing and working **behind** Rnd 4, remove safety pin from Rnd 3 and place loop onto hook; ch 2, sc in ch-1 sp in **front** of ch-2, ch 1, (sc, ch 2, sc) in next corner ch-2 sp, ch 1, ★ (sc in next ch-1 sp, ch 1) across to next corner ch-2 sp, (sc, ch 2, sc) in corner ch-2 sp, ch 1; repeat from ★ 2 times **more**, (sc in next ch-1 sp, ch 1) across; join with slip st to first sc, finish off: 280 sc and 280 sps.

Rnd 6: With **wrong** side facing, remove safety pin from Rnd 4 and place loop onto hook; ch 2, sc in ch-1 sp **behind** ch-2, ch 1, ★ (sc in next ch-1 sp, ch 1) across to next corner ch-2 sp, (sc, ch 2, sc) in corner ch-2 sp, ch 1; repeat from ★ 3 times **more**, (sc in next ch-1 sp, ch 1) twice; join with slip st to first sc: 284 sc and 284 sps.

Rnd 7: Ch 1, turn; ★ (slip st in next ch-1 sp, ch 1) across to next corner ch-2 sp, (slip st, ch 2, slip st) in corner ch-2 sp, ch 1; repeat from ★ 3 times **more**, (slip st in next ch-1 sp, ch 1) across; join with slip st to first slip st, finish off.

WINTER

Winter falls softly with frosty flurries and twinkling holiday
lights. Celebrate the season by curling up near the hearth with a
mug of eggnog and one of our toasty throws. The quick-to-stitch
seasonal patterns make handsome choices for handmade
holiday presents. And don't forget to start the year off right
by gifting yourself with one of these winter wonders!

GIFT OF LOVE

This keepsake afghan is adorned with symbols of love's most cherished gifts — hugs and kisses. Cluster stitches create the dimensional X's and O's on this tender coverlet.

Finished Size: 38" x 55" (98 cm x 139.5 cm)

MATERIALS
Worsted Weight Yarn:
Rose - 27 ounces, 1,850 yards
(770 grams, 1,691.5 meters)
Lt Rose - 20 ounces, 1,370 yards
(570 grams, 1,252.5 meters)
Crochet hook, size I (5.5 mm) **or** size needed
for gauge

GAUGE: Sc, (ch 1, sc) 8 times and
16 rows = 4^1/$_4$" (10.75 cm)

Gauge Swatch: 4^1/$_4$" (10.75 cm) square
Ch 18 **loosely.**
Row 1: Sc in second ch from hook, ★ ch 1, skip next ch, sc in next ch; repeat from ★ across: 9 sc and 8 ch-1 sps.
Rows 2-16: Ch 1, turn; sc in first sc, (ch 1, sc in next sc) across.
Finish off.

Note: Each row is worked across length of Afghan. When joining yarn and finishing off, leave an 8" (20.25 cm) length to be worked into fringe.

STITCH GUIDE

CLUSTER (uses one ch)
Ch 3, YO, insert hook in third ch from hook, YO and pull up a loop, YO and draw through 2 loops on hook, ★ YO, insert hook in **same** ch, YO and pull up a loop, YO and draw through 2 loops on hook; repeat from ★ once **more**, YO and draw through all 4 loops on hook *(Figs. 10a & b, page 139)*.

AFGHAN BODY
With Lt Rose, ch 222 **loosely.**
Row 1 (Right side)**:** Sc in second ch from hook, ★ ch 1, skip next ch, sc in next ch; repeat from ★ across; finish off: 111 sc.
Note: Loop a short piece of yarn around any stitch to mark Row 1 as **right** side.

Row 2: With **wrong** side facing, join Rose with sc in first sc *(see Joining With Sc, page 140)*; ★ work Cluster, ch 1, skip next sc, sc in next sc; repeat from ★ across; finish off: 55 Clusters and 56 sc.
Row 3: With **right** side facing, join Lt Rose with sc in first sc; ★ ch 1, working **behind** next Cluster *(Fig. 18, page 141)*, dc in skipped sc one row **below** Cluster, ch 1, sc in next sc; repeat from ★ across; finish off: 111 sts.
Row 4: With **wrong** side facing, join Rose with sc in first sc; work Cluster, ch 1, skip next dc, sc in next sc, ★ (ch 1, skip next ch-1 sp, sc in next st) 10 times, work Cluster, ch 1, skip next dc, sc in next sc; repeat from ★ across; finish off: 10 Clusters and 101 sc.
Row 5: With **right** side facing, join Lt Rose with sc in first sc; ch 1, working **behind** next Cluster, dc in skipped dc one row **below** Cluster, ch 1, sc in next sc, ★ ch 1, (sc in next sc, ch 1) 10 times, working **behind** next Cluster, dc in skipped dc one row **below** Cluster, ch 1, sc in next sc; repeat from ★ across; finish off: 111 sts.
Rows 6 and 7: Repeat Rows 4 and 5.
Row 8: With **wrong** side facing, join Rose with sc in first sc; work Cluster, ★ † [ch 1, skip next 2 ch-1 sps, sc in next st, (ch 1, skip next ch-1 sp, sc in next st) twice, work Cluster] 3 times, ch 1, skip next dc, sc in next sc †, (ch 1, skip next ch-1 sp, sc in next st) 3 times, (work Cluster, ch 1, skip next 2 ch-1 sps, sc in next st) twice, (ch 1, sc in next sc) 3 times, work Cluster; repeat from ★ 3 times **more**, then repeat from † to † once; finish off: 28 Clusters and 83 sc.
Row 9: With **right** side facing, join Lt Rose with sc in first sc; ch 1, working **behind** next Cluster, dc in skipped dc one row **below** Cluster, ch 1, (sc in next sc, ch 1) 3 times, [working **behind** next Cluster, dc in skipped sc one row **below** Cluster, ch 1, (sc in next sc, ch 1) 3 times] twice, working **behind** next Cluster, dc in skipped dc one row **below** Cluster, ch 1, ★ (sc in next sc, ch 1) 4 times, working **behind** next Cluster, dc in skipped sc one row **below** Cluster, ch 1, sc in next sc, ch 1, working **behind** next Cluster, dc in skipped sc one row **below** Cluster, ch 1, (sc in next sc, ch 1) 4 times, working **behind** next Cluster, dc in skipped dc one row **below** Cluster, ch 1, (sc in next sc, ch 1) 3 times, [working **behind** next Cluster, dc in skipped sc one row **below** Cluster, ch 1, (sc in next sc, ch 1) 3 times] twice, working **behind** next Cluster, dc in skipped dc one row **below** Cluster, ch 1; repeat from ★ 3 times **more**, sc in last sc; finish off: 111 sts.

Row 10: With **wrong** side facing, join Rose with sc in first sc; work Cluster, ★ † ch 1, skip next dc, sc in next sc, (ch 1, skip next ch-1 sp, sc in next st) 3 times, (work Cluster, ch 1, skip next 2 ch-1 sps, sc in next st) twice, (ch 1, sc in next sc) 3 times, work Cluster †, [ch 1, skip next 2 ch-1 sps, sc in next st, (ch 1, skip next ch-1 sp, sc in next st) twice, work Cluster] 3 times; repeat from ★ 3 times **more**, then repeat from † to † once, ch 1, skip next dc, sc in last sc; finish off: 28 Clusters and 83 sc.

Continued on page 108.

Row 11: With **right** side facing, join Lt Rose with sc in first sc; ch 1, ★ † working **behind** next Cluster, dc in skipped dc one row **below** Cluster, ch 1, (sc in next sc, ch 1) 4 times, working **behind** next Cluster, dc in skipped sc one row **below** Cluster, ch 1, sc in next sc, ch 1, working **behind** next Cluster, dc in skipped sc one row **below** Cluster, ch 1, (sc in next sc, ch 1) 4 times, working **behind** next Cluster, dc in skipped dc one row **below** Cluster, ch 1 †, (sc in next sc, ch 1) 3 times, [working **behind** next Cluster, dc in skipped sc one row **below** Cluster, ch 1, (sc in next sc, ch 1) 3 times] twice; repeat from ★ 3 times **more**, then repeat from † to † once, sc in last sc; finish off: 111 sts.

Row 12: With **wrong** side facing, join Rose with sc in first sc; work Cluster, ch 1, [skip next 2 ch-1 sps, sc in next sc, (ch 1, skip next ch-1 sp, sc in next st) 4 times, work Cluster, ch 1] twice, ★ [skip next dc, sc in next sc, (ch 1, sc in next sc) twice, work Cluster, ch 1] 3 times, [skip next 2 ch-1 sps, sc in next sc, (ch 1, skip next ch-1 sp, sc in next st) 4 times, work Cluster, ch 1] twice; repeat from ★ 3 times **more**, skip next dc, sc in last sc; finish off: 23 Clusters and 88 sc.

Row 13: With **right** side facing, join Lt Rose with sc in first sc; ch 1, working **behind** next Cluster, dc in skipped dc one row **below** Cluster, ch 1, ★ † (sc in next sc, ch 1) 5 times, working **behind** next Cluster, dc in skipped sc one row **below** Cluster, ch 1, (sc in next sc, ch 1) 5 times, working **behind** next Cluster, dc in skipped dc one row **below** Cluster, ch 1 †, [(sc in next sc, ch 1) 3 times, working **behind** next Cluster, dc in skipped dc one row **below** Cluster, ch 1] 3 times; repeat from ★ 3 times **more**, then repeat from † to † once, sc in last sc; finish off: 111 sts.

Row 14: Repeat Row 10: 28 Cluster and 83 sc.

Row 15: With **right** side facing, join Lt Rose with sc in first sc; ch 1, working **behind** next Cluster, dc in skipped dc one row **below** Cluster, ch 1, ★ † (sc in next sc, ch 1) 4 times, working **behind** next Cluster, dc in skipped sc one row **below** Cluster, ch 1, sc in next sc, ch 1, working **behind** next Cluster, dc in skipped sc one row **below** Cluster, ch 1, (sc in next sc, ch 1) 4 times, working **behind** next Cluster, dc in skipped dc one row **below** Cluster, ch 1 †, [(sc in next sc, ch 1) 3 times, working **behind** next Cluster, dc in skipped dc one row **below** Cluster, ch 1] 3 times; repeat from ★ 3 times **more**, then repeat from † to † once, sc in last sc; finish off: 111 sts.

Rows 16 and 17: Repeat Rows 8 and 9.

Rows 18-21: Repeat Rows 4 and 5 twice.

Row 22: With **wrong** side facing, join Rose with sc in first sc; ★ work Cluster, ch 1, skip next 2 ch-1 sps, sc in next sc; repeat from ★ across; finish off: 55 Clusters and 56 sc.

108

Row 23: With **right** side facing, join Lt Rose with sc in first sc; ch 1, working **behind** next Cluster, dc in skipped dc one row **below** Cluster, ch 1, ★ sc in next sc, ch 1, (working **behind** next Cluster, dc in skipped sc one row **below** next Cluster, ch 1, sc in next sc, ch 1) 5 times, working **behind** next Cluster, dc in skipped dc one row **below** Cluster, ch 1; repeat from ★ across to last sc, sc in last sc; finish off: 111 sts.

Rows 24-27: Repeat Rows 4 and 5 twice.

Rows 28 and 29: Repeat Rows 10 and 11.

Rows 30 and 31: Repeat Rows 8 and 9.

Row 32: With **wrong** side facing, join Rose with sc in first sc; ★ † work Cluster, ch 1, skip next dc, sc in next sc, [(ch 1, sc in next sc) twice, work Cluster, ch 1, skip next dc, sc in next sc] 3 times †, (ch 1, skip next ch-1 sp, sc in next st) 4 times, work Cluster, ch 1, skip next 2 ch-1 sps, sc in next st, (ch 1, sc in next sc) 4 times; repeat from ★ 3 times **more**, then repeat from † to † once; finish off: 24 Clusters and 87 sc.

Row 33: With **right** side facing, join Lt Rose with sc in first sc; ch 1, working **behind** next Cluster, dc in skipped dc one row **below** Cluster, ch 1, ★ † [(sc in next sc, ch 1) 3 times, working **behind** next Cluster, dc in skipped dc one row **below** Cluster, ch 1] 3 times †, [(sc in next sc, ch 1) 5 times, working **behind** next Cluster, dc in skipped st one row **below** Cluster, ch 1] twice; repeat from ★ 3 times **more**, then repeat from † to † once, sc in last sc; finish off: 111 sts.

Rows 34-37: Repeat Rows 8-11.

Rows 38-41: Repeat Rows 4 and 5 twice.

Rows 42 and 43: Repeat Rows 22 and 23.

Rows 44-143: Repeat Rows 4-43 twice, then repeat Rows 4-23 once **more**.

EDGING
FIRST SIDE

With **right** side facing, join Lt Rose with slip st in first sc on Row 143; slip st in next ch-1 sp, (ch 1, slip st in next ch-1 sp) across to last sc, slip st in last sc; finish off.

SECOND SIDE

With **right** side facing, working in sps and in free loops of beginning ch *(Fig. 17b, page 141)*, join Lt Rose with slip st in first ch; slip st in next sp, (ch 1, slip st in next sp) across to last ch, slip st in last ch; finish off.

Holding 2 strands of Lt Rose and 2 strands of Rose together, each 18" (45.5 cm) long, add additional fringe in every other row across short edges of Afghan *(Figs. 22b & d, page 142)*.

STAINED GLASS

Radiant hues give this breathtaking blanket the brilliance of sunlit stained glass windows. Choose scrap colors to make your comforter elegant and distinguished or wild and wacky.

Finished Size: 52" x 64¹/₂" (132 cm x 164 cm)

MATERIALS

Worsted Weight Yarn:
Black - 21 ounces, 1,185 yards
(600 grams, 1,083.5 meters)
Scraps - 38 ounces, 2,145 yards
(1,080 grams, 1,961.5 meters) **total**
Note: We used 13 different colors.
Crochet hook, size H (5 mm) **or** size needed
for gauge

GAUGE: Each Strip = 5" (12.75 cm) wide
In pattern,
sc, (ch 1, sc) 5 times = 2³/₄" (7 cm);
14 rows = 4" (10 cm)

Gauge Swatch: 4¹/₂"w x 4"h (11.5 cm x 10 cm)
Work same as Strip A Center through Row 14.

STITCH GUIDE

FRONT POST SINGLE CROCHET
(abbreviated FPsc)
Insert hook from **front** to **back** around post of sc
indicated **(Fig. 9, page 139)**, YO and pull up a
loop, YO and draw through both loops on hook.
BACK POST SINGLE CROCHET
(abbreviated BPsc)
Insert hook from **back** to **front** around post of st
indicated **(Fig. 9, page 139)**, YO and pull up a
loop, YO and draw through both loops on hook.

STRIP A (Make 5)
CENTER

With Scrap color, ch 18.
Row 1 (Right side)**:** Sc in second ch from hook,
★ ch 1, skip next ch, sc in next ch; repeat from ★
across: 9 sc and 8 ch-1 sps.
Note: Loop a short piece of yarn around any stitch
to mark Row 1 as **right** side and bottom edge.
Row 2: Ch 1, turn; sc in first sc, (sc in next ch-1 sp,
ch 1) across to last ch-1 sp, sc in last ch-1 sp and in
last sc: 10 sc and 7 ch-1 sps.

Row 3: Ch 1, turn; sc in first sc, ch 1, (sc in next
ch-1 sp, ch 1) across to last 2 sc, skip next sc, sc in
last sc: 9 sc and 8 ch-1 sps.
Rows 4-14: Repeat Rows 2 and 3, 5 times; then
repeat Row 2 once **more**.
Finish off.
Row 15: With **right** side facing, join Black with sc in
first sc *(see Joining With Sc, page 140)*; sc in next sc
and in each ch-1 sp and each sc across: 17 sc.
Row 16: Ch 1, turn; work FPsc around each sc
across; finish off.
Row 17: With **right** side facing, join next Scrap color
with sc in first FPsc; ★ ch 1, skip next FPsc, sc in
next FPsc; repeat from ★ across: 9 sc and 8 ch-1 sps.
Rows 18-36: Repeat Rows 2 and 3, 9 times; then
repeat Row 2 once **more**.
Finish off.
Rows 37-39: Repeat Rows 15-17.
Rows 40-46: Repeat Rows 2 and 3, 3 times; then
repeat Row 2 once **more**.
Finish off.
Rows 47-49: Repeat Rows 15-17.
Rows 50-56: Repeat Rows 2 and 3, 3 times; then
repeat Row 2 once **more**.
Finish off.
Rows 57-59: Repeat Rows 15-17.
Rows 60-72: Repeat Rows 2 and 3, 6 times; then
repeat Row 2 once **more**.
Finish off.
Rows 73-75: Repeat Rows 15-17.
Rows 76-86: Repeat Rows 2 and 3, 5 times; then
repeat Row 2 once **more**.
Finish off.
Rows 87-89: Repeat Rows 15-17.
Rows 90-100: Repeat Rows 2 and 3, 5 times; then
repeat Row 2 once **more**.
Finish off.
Rows 101-103: Repeat Rows 15-17.
Rows 104-106: Repeat Rows 2 and 3 once, then
repeat Row 2 once **more**.
Finish off.
Rows 107-109: Repeat Rows 15-17.
Rows 110-124: Repeat Rows 2 and 3, 7 times; then
repeat Row 2 once **more**.
Finish off.
Rows 125-127: Repeat Rows 15-17.

Continued on page 110.

Rows 128-138: Repeat Rows 2 and 3, 5 times; then repeat Row 2 once **more**.
Finish off.
Rows 139-141: Repeat Rows 15-17.
Rows 142-162: Repeat Rows 2 and 3, 10 times; then repeat Row 2 once **more**.
Finish off.
Rows 163-165: Repeat Rows 15-17.
Rows 166-174: Repeat Rows 2 and 3, 4 times; then repeat Row 2 once **more**.
Finish off.
Rows 175-177: Repeat Rows 15-17.
Rows 178-188: Repeat Rows 2 and 3, 5 times; then repeat Row 2 once **more**.
Finish off.
Rows 189-191: Repeat Rows 15-17.
Rows 192-196: Repeat Rows 2 and 3 twice, then repeat Row 2 once **more**.
Finish off.
Rows 197-199: Repeat Rows 15-17.
Rows 200-208: Repeat Rows 2 and 3, 4 times; then repeat Row 2 once **more**.
Finish off.
Rows 209-211: Repeat Rows 15-17.
Rows 212-220: Repeat Rows 2 and 3, 4 times; then repeat Row 2 once **more**.
Finish off.

BORDER

With **right** side facing and working in end of rows, join Black with sc in end of Row 1; sc in end of each row across; working in sts and in sps across Row 220, 3 sc in first sc, sc in each sc and in each ch-1 sp across to last sc, 3 sc in last sc; sc in end of each row across; working in free loops *(Fig. 17b, page 141)* and in sps across beginning ch, 3 sc in ch at base of first sc, sc in next sp, (sc in next ch and in next sp) 7 times, 3 sc in last ch; join with slip st to first sc, finish off: 482 sc.

STRIP B (Make 5)

With Scrap color, ch 18.
Row 1 (Right side): Sc in second ch from hook, ★ ch 1, skip next ch, sc in next ch; repeat from ★ across: 9 sc and 8 ch-1 sps.
Note: Mark Row 1 as **right** side and bottom edge.
Row 2: Ch 1, turn; sc in first sc, (sc in next ch-1 sp, ch 1) across to last ch-1 sp, sc in last ch-1 sp and in last sc: 10 sc and 7 ch-1 sps.
Row 3: Ch 1, turn; sc in first sc, ch 1, (sc in next ch-1 sp, ch 1) across to last 2 sc, skip next sc, sc in last sc: 9 sc and 8 ch-1 sps.
Rows 4-8: Repeat Rows 2 and 3 twice, then repeat Row 2 once **more**.
Finish off.
110

Row 9: With **right** side facing, join Black with sc in first sc; sc in next sc and in each ch-1 sp and each sc across: 17 sc.
Row 10: Ch 1, turn; work FPsc around each sc across; finish off.
Row 11: With **right** side facing, join next Scrap color with sc in first FPsc; ★ ch 1, skip next FPsc, sc in next FPsc; repeat from ★ across: 9 sc and 8 ch-1 sps.
Rows 12-18: Repeat Rows 2 and 3, 3 times; then repeat Row 2 once **more**.
Finish off.
Rows 19-21: Repeat Rows 9-11.
Rows 22-30: Repeat Rows 2 and 3, 4 times; then repeat Row 2 once **more**.
Finish off.
Rows 31-33: Repeat Rows 9-11.
Rows 34-42: Repeat Rows 2 and 3, 4 times; then repeat Row 2 once **more**.
Finish off.
Rows 43-45: Repeat Rows 9-11.
Rows 46-52: Repeat Rows 2 and 3, 3 times; then repeat Row 2 once **more**.
Finish off.
Rows 53-55: Repeat Rows 9-11.
Rows 56-68: Repeat Rows 2 and 3, 6 times; then repeat Row 2 once **more**.
Finish off.
Rows 69-71: Repeat Rows 9-11.
Rows 72-82: Repeat Rows 2 and 3, 5 times; then repeat Row 2 once **more**.
Finish off.
Rows 83-85: Repeat Rows 9-11.
Rows 86-96: Repeat Rows 2 and 3, 5 times; then repeat Row 2 once **more**.
Finish off.
Rows 97-99: Repeat Rows 9-11.
Rows 100-104: Repeat Rows 2 and 3 twice, then repeat Row 2 once **more**.
Finish off.
Rows 105-107: Repeat Rows 9-11.
Rows 108-118: Repeat Rows 2 and 3, 5 times; then repeat Row 2 once **more**.
Finish off.
Rows 119-121: Repeat Rows 9-11.
Rows 122-132: Repeat Rows 2 and 3, 5 times; then repeat Row 2 once **more**.
Finish off.
Rows 133-135: Repeat Rows 9-11.
Rows 136-146: Repeat Rows 2 and 3, 5 times; then repeat Row 2 once **more**.
Finish off.
Rows 147-149: Repeat Rows 9-11.
Rows 150-154: Repeat Rows 2 and 3 twice, then repeat Row 2 once **more**.
Finish off.

Continued on page 112.

Rows 155-157: Repeat Rows 9-11.
Rows 158-166: Repeat Rows 2 and 3, 4 times; then repeat Row 2 once **more**.
Finish off.
Rows 167-169: Repeat Rows 9-11.
Rows 170-174: Repeat Rows 2 and 3 twice, then repeat Row 2 once **more**.
Finish off.
Rows 175-177: Repeat Rows 9-11.
Rows 178-192: Repeat Rows 2 and 3, 7 times; then repeat Row 2 once **more**.
Finish off.
Rows 193-195: Repeat Rows 9-11.
Rows 196-204: Repeat Rows 2 and 3, 4 times; then repeat Row 2 once **more**.
Finish off.
Rows 205-207: Repeat Rows 9-11.
Rows 208-220: Repeat Rows 2 and 3, 6 times; then repeat Row 2 once **more**.
Finish off.

BORDER
Work same as Strip A: 482 sc.

ASSEMBLY
Afghan is assembled by joining Strips in the following sequence: (Strip A, Strip B) 5 times. With **wrong** sides together, bottom edges at same end, and working through inside loops only, join Black with sc in center sc of first corner 3-sc group; sc in each sc across ending in center sc of next corner 3-sc group; finish off.

EDGING
Rnd 1: With **right** side facing and working across long edge of Afghan, join Black with sc in center sc of first corner 3-sc group; 2 sc in same st, † sc in next sc and in each sc across to center sc of next corner 3-sc group, 3 sc in center sc, sc in next 17 sc, (sc in same st as joining on same Strip and on next Strip, sc in next 17 sc) 9 times †, 3 sc in next sc, repeat from † to † once; join with slip st to first sc: 832 sc.
Rnd 2: Ch 1, work BPsc around same st, (ch 1, work BPsc around next sc) twice, ★ work BPsc around next sc and each sc across to center sc of next corner 3-sc group, (ch 1, work BPsc around next sc) twice; repeat from ★ 2 times **more**, work BPsc around next sc and each sc across; join with slip st to first BPsc, finish off.

CUPID'S MARK

This heartwarming throw is a sweet reminder that your life will never be the same once Cupid has made his mark. Crochet in pink or red for a lovely Valentine's Day surprise.

Finished Size: 45¹/₂" x 60" (115.5 cm x 152.5 cm)

MATERIALS
Brushed Acrylic Worsted Weight Yarn:
   44 ounces, 2,230 yards
     (1,250 grams, 2,039 meters)
Crochet hook, size I (5.5 mm) **or** size needed
   for gauge
Yarn needle

GAUGE: Each Square = 7" (17.75 cm)

Gauge Swatch: 4¹/₄" (10.75 cm) square
Work same as Square through Rnd 4.

STITCH GUIDE

FRONT POST SINGLE CROCHET
  (abbreviated FPsc)
Insert hook from **front** to **back** around post of st indicated *(Fig. 9, page 139)*, YO and pull up a loop, YO and draw through both loops on hook.
ADDING HALF DOUBLE CROCHET
  (abbreviated add hdc)
YO, insert hook in side of last st made, YO and pull up a loop, YO and draw through all 3 loops on hook **(counts as one hdc)**.
PICOT
Ch 3, slip st in second ch from hook and in next ch.

Continued on page 114.

SQUARE (Make 48)

Ch 4; join with slip st to form a ring.

Rnd 1 (Right side): Ch 6 **(counts as first dc plus ch 3)**, (3 dc in ring, ch 3) 3 times, 2 dc in ring; join with slip st to first dc: 12 dc and 4 ch-3 sps.

Note: Loop a short piece of yarn around any stitch to mark Rnd 1 as **right** side.

Rnd 2: Slip st in first corner ch-3 sp, ch 1, (sc, ch 3, sc) in same sp, working from **top** to **bottom**, work 3 FPsc around next dc, ch 1, skip next dc, working from **bottom** to **top**, work 3 FPsc around next dc, ★ (sc, ch 3, sc) in next corner ch-3 sp, working from **top** to **bottom**, work 3 FPsc around next dc, ch 1, skip next dc, working from **bottom** to **top**, work 3 FPsc around next dc; repeat from ★ 2 times **more**; join with slip st to first sc: 32 sts and 4 ch-3 sps.

Rnd 3: Working **behind** sts on Rnd 2 and in skipped dc and in corner ch-3 sps on Rnd 1, slip st in corner ch-3 sp (between sc), ch 3 **(counts as first dc, now and throughout)**, (dc, ch 3, 2 dc) in same sp, ch 1, dc in next skipped dc, ch 1, ★ (2 dc, ch 3, 2 dc) in next corner ch-3 sp (between sc), ch 1, dc in next skipped dc, ch 1; repeat from ★ 2 times **more**; join with slip st to first dc: 20 dc and 12 sps.

Rnd 4: Slip st in next dc and in next corner ch-3 sp, ch 3, (dc, ch 3, 2 dc) in same sp, ch 1, skip next dc, (dc in next dc, ch 1) 3 times, ★ (2 dc, ch 3, 2 dc) in next corner ch-3 sp, ch 1, skip next dc, (dc in next dc, ch 1) 3 times; repeat from ★ 2 times **more**; join with slip st to first dc: 28 dc and 20 sps.

Rnd 5: Slip st in next dc and in next corner ch-3 sp, ch 3, (dc, ch 3, 2 dc) in same sp, ch 1, skip next dc, (dc in next dc, ch 1) 5 times, ★ (2 dc, ch 3, 2 dc) in next corner ch-3 sp, ch 1, skip next dc, (dc in next dc, ch 1) 5 times; repeat from ★ 2 times **more**; join with slip st to first dc: 36 dc and 28 sps.

Rnd 6: Slip st in next dc and in next corner ch-3 sp, ch 3, (dc, add 3 hdc, 2 dc) in same sp, ch 1, skip next dc, (dc in next dc, ch 1) 7 times, ★ (2 dc, add 3 hdc, 2 dc) in next corner ch-3 sp, ch 1, skip next dc, (dc in next dc, ch 1) 7 times; repeat from ★ 2 times **more**; join with slip st to first dc: 44 dc and 4 3-hdc groups.

Rnd 7: Ch 1, sc in same st, ch 1, working from **top** to **bottom**, work 3 FPsc around next dc, work Picot, working from **bottom** to **top**, work 3 FPsc around next dc, ch 1, sc in next dc, ★ (sc in next ch-1 sp and in next dc) 8 times, ch 1, working from **top** to **bottom**, work 3 FPsc around next dc, work Picot, working from **bottom** to **top**, work 3 FPsc around next dc, ch 1, sc in next dc; repeat from ★ 2 times **more**, sc in next ch-1 sp, (sc in next dc and in next ch-1 sp) 7 times; join with slip st to first sc, finish off.

ASSEMBLY

With **wrong** Sides together and working through inside loops only. Whipstitch Squares together forming 6 vertical strips of 8 Squares each *(Fig. 21a, page 142)*, beginning in center hdc of first corner 3-hdc group on Rnd 6, working across hdc on Rnd 6 **and** in sc between ch-1 sps on Rnd 7, ending in center hdc of next corner 3-hdc group on Rnd 6; then whipstitch strips together in same manner.

EDGING

Rnd 1: With **right** side facing and working in Back Loops Only *(Fig. 15, page 140)*, join yarn with dc in center hdc of corner 3-hdc group at upper right corner *(see Joining With Dc, page 140)*; dc in same st, † work 141 dc evenly spaced across to center hdc of next corner 3-hdc group, (2 dc, ch 3, 2 dc) in center hdc, work 189 dc evenly spaced across to center hdc of next corner 3-hdc group †, (2 dc, ch 3, 2 dc) in center hdc, repeat from † to † once, 2 dc in same st as first dc, ch 1, hdc in first dc to form last ch-3 sp: 676 dc and 4 ch-3 sps.

Rnd 2: Ch 3, turn; dc in last ch-3 sp, dc in Front Loop Only of each dc across to next corner ch-3 sp, ★ (2 dc, ch 3, 2 dc) in corner ch-3 sp, dc in Front Loop Only of each dc across to next corner ch-3 sp; repeat from ★ 2 times **more**, 2 dc in same sp as first dc, ch 2, sc in first dc to form last ch-3 sp; do **not** finish off.

BORDER
TOP

Row 1: Ch 1, turn; working in both loops, sc in first ch, ch 3, skip next ch, sc in next dc, ch 3, ★ skip next dc, sc in next dc, ch 3; repeat from ★ across to next corner ch-3, skip next ch, sc in next ch, leave remaining sts unworked.

Row 2: Ch 1, turn; 2 sc in each ch-3 sp across; finish off.

BOTTOM

Row 1: With **right** side facing, join yarn with sc in center ch of lower left corner ch-3 *(see Joining With Sc, page 140)*; ch 3, skip next ch, sc in next dc, ch 3, ★ skip next dc, sc in next dc, ch 3; repeat from ★ across to next corner ch-3, skip next ch, sc in next ch, leave remaining sts unworked.

Row 2: Ch 1, turn; 2 sc in each ch-3 sp across; finish off.

ANGELS AMONG US

Though you may not see them, this heavenly coverlet reminds us there are angels everywhere. Cluster stitches form the heads of these celestial spirits.

Finished Size: 48" x 61" (122 cm x 155 cm)

MATERIALS
Worsted Weight Yarn:
45 ounces, 2,025 yards
(1,280 grams, 1,851.5 meters)
Crochet hook, size G (4 mm) **or** size needed
for gauge

GAUGE: 15 dc and 8 rows = 4" (10 cm)

Gauge Swatch: 4" (10 cm) square
Ch 17 **loosely**.
Row 1: Dc in fourth ch from hook **(3 skipped chs count as first dc)** and in each ch across: 15 dc.
Rows 2-8: Ch 3 **(counts as first dc)**, turn; dc in next dc and in each dc across.
Finish off.

STITCH GUIDE

CLUSTER
★ YO twice, insert hook from **front** to **back** around post of dc indicated *(Fig. 9, page 139)*, YO and pull up a loop, (YO and draw through 2 loops on hook) twice; repeat from ★ 5 times **more**, YO and draw through all 7 loops on hook.

AFGHAN BODY

Ch 181 **loosely**, place marker in third ch from hook for stitch placement.
Row 1 (Right side): Dc in fourth ch from hook **(3 skipped chs count as first dc)** and in each ch across: 179 dc.
Row 2: Ch 3 **(counts as first dc, now and throughout)**, turn; dc in next 2 dc, ch 2, skip next dc, sc in next dc, ch 2, skip next dc, dc in next 3 dc, ★ ch 1, skip next dc, (dc in next dc, ch 1, skip next dc) 12 times, dc in next 3 dc, ch 2, skip next dc, sc in next dc, ch 2, skip next dc, dc in next 3 dc; repeat from ★ across: 102 sts and 77 sps.
Row 3: Ch 3, turn; dc in next 2 dc, ch 3, skip next sc, dc in next 3 dc, ★ (ch 1, dc in next dc) 6 times, dc in next ch-1 sp and in next dc, ch 1, (dc in next dc, ch 1) 5 times, dc in next 3 dc, ch 3, skip next sc, dc in next 3 dc; repeat from ★ across: 101 dc and 66 sps.

Row 4: Ch 3, turn; dc in next 2 dc, ch 2, skip next ch, sc in next ch, ch 2, dc in next 3 dc, ★ ch 1, (dc in next dc, ch 1) twice, (dc in next dc and in next ch-1 sp) 3 times, dc in next 3 dc, (dc in next ch-1 sp and in next dc) 3 times, ch 1, (dc in next dc, ch 1) twice, dc in next 3 dc, ch 2, skip next ch, sc in next ch, ch 2, dc in next 3 dc; repeat from ★ across: 137 sts and 42 sps.
Row 5: Ch 3, turn; dc in next 2 dc, ch 3, skip next sc, dc in next 3 dc, ★ ch 1, (dc in next dc, ch 1) twice, dc in next 15 dc, ch 1, (dc in next dc, ch 1) twice, dc in next 3 dc, ch 3, skip next sc, dc in next 3 dc; repeat from ★ across: 131 dc and 36 sps.
Row 6: Ch 3, turn; dc in next 2 dc, ch 2, skip next ch, sc in next ch, ch 2, dc in next 3 dc, ★ ch 1, (dc in next dc, ch 1) twice, dc in next 15 dc, ch 1, (dc in next dc, ch 1) twice, dc in next 3 dc, ch 2, skip next ch, sc in next ch, ch 2, dc in next 3 dc; repeat from ★ across: 137 sts and 42 sps.
Row 7: Ch 3, turn; dc in next 2 dc, ch 3, skip next sc, dc in next 3 dc, ★ ch 1, (dc in next dc, ch 1) 3 times, skip next dc, dc in next 11 dc, ch 1, skip next dc, (dc in next dc, ch 1) 3 times, dc in next 3 dc, ch 3, skip next sc, dc in next 3 dc; repeat from ★ across: 121 dc and 46 sps.
Row 8: Ch 3, turn; dc in next 2 dc, ch 2, skip next ch, sc in next ch, ch 2, dc in next 3 dc, ★ ch 1, (dc in next dc, ch 1) 3 times, dc in next 11 dc, ch 1, (dc in next dc, ch 1) 3 times, dc in next 3 dc, ch 2, skip next ch, sc in next ch, ch 2, dc in next 3 dc; repeat from ★ across: 127 sts and 52 sps.
Row 9: Ch 3, turn; dc in next 2 dc, ch 3, skip next sc, dc in next 3 dc, ★ (ch 1, dc in next dc) 3 times, dc in next ch-1 sp and in next dc, ch 1, skip next dc, dc in next 7 dc, ch 1, skip next dc, dc in next dc and in next ch-1 sp, (dc in next dc, ch 1) 3 times, dc in next 3 dc, ch 3, skip next sc, dc in next 3 dc; repeat from ★ across: 121 dc and 46 sps.
Row 10: Ch 3, turn; dc in next 2 dc, ch 2, skip next ch, sc in next ch, ch 2, dc in next 3 dc, ★ (ch 1, dc in next dc) twice, dc in next ch-1 sp and in next dc, ch 1, skip next dc, dc in next dc, ch 1, dc in next 7 dc, ch 1, dc in next dc, ch 1, skip next dc, dc in next dc and in next ch-1 sp, (dc in next dc, ch 1) twice, dc in next 3 dc, ch 2, skip next ch, sc in next ch, ch 2, dc in next 3 dc; repeat from ★ across: 127 sts and 52 sps.

Continued on page 116.

Row 11: Ch 3, turn; dc in next 2 dc, ch 3, skip next sc, dc in next 3 dc, ★ ch 1, dc in next dc, dc in next ch-1 sp and in next dc, ch 1, skip next dc, (dc in next dc, ch 1) 3 times, skip next dc, dc in next 3 dc, ch 1, skip next dc, (dc in next dc, ch 1) 3 times, skip next dc, dc in next dc, dc in next ch-1 sp and in next dc, ch 1, dc in next 3 dc, ch 3, skip next sc, dc in next 3 dc; repeat from ★ across: 111 dc and 56 sps.

Row 12: Ch 3, turn; dc in next 2 dc, ch 2, skip next ch, sc in next ch, ch 2, dc in next 3 dc, ★ ch 1, dc in next 3 dc, (ch 1, dc in next dc) twice, dc in next ch-1 sp and in next dc, ch 2, skip next dc, dc in next dc, ch 2, skip next dc, dc in next dc and in next ch-1 sp, (dc in next dc, ch 1) twice, dc in next 3 dc, ch 1, dc in next 3 dc, ch 2, skip next ch, sc in next ch, ch 2, dc in next 3 dc; repeat from ★ across: 117 sts and 52 sps.

Row 13: Ch 3, turn; dc in next 2 dc, ch 3, skip next sc, dc in next 3 dc, ★ ch 1, dc in next dc, ch 1, skip next dc, dc in next dc, (dc in next ch-1 sp and in next dc) twice, ch 1, skip next dc, dc in next dc, ch 2, work Cluster around next dc, ch 2, dc in next dc, ch 1, skip next dc, dc in next dc, (dc in next ch-1 sp and in next dc) twice, ch 1, skip next dc, dc in next dc, ch 1, dc in next 3 dc, ch 3, skip next sc, dc in next 3 dc; repeat from ★ across: 5 Clusters, 106 dc, and 46 sps.

Row 14: Ch 3, turn; dc in next 2 dc, ch 2, skip next ch, sc in next ch, ch 2, dc in next 3 dc, ★ ch 1, (dc in next dc, ch 1) twice, (skip next dc, dc in next dc, ch 1) twice, dc in next dc, [dc, (ch 1, dc) twice] in next Cluster, (dc in next dc, ch 1) twice, (skip next dc, dc in next dc, ch 1) twice, dc in next dc, ch 1, dc in next 3 dc, ch 2, skip next ch, sc in next ch, ch 2, dc in next 3 dc; repeat from ★ across: 107 sts and 72 sps.

Row 15: Ch 3, turn; dc in next 2 dc, ch 3, skip next sc, dc in next 3 dc, ★ ch 1, (dc in next dc, ch 1) 5 times, (dc in next ch-1 sp, ch 1) twice, skip next dc, (dc in next dc, ch 1) 5 times, dc in next 3 dc, ch 3, skip next sc, dc in next 3 dc; repeat from ★ across: 96 dc and 71 sps.

Row 16: Ch 3, turn; dc in next 2 dc, ch 2, skip next ch, sc in next ch, ch 2, dc in next 3 dc, ★ ch 1, (dc in next dc, ch 1) 12 times, dc in next 3 dc, ch 2, skip next ch, sc in next ch, ch 2, dc in next 3 dc; repeat from ★ across: 102 sts and 77 sps.

Rows 17-113: Repeat Rows 3-16, 6 times; then repeat Rows 3-15 once **more**.

Row 114: Ch 3, turn; dc in next dc and in each dc and each ch across; do **not** finish off: 179 dc.

EDGING

Rnd 1: Ch 1, turn; 2 sc in first dc, sc in each dc across to last dc, 3 sc in last dc; † working in end of rows, 2 sc in first row and in each row across to last row, sc in last row †; working in free loops of beginning ch (*Fig. 17b, page 140*), 3 sc in first ch, sc in each ch across to marked ch, 3 sc in marked ch; repeat from † to † once, sc in same st as first sc; join with slip st to first sc: 820 sc.

Rnd 2: Ch 1, (sc in same st, ch 2) twice, ★ skip next sc, (sc in next sc, ch 2, skip next sc) across to center sc of next corner 3-sc group, (sc, ch 2) twice in center sc; repeat from ★ 2 times **more**, skip next sc, (sc in next sc, ch 2, skip next sc) across; join with slip st to first sc, finish off.

WINTRY WINDOWS

Nature's lacy frost creates lovely designs on winter windows. Six shades of blue are used to mimic that icy view in this eye-catching afghan.

Finished Size: 43" x 64" (109 cm x 162.5 cm)

MATERIALS

Worsted Weight Yarn:

Navy - 20 ounces, 1,130 yards
(570 grams, 1,033.5 meters)

Dk Blue - 10 ounces, 565 yards
(280 grams, 516.5 meters)

Blue - 8¹/₂ ounces, 480 yards
(240 grams, 439 meters)

Periwinkle - 6 ounces, 340 yards
(170 grams, 311 meters)

Pale Blue - 4¹/₂ ounces, 255 yards
(130 grams, 233 meters)

Lt Blue - 4 ounces, 225 yards
(110 grams, 205.5 meters)

White - 3¹/₂ ounces, 200 yards
(100 grams, 183 meters)

Crochet hook, size H (5 mm) **or** size needed for gauge

Yarn needle

GAUGE: Each Square = 5¹/₄" (13.25 cm)

Gauge Swatch: 1¹/₄" (3.25 cm) square
Work same as Square through Rnd 2.

To work **color change**, work last sc to within one step of completion, hook new yarn **(Fig. 19, page 141)** and draw through both loops on hook.

SQUARE (Make 96)

Rnd 1 (Right side): With White, ch 2 **loosely**, 8 sc in second ch from hook; join with slip st to first sc.
Note: Loop a short piece of yarn around any stitch to mark Rnd 1 as **right** side.
Rnd 2: Ch 3, sc in same st, ch 1, skip next sc, ★ (sc, ch 2, sc) in next sc, ch 1, skip next sc; repeat from ★ 2 times **more**; join with slip st in first ch-3 sp: 7 sc and 8 sps.
Note: Begin working in rows.
Row 1: Ch 2, sc in same sp, ch 1, sc in next ch-1 sp, ch 1, (sc, ch 2, sc) in next ch-2 sp, (ch 1, sc in next sp) twice changing to Lt Blue in last sc **(Fig. 19, page 141)**, leave remaining sps unworked: 6 sc and 6 sps.

Rows 2-4: Ch 2, turn; (sc in next ch-1 sp, ch 1) across to next ch-2 sp, (sc, ch 2, sc) in ch-2 sp, (ch 1, sc in next sp) across, changing to Pale Blue in last sc on Row 4: 9 sps.
Rows 5-7: Ch 2, turn; (sc in next ch-1 sp, ch 1) across to next ch-2 sp, (sc, ch 2, sc) in ch-2 sp, (ch 1, sc in next sp) across, changing to Periwinkle in last sc on Row 7; do **not** finish off: 12 sps.
Rows 8-10: Ch 2, turn; (sc in next ch-1 sp, ch 1) across to next ch-2 sp, (sc, ch 2, sc) in ch-2 sp, (ch 1, sc in next sp) across, changing to Blue in last sc on Row 10: 15 sps.
Rows 11-13: Ch 2, turn; (sc in next ch-1 sp, ch 1) across to next ch-2 sp, (sc, ch 2, sc) in ch-2 sp, (ch 1, sc in next sp) across, changing to Dk Blue in last sc on Row 13: 18 sps.
Rows 14-16: Ch 2, turn; (sc in next ch-1 sp, ch 1) across to next ch-2 sp, (sc, ch 2, sc) in ch-2 sp, (ch 1, sc in next sp) across, changing to Navy in last sc on Row 16: 21 sps.
Note: Begin working in rounds.
Rnd 1: Ch 2, turn; (sc in next ch-1 sp, ch 1) 10 times, (sc, ch 2, sc) in next ch-2 sp, ch 1, (sc in next ch-1 sp, ch 1) 9 times, (sc, ch 2, sc) in next ch-2 sp, ch 1; working in end of rows and in sps on Rnd 2, skip next row, (sc in next row, ch 1, skip next row) 7 times, (sc in next sp, ch 1) twice, (sc, ch 2, sc) in next ch-2 sp, ch 1, sc in next sp, ch 1, skip next slip st, (sc in next row, ch 1, skip next row) 8 times; join with slip st in first ch-2 sp: 44 sps.
Rnd 2: Ch 1, do **not** turn; (sc, ch 2, sc) in same sp, ch 1, (sc in next ch-1 sp, ch 1) 10 times, ★ (sc, ch 2, sc) in next corner ch-2 sp, ch 1, (sc in next ch-1 sp, ch 1) 10 times; repeat from ★ 2 times **more**; join with slip st to first sc, finish off: 48 sps.

ASSEMBLY

With Navy, using photo as guide for placement, page 119, and working through inside loops only, whipstitch Squares together forming 8 vertical strips of 12 Squares each **(Fig. 21a, page 142)**, beginning in second ch of first corner ch-2 and ending in first ch of next corner ch-2; then whipstitch Strips together in same manner.

EDGING

Rnd 1: With **right** side facing and working across top edge, join Navy with sc in first corner ch-2 sp *(see Joining With Sc, page 140)*; ch 2, sc in same sp, ch 1, ★ (sc in next sp, ch 1) across to next corner ch-2 sp, (sc, ch 2, sc) in corner ch-2 sp, ch 1; repeat from ★ 2 times **more**, (sc in next sp, ch 1) across; join with slip st to first sc: 520 sps.

Rnd 2: Slip st in next corner ch-2 sp, ch 1, (sc, ch 2, sc) in same sp, ch 1, ★ (sc in next ch-1 sp, ch 1) across to next corner ch-2 sp, (sc, ch 2, sc) in corner ch-2 sp, ch 1; repeat from ★ 2 times **more**, (sc in next ch-1 sp, ch 1) across; join with slip st to first sc, finish off.

HOT COCOA

After a long day at work, it's time to unwind with a steaming mug of hot cocoa.
Thick ripples make this toasty wrap a stylish statement in a den or study.

Finished Size: 50" x 64½" (127 cm x 164 cm)

MATERIALS

Worsted Weight Yarn:
   50 ounces, 3,280 yards
      (1,420 grams, 2,999 meters)
Crochet hook, size H (5 mm) **or** size needed
   for gauge

GAUGE: In pattern, one repeat from point to point
   and 5 rows = 4½" (11.5 cm);

Gauge Swatch: 9"w x 6½"h (22.75 cm x 16.5 cm)
Ch 51 **loosely**.
Work same as Afghan Body for 5 rows.
Finish off.

STITCH GUIDE

TREBLE CROCHET (abbreviated tr)
YO twice, insert hook in sc indicated, YO and
pull up a loop (4 loops on hook), (YO and draw
through 2 loops on hook) 3 times.

FRONT POST DOUBLE CROCHET
   (abbreviated FPdc)
YO, insert hook from **front** to **back** around post
of dc indicated (*Fig. 9, page 139*), YO and pull
up a loop (3 loops on hook), (YO and draw
through 2 loops on hook) twice.

BACK POST DOUBLE CROCHET
   (abbreviated BPdc)
YO, insert hook from **back** to **front** around post
of dc indicated (*Fig. 9, page 139*), YO and pull
up a loop (3 loops on hook), (YO and draw
through 2 loops on hook) twice.

SPLIT FRONT POST TREBLE CROCHET
   (abbreviated Split FPtr)
† YO twice, insert hook from **front** to **back**
around post of **next** BPdc (*Fig. 9, page 139*), YO
and pull up a loop, (YO and draw through
2 loops on hook) twice †, skip next 5 sts, repeat
from † to † once, YO and draw through all
3 loops on hook.

SPLIT BACK POST TREBLE CROCHET
   (abbreviated Split BPtr)
First Leg: YO twice, insert hook from **back** to
front around post of st indicated (*Fig. 9,
page 139*), YO and pull up a loop (4 loops on
hook), (YO and draw through 2 loops on hook)
twice (2 loops remaining on hook).
Second Leg: YO twice, insert hook from **back** to
front around post of st indicated, YO and pull
up a loop, (YO and draw through 2 loops on
hook) twice, YO and draw through all 3 loops
on hook.
DECREASE
Pull up a loop in next 3 sts, YO and draw
through all 4 loops on hook.

AFGHAN BODY

Ch 258 **loosely**.
Row 1 (Right side): (Tr, dc) in fifth ch from hook
(4 skipped chs count as first tr), 2 dc in next ch, dc
in next 3 chs, ch 2, skip next 2 chs, dc in next 3 chs,
skip next 4 chs, dc in next 3 chs, ch 2, ★ skip next
2 chs, dc in next 2 chs, 2 dc in each of next 2 chs, 3 tr
in next ch, 2 dc in each of next 2 chs, dc in next
2 chs, ch 2, skip next 2 chs, dc in next 3 chs, skip
next 4 chs, dc in next 3 chs, ch 2; repeat from ★
9 times **more**, skip next 2 chs, dc in next 3 chs, 2 dc
in next ch, (dc, 2 tr) in last ch: 232 sts and
22 ch-2 sps.
Note: Loop a short piece of yarn around any stitch
to mark Row 1 as **right** side.
Row 2: Ch 4 **(counts as first tr, now and
throughout)**, turn; (tr, dc) in same st, 2 dc in next tr,
dc in next 3 dc, ★ † ch 2, skip next 2 dc, work BPdc
around next dc, 2 dc in next ch-2 sp, work First Leg
of Split BPtr around next dc, skip next 4 dc, work
Second Leg of Split BPtr around next dc, 2 dc in next
ch-2 sp, work BPdc around next dc, ch 2, skip next
2 dc †, dc in next 2 dc, 2 dc in each of next 2 sts, 3 tr
in next tr, 2 dc in each of next 2 sts, dc in next 2 dc;
repeat from ★ 9 times **more**, then repeat from † to †
once, dc in next 3 dc, 2 dc in next tr, (dc, 2 tr) in last
tr: 243 sts and 22 ch-2 sps.

Continued on page 122.

Row 3: Ch 4, turn; (tr, dc) in same st, 2 dc in next tr, dc in next 3 dc, ch 2, skip next 2 dc, work FPdc around next dc, 2 dc in next ch-2 sp, work Split FPtr, 2 dc in next ch-2 sp, work FPdc around next dc, ch 2, ★ skip next 2 dc, dc in next 2 dc, 2 dc in each of next 2 sts, 3 tr in next tr, 2 dc in each of next 2 sts, dc in next 2 dc, ch 2, skip next 2 dc, work FPdc around next dc, 2 dc in next ch-2 sp, work Split FPtr, 2 dc in next ch-2 sp, work FPdc around next dc, ch 2; repeat from ★ 9 times **more**, skip next 2 dc, dc in next 3 dc, 2 dc in next tr, (dc, 2 tr) in last tr.

Row 4: Ch 4, turn; (tr, dc) in same st, 2 dc in next tr, dc in next 3 dc, ★ † ch 2, skip next 2 dc, work BPdc around next dc, 2 dc in next ch-2 sp, work First Leg of Split BPtr around next FPdc, skip next 5 sts, work Second Leg of Split BPtr around next FPdc, 2 dc in next ch-2 sp, work BPdc around next dc, ch 2, skip next 2 dc †, dc in next 2 dc, 2 dc in each of next 2 sts, 3 tr in next tr, 2 dc in each of next 2 sts, dc in next 2 dc; repeat from ★ 9 times **more**, then repeat from † to † once, dc in next 3 dc, 2 dc in next tr, (dc, 2 tr) in last tr.

Repeat Rows 3 and 4 until Afghan Body measures approximately 64" (162.5 cm), ending by working Row 3; do **not** finish off.

EDGING

Ch 1, do **not** turn; sc evenly across end of rows; working in sps and in free loops of beginning ch **(Fig. 17b, page 141)**, sc in first 5 chs, 2 sc in next sp, sc in next 3 chs, 5 sc in next sp, sc in next 3 chs, 2 sc in next sp, ★ sc in next 3 chs, decrease, sc in next 3 chs, 2 sc in next sp, sc in next 3 chs, 5 sc in next sp, sc in next 3 chs, 2 sc in next sp; repeat from ★ 9 times **more**, sc in next 6 chs; sc evenly across end of rows; working in sts and sps across last row, 3 sc in first tr, † sc in next 7 sts, 2 sc in next ch-2 sp, sc in next 2 sts, decrease, sc in next 2 sts, 2 sc in next ch-2 sp, sc in next 7 sts, 3 sc in next tr †; repeat from † to † across; join with slip st to first sc, finish off.

Holding 12 strands of yarn together, each 16" (40.5 cm) long, add fringe in each point across short edges of Afghan **(Figs. 22a & c, page 142)**.

SNOW STARS

This whimsical winter throw is sure to have you wishing for snow. The clever design uses only three colors to create eight unique star-shaped "snowflakes."

Finished Size: 58" x 70" (147.5 cm x 178 cm)

MATERIALS
Worsted Weight Yarn:
Lt Blue - 21 ounces, 1,370 yards
(600 grams, 1,252.5 meters)
Blue - 18^1/$_2$ ounces, 1,205 yards
(530 grams, 1,102 meters)
White - 12 ounces, 780 yards
(340 grams, 713 meters)
Crochet hook, size I (5.5 mm) **or** size needed for gauge
Yarn needle

GAUGE SWATCH: 3" (7.5 cm) square
Work same as Square A.

Referring to the Key, page 124, make the number of Squares specified in the colors indicated.

SQUARE A

With color indicated, ch 4; join with slip st to form a ring.

Rnd 1 (Right side): Ch 3 **(counts as first dc, now and throughout)**, 2 dc in ring, (ch 2, 3 dc in ring) 3 times, hdc in first dc to form last ch-2 sp: 12 dc and 4 ch-2 sps.

Note: Loop a short piece of yarn around any stitch to mark Rnd 1 as **right** side.

Rnd 2: Ch 3, (2 dc, ch 2, 3 dc) in last ch-2 sp made, ch 1, ★ (3 dc, ch 2, 3 dc) in next ch-2 sp, ch 1; repeat from ★ 2 times **more**; join with slip st to first dc, finish off: 24 dc and 8 sps.

Continued on page 124.

SQUARE B

With first color indicated, ch 4; join with slip st to form a ring.

Rnd 1 (Right side)**:** Ch 5 **(counts as first dc plus ch 2)**, 3 dc in ring, cut first color, with second color indicated, YO and draw through, ch 1, (3 dc, ch 2, 3 dc) in ring, cut second color, with first color, YO and draw through, ch 1, 2 dc in ring; join with slip st to first dc: 12 dc and 4 ch-2 sps.

Note: Mark Rnd 1 as **right** side.

Rnd 2: Slip st in first ch-2 sp, ch 3, (2 dc, ch 2, 3 dc) in same sp, ch 1, 3 dc in next ch-2 sp, cut first color, with second color, YO and draw through, ch 1, 3 dc in same sp, ch 1, (3 dc, ch 2, 3 dc) in next ch-2 sp, ch 1, 3 dc in next ch-2 sp, cut second color, with first color, YO and draw through, ch 1, 3 dc in same sp, ch 1; join with slip st to first dc, finish off: 24 dc and 8 sps.

ASSEMBLY

With matching color, using Placement Diagram as a guide and working through inside loops only, whipstitch Squares together forming 18 vertical strips of 22 Squares each *(Fig. 21a, page 142)*; then whipstitch strips together in same manner.

EDGING

Rnd 1: With **right** side facing, join Blue with sc in any corner ch-2 sp *(see Joining With Sc, page 140)*; (sc in next 3 dc and in next sp) twice, hdc in joining, (sc in next sp and in next 3 dc) twice, [sc in next sp, hdc in joining, (sc in next sp and in next 3 dc) twice] across to next corner ch-2 sp, ★ (sc, ch 2, sc) in corner ch-2 sp, (sc in next 3 dc and in next sp) twice, hdc in joining, (sc in next sp and in next 3 dc) twice, [sc in next sp, hdc in joining, (sc in next sp and in next 3 dc) twice] across to next corner ch-2 sp; repeat from ★ 2 times **more**, sc in same sp as first sc, ch 1, sc in first sc to form last ch-2 sp: 796 sts and 4 ch-2 sps.

Rnd 2: Ch 3, 2 dc in last ch-2 sp made, dc in each st across to next corner ch-2 sp, ★ (3 dc, ch 2, 3 dc) in corner ch-2 sp, dc in each st across to next corner ch-2 sp; repeat from ★ 2 times **more**, 3 dc in same sp as first dc, ch 1, sc in first dc to form last ch-2 sp: 820 dc and 4 ch-2 sps.

Rnd 3: Ch 4 **(counts as first dc plus ch 1)**, skip next dc, (dc in next dc, ch 1, skip next dc) across to next corner ch-2 sp, ★ (dc, ch 2, dc) in corner ch-2 sp, ch 1, skip next dc, (dc in next dc, ch 1, skip next dc) across to next corner ch-2 sp; repeat from ★ 2 times **more**, dc in same sp as first dc, ch 1, sc in first dc to form last ch-2 sp: 416 sts and 416 sps.

Rnd 4: Ch 3, 2 dc in last ch-2 sp made, dc in next dc, (dc in next ch-1 sp and in next dc) across to next corner ch-2 sp, ★ (3 dc, ch 2, 3 dc) in corner ch-2 sp, dc in next dc, (dc in next ch-1 sp and in next dc) across to next corner ch-2 sp; repeat from ★ 2 times **more**, 3 dc in same sp as first dc, hdc in first dc to form last ch-2 sp: 852 dc and 4 ch-2 sps.

Rnd 5: Ch 1, sc in last ch-2 sp made, ch 2, skip next dc, (sc in next dc, ch 2, skip next dc) across to next corner ch-2 sp, ★ sc in corner ch-2 sp, ch 2, skip next dc, (sc in next dc, ch 2, skip next dc) across to next corner ch-2 sp; repeat from ★ 2 times **more**; join with slip st to first sc, finish off.

PLACEMENT DIAGRAM

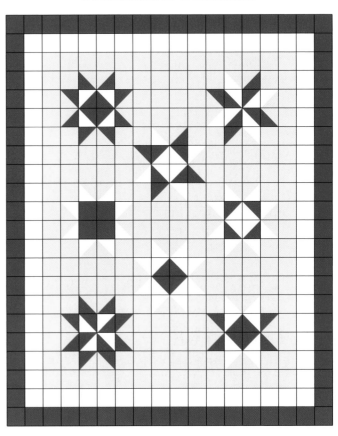

KEY

Square A
☐ - Lt Blue (Make 156)
■ - Blue (Make 80)
☐ - White (Make 68)
Square B
☐ - White & Lt Blue (Make 36)
◪ - Blue & Lt Blue (Make 28)
◪ - White & Blue (Make 28)

124

CHEERY POINSETTIAS

These pretty poinsettias will add a cheery splash of color to your décor this Noel. The square motifs are joined as you go, and the blanket is finished with picots that enhance the petal edging.

Finished Size: 43" x 65" (109 cm x 165 cm)

MATERIALS
Worsted Weight Yarn:
    Green - 21 ounces, 1,185 yards
        (600 grams, 1,083.5 meters)
    Red - 10 ounces, 565 yards
        (280 grams, 516.5 meters)
    Aran - 9$\frac{1}{2}$ ounces, 535 yards
        (270 grams, 489 meters)
    Gold - 3 ounces, 170 yards
        (90 grams, 155.5 meters)
Crochet hook, size I (5.5 mm) **or** size needed
    for gauge

GAUGE: Each Square = 5$\frac{1}{2}$" (14 cm)

STITCH GUIDE

PETAL
Ch 5 **loosely**, working in back ridge of chs *(Fig. 2b, page 137)*, sc in second ch from hook, hdc in next ch, dc in last 2 chs.
PICOT
Ch 3, slip st in back ridge of third ch from hook *(Fig. 2b, page 137)*.

FIRST SQUARE

Rnd 1 (Right side): With Gold, ch 5, dc in fifth ch from hook **(4 skipped chs count as first dc plus ch 1)**, ch 1, (dc in same ch, ch 1) 6 times; join with slip st to first dc, finish off: 8 ch-1 sps.
Note: Loop a short piece of yarn around any stitch to mark Rnd 1 as **right** side.
Rnd 2: With **right** side facing, join Red with sc in any ch-1 sp *(see Joining With Sc, page 140)*; work Petal, (sc in next ch-1 sp, work Petal) around; join with slip st to first sc, finish off: 8 Petals.
Rnd 3: With **right** side facing, join Green with sc in ch at tip of any Petal; ch 3, skip next 4 sts on Petal, dc in next sc, ch 3, ★ sc in ch at tip of next Petal, ch 3, skip next 4 sts on Petal, dc in next sc, ch 3; repeat from ★ around; join with slip st to first sc, do **not** finish off: 8 sc and 8 dc.

Rnd 4: Ch 3 **(counts as first dc, now and throughout)**, (2 dc, ch 2, 3 dc) in same st, ch 1, 3 dc in next dc, sc in next sc, 3 dc in next dc, ch 1, ★ (3 dc, ch 2, 3 dc) in next sc, ch 1, 3 dc in next dc, sc in next sc, 3 dc in next dc, ch 1; repeat from ★ 2 times **more**; join with slip st to first dc, finish off: 52 sts and 12 sps.
Rnd 5: With **right** side facing, join Aran with sc in any corner ch-2 sp; ch 3, sc in same sp, ch 3, sc in next ch-1 sp, ch 3, skip next 3 dc, sc in next sc, ch 3, sc in next ch-1 sp, ch 3, ★ (sc, ch 3) twice in next corner ch-2 sp, sc in next ch-1 sp, ch 3, skip next 3 dc, sc in next sc, ch 3, sc in next ch-1 sp, ch 3; repeat from ★ 2 times **more**; join with slip st to first sc, finish off: 20 sc and 20 ch-3 sps.

ADDITIONAL SQUARES
The method used to connect the Squares is a no-sew joining also know as "join-as-you-go." After the First Square is made, each remaining Square is worked through Rnd 6, then crocheted together as Rnd 7 is worked across the last side(s), working One Side or Two Side Joining. Holding Squares with **wrong** sides together, work slip st into spaces as indicated.

Work same as First Square through Rnd 4: 52 sts and 12 sps.

Note: When joining to a Square that has already been joined, slip st in joining slip st.

Rnd 5 (Joining rnd): Work One Side or Two Side Joining as needed, arranging Squares into 7 vertical rows of 11 Squares each.

Continued on page 126.

ONE SIDE JOINING

Rnd 5 (Joining rnd): With **right** side facing, join Aran with sc in any corner ch-2 sp; ch 3, ★ † sc in next ch-1 sp, ch 3, skip next 3 dc, sc in next sc, ch 3, sc in next ch-1 sp, ch 3 †, (sc, ch 3) twice in next corner ch-2 sp; repeat from ★ once **more**, then repeat from † to † once, sc in next corner ch-2 sp, ch 1, holding Squares with **wrong** sides together, slip st in corresponding corner ch-3 sp on **adjacent Square**, ch 1, sc in same sp on **new Square**, ch 1, slip st in next ch-3 sp on **adjacent Square**, ch 1, sc in next ch-1 sp on **new Square**, ch 1, slip st in next ch-3 sp on **adjacent Square**, ch 1, skip next 3 dc on **new Square**, sc in next sc, ch 1, slip st in next ch-3 sp on **adjacent Square**, ch 1, sc in next ch-1 sp on **new Square**, ch 1, slip st in next ch-3 sp on **adjacent Square**, ch 1, sc in same sp as first sc on **new Square**, ch 1, slip st in next corner ch-3 sp on **adjacent Square**, ch 1; join with slip st to first sc, finish off.

TWO SIDE JOINING

Rnd 5 (Joining rnd): With **right** side facing, join Aran with sc in any corner ch-2 sp; ch 3, † sc in next ch-1 sp, ch 3, skip next 3 dc, sc in next sc, ch 3, sc in next ch-1 sp, ch 3 †, (sc, ch 3) twice in next corner ch-2 sp, repeat from † to † once, sc in next corner ch-2 sp, ch 1, holding Squares with **wrong** sides together, slip st in corresponding corner ch-3 sp on **adjacent Square**, ♥ ch 1, sc in same sp on **new Square**, ch 1, slip st in next ch-3 sp on **adjacent Square**, ch 1, sc in next ch-1 sp on **new Square**, ch 1, slip st in next ch-3 sp on **adjacent Square**, ch 1, skip next 3 dc on **new Square**, sc in next sc, ch 1, slip st in next ch-3 sp on **adjacent Square**, ch 1, sc in next ch-1 sp on **new Square**, ch 1, slip st in next ch-3 sp on **adjacent Square**, ch 1 ♥, sc in next corner ch-2 sp on **new Square**, ch 1, slip st in next corner ch-3 sp on **adjacent Square**, repeat from ♥ to ♥ once, sc in same sp as first sc on **new Square**, ch 1, slip st in next ch-3 sp on **adjacent Square**, ch 1; join with slip st to first sc, finish off.

EDGING

Rnd 1: With **right** side facing, join Aran with slip st in any corner ch-3 sp; ch 3, (2 dc, ch 2, 3 dc) in same sp, ★ 3 dc in each of next 4 ch-3 sps, † dc in next sp, dc around next joining slip st, dc in next sp, 3 dc in each of next 4 ch-3 sps †; repeat from † to † across to next corner ch-3 sp, (3 dc, ch 2, 3 dc) in corner ch-3 sp; repeat from ★ 2 times **more**, 3 dc in each of next 4 ch 3 sps, repeat from † to † across; join with slip st to first dc, finish off: 184 3-dc groups and 4 ch-2 sps.

Rnd 2: With **right** side facing, join Green with sc in any corner ch-2 sp; work Petal, sc in same sp, work Petal, ★ † skip next 3 dc, (sc in sp **before** next dc, work Petal, skip next 3 dc) across to next corner ch-2 sp †, (sc, work Petal) twice in corner ch-2 sp; repeat from ★ 2 times **more**, then repeat from † to † once; join with slip st to first sc, finish off.

Rnd 3: With **right** side facing, join Aran with sc in ch at tip of any Petal; work Picot, sc in same st, ch 3, skip next 4 sts on Petal, sc in next sc, ch 3, ★ (sc, work Picot, sc) in ch at tip of next Petal, ch 3, skip next 4 sts on Petal, sc in next sc, ch 3; repeat from ★ around; join with slip st to first sc, finish off.

CABLED COMFORTER

Whenever you dive into a novel adventure on the high seas, you'll feel warm and secure in our made-for-comfort wrap. Fisherman cables and picots create this handsome throw's toasty texture.

Finished Size: 43^1/$_2$" x 51" (110.5 cm x 129.5 cm)

MATERIALS
Worsted Weight Yarn:
38^1/$_2$ ounces, 2,175 yards
(1,090 grams, 1,989 meters)
Crochet hook, size J (6 mm) **or** size needed
for gauge

GAUGE: 11 sc = 3" (7.5 cm); in pattern,
one repeat (8 rows) = 2^3/$_8$" (6 cm)

Note: Each row is worked across length of Afghan.

STITCH GUIDE

CABLE (uses next 3 sc)
Ch 3 **loosely**, skip next 2 sc, sc in next sc, **turn**;
sc in next 3 chs *(Fig. 1a)*, slip st in next sc (sc
made before ch-3) *(Fig. 1b)*.

Fig. 1a   **Fig. 1b**

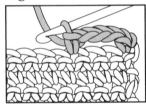   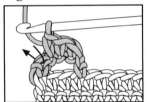

PICOT
Ch 3, sc in third ch from hook.

AFGHAN BODY
Ch 163 **loosely**.
Row 1: Sc in second ch from hook and in each ch
across: 162 sc.
Row 2 (Right side): Ch 1, turn; sc in first 2 sc,
★ work Cable, **turn**; working **behind** Cable, sc in
2 skipped sc *(Fig. 2)*; repeat from ★ across to last sc,
2 sc in last sc: 53 Cables and 110 sc behind Cables.

Fig. 2

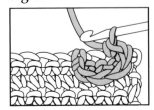

Row 3: Ch 1, turn; working in **front** of Cables, sc in
first 4 sc, ★ skip next Cable, 2 sc in next sc (same sc
as Cable slip st), sc in next sc; repeat from ★ across
to last Cable and last 2 sc, skip last Cable, sc in next
sc (same sc as Cable slip st), sc in last sc: 162 sc.
Row 4: Ch 1, turn; sc in each sc across.
Row 5: Ch 1, turn; sc in first 2 sc, work Picot, ★ skip
next 2 sc, sc in next sc, work Picot; repeat from ★
across to last 4 sc, skip next 2 sc, sc in last 2 sc: 56 sc
and 53 Picots.
Row 6: Ch 2 **(counts as first hdc)**, turn; hdc in next
sc, ch 2, ★ skip next Picot, hdc in next sc, ch 2; repeat
from ★ across to last Picot and last 2 sc, skip last
Picot, hdc in last 2 sc: 56 hdc and 53 ch-2 sps.
Row 7: Ch 1, turn; sc in first 2 hdc, 2 sc in next
ch-2 sp, (sc in next hdc, 2 sc in next ch-2 sp) across to
last 2 hdc, sc in last 2 hdc: 162 sc.
Rows 8 and 9: Ch 1, turn; sc in each sc across.
Row 10: Ch 1, turn; sc in first 2 sc, ★ work Cable,
turn; working **behind** Cable, sc in 2 skipped sc;
repeat from ★ across to last sc, 2 sc in last sc:
53 Cables and 110 sc behind Cables.
Rows 11-123: Repeat Rows 3-10, 14 times; then
repeat Row 3 once **more**; do **not** finish off.

EDGING
Rnd 1: Ch 1, turn; 2 sc in each of first 2 sc, sc in each
sc across to last 2 sc, 2 sc in next sc, 3 sc in last sc;
work 135 sc evenly spaced across end of rows;
working in free loops of beginning ch *(Fig. 17b,
page 141)*, 3 sc in ch at base of first sc, 2 sc in next ch,
sc in each ch across to last 2 chs, 2 sc in next ch, 3 sc
in last ch; work 135 sc evenly spaced across end of
rows, sc in same st as first sc; join with slip st to first
sc: 606 sc.
Rnd 2: Ch 4 **(counts as first hdc plus ch 2, now and
throughout)**, do **not** turn; hdc in same st, ch 2,
★ † skip next 2 sc, (hdc in next sc, ch 2, skip next
2 sc) across to center sc of next corner 3-sc group †,
(hdc, ch 2) 3 times in center sc; repeat from ★ 2 times
more, then repeat from † to † once, hdc in same st as
first hdc, ch 2; join with slip st to first hdc: 210 hdc.
Rnd 3: Ch 1, sc in same st, work Picot, (sc in next
hdc, work Picot) around; join with slip st to first sc.

Rnd 4: Ch 4, hdc in same st, ch 2, ★ † skip next Picot, (hdc in next sc, ch 2, skip next Picot) across to next corner sc †, (hdc, ch 2) 3 times in corner sc; repeat from ★ 2 times **more**, then repeat from † to † once, hdc in same st as first hdc, ch 2; join with slip st to first hdc: 218 hdc.

Rnds 5-9: Repeat Rnds 3 and 4 twice, then repeat Rnd 3 once **more**.
Finish off.

PATCHWORK STARS

Quilt-like patchwork stars dance over this cheerful coverlet. Its bright colors make it an inviting addition to any room in your home, as well as a thoughtful gift!

Finished Size: 47" x 62" (119.5 cm x 157.5 cm)

MATERIALS
Worsted Weight Yarn:
Navy - 17 ounces, 1,165 yards
(480 grams, 1,065.5 meters)
Red - 15 ounces, 1,030 yards
(430 grams, 942 meters)
Gold - $11^1/2$ ounces, 790 yards
(330 grams, 722.5 meters)
Off-White - $11^1/2$ ounces, 790 yards
(330 grams, 722.5 meters)
Crochet hook, size G (4 mm) **or** size needed
for gauge
Yarn needle

GAUGE SWATCH: 5" (12.75 cm) square
Work same as Solid Square.

SOLID SQUARE (Make 12)
With Navy, ch 5; join with slip st to form a ring.
Rnd 1 (Right side): Ch 3 **(counts as first dc, now and throughout)**, 2 dc in ring, (ch 2, 3 dc in ring) 3 times, ch 1, sc in first dc to form last ch-2 sp: 12 dc and 4 ch-2 sps.
Note: Loop a short piece of yarn around any stitch to mark Rnd 1 as **right** side.
Rnd 2: Ch 3, turn; 2 dc in last ch-2 sp made, ch 1, ★ (3 dc, ch 2, 3 dc) in next ch-2 sp, ch 1; repeat from ★ 2 times **more**, 3 dc in same sp as first dc, ch 1, sc in first dc to form last ch-2 sp: 24 dc and 8 sps.
Rnd 3: Ch 3, turn; 2 dc in last ch-2 sp made, ch 1, 3 dc in next ch-1 sp, ch 1, ★ (3 dc, ch 2, 3 dc) in next corner ch-2 sp, ch 1, 3 dc in next ch-1 sp, ch 1; repeat from ★ 2 times **more**, 3 dc in same sp as first dc, ch 1, sc in first dc to form last ch-2 sp: 36 dc and 12 sps.
Rnds 4 and 5: Ch 3, turn; 2 dc in last ch-2 sp made, ch 1, (3 dc in next ch-1 sp, ch 1) across to next corner ch-2 sp, ★ (3 dc, ch 2, 3 dc) in corner ch-2 sp, ch 1, (3 dc in next ch-1 sp, ch 1) across to next corner ch-2 sp; repeat from ★ 2 times **more**, 3 dc in same sp as first dc, ch 1, sc in first dc to form last ch-2 sp: 60 dc and 20 sps.
Finish off leaving a long end for sewing.

TRIANGLE
Make 48 **each** of Navy, Red, Gold, and Off-White.
Row 1 (Right side): Ch 4, 2 dc in fourth ch from hook: 3 sts.
Note: Mark Row 1 as **right** side.
Row 2: Ch 4, turn; 2 dc in fourth ch from hook, ch 1, skip next 2 dc, 3 dc in next ch: 6 sts and one sp.
Row 3: Ch 4, turn; 2 dc in fourth ch from hook, ch 1, 3 dc in next ch-1 sp, ch 1, skip next 2 dc, 3 dc in next ch: 9 sts and 2 sps.
Rows 4-7: Ch 4, turn; 2 dc in fourth ch from hook, ch 1, (3 dc in next ch-1 sp, ch 1) across to last 2 dc, skip last 2 dc, 3 dc in next ch: 21 sts and 6 sps.
Finish off leaving a long end for sewing.

ASSEMBLY
With matching color and working through both loops of each stitch on last row of Triangles, whipstitch Triangles together to form 48 Navy and Gold squares and 48 Red and Off-White squares *(Fig. 21b, page 142)*. Using Block Diagram as a guide, whipstitch squares together to form blocks, working in end of rows on Triangles and through both loops of each stitch across sides of Solid Squares. Whipstitch blocks together in same manner to form 3 vertical strips of 4 blocks each; then whipstitch strips together.

BLOCK DIAGRAM

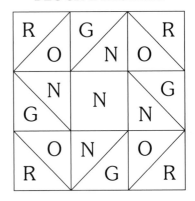

KEY

N - Navy
R - Red
G - Gold
O - Off-White

EDGING

Rnd 1: With **right** side facing, join Red with slip st in free loop of ch at any corner *(Fig. 17b, page 141)*; ch 2 **(counts as first hdc)**, 2 hdc in same st, hdc evenly around working 3 hdc in each corner ch; join with slip st to first hdc.

Rnds 2 and 3: Ch 3, dc in each st around working 5 dc in center st of each corner group; join with slip st to first dc.
Finish off.

TWEEDY STRIPES

Our clever striped afghan is a handsome gift for a man in your life. Made of crossed stitches worked with two strands of yarn, this tweedy blanket is quick to finish.

Finished Size: 48" x 65" (122 cm x 165 cm)

MATERIALS

Worsted Weight Yarn:
   Black - 25 ounces, 1,410 yards
      (710 grams, 1,289.5 meters)
   Peach - 9 ounces, 510 yards
      (260 grams, 466.5 meters)
   Lilac and Green - 8 ounces, 450 yards
      (230 grams, 411.5 meters) **each**
   Yellow and Lavender - 7 ounces, 395 yards
      (200 grams, 361 meters) **each**
   Rose, Dk Rose, and Lt Green -
      4$\frac{1}{2}$ ounces, 255 yards
      (130 grams, 233 meters) **each**
   Crochet hook, size K (6.5 mm) **or** size needed
      for gauge

STITCH GUIDE

TREBLE CROCHET *(abbreviated tr)*
YO twice, insert hook in sc indicated, YO and pull up a loop (4 loops on hook), (YO and draw through 2 loops on hook) 3 times.

Note: Each row is worked across length of Afghan holding two strands of yarn together. When joining yarn and finishing off, leave a 9" (23 cm) end to be worked into fringe.

GAUGE: In pattern, 12 sts = 4$\frac{1}{2}$" (11.5 cm);
            6 rows = 4" (10 cm)

Gauge Swatch: 5$\frac{1}{2}$"w x 4"h (14 cm x 10 cm)
Holding two strands of Black together, ch 15.
Work same as Afghan Body for 6 rows.

COLOR SEQUENCE

Work one row each: ★ one strand Green and one strand Lilac, two strands Black, one strand Rose and one strand Peach, two strands Black, one strand Lavender and one strand Yellow, one strand Lt Green and one strand Peach, two strands Black, one strand Dk Rose and one strand Lilac, two strands Black, one strand Green and one strand Yellow, two strands Black, one strand Lavender and one strand Peach, two strands Black, one strand Lilac and one strand Yellow, two strands Black, one strand Rose and one strand Lt Green, two strands Black, one strand Lavender and one strand Green, two strands Black, one strand Dk Rose and one strand Peach, two strands Black; repeat from ★ for sequence.

AFGHAN BODY

Holding two strands of Black together, ch 174.
Row 1 (Wrong side)**:** Sc in second ch from hook and in next ch, ★ ch 1, skip next ch, sc in next 2 chs; repeat from ★ across; finish off.
Note: Loop a short piece of yarn around **back** of any stitch on Row 1 to mark **right** side.
Begin working in Color Sequence.
Row 2: With **right** side facing, join yarn indicated with slip st in first sc; ch 3 **(counts as first dc)**, ★ skip next sc and next ch, tr in next sc, ch 1, working in **front** of tr just made *(Fig. 18, page 141)*, tr in skipped sc; repeat from ★ across to last sc, dc in last sc; finish off.
Row 3: With **wrong** side facing, join Black with sc in first dc *(see Joining With Sc, page 140)*; sc in next tr, (ch 1, skip next ch, sc in next 2 sts) across; finish off.
Repeat Rows 2 and 3 for pattern until Afghan Body measures approximately 47$\frac{1}{2}$" (120.5 cm) from beginning ch, ending by working Row 3.

EDGING
TOP

With **right** side facing and holding two strands of Black together, join yarn with slip st in first sc; ch 2, (slip st in next sp, ch 2) across, skip next sc, slip st in last sc; finish off.

BOTTOM

With **right** side facing, holding two strands of Black together, and working in sps and in free loops *(Fig. 17b, page 141)* across beginning ch, join yarn with slip st in ch at base of first sc; ch 2, (slip st in next sp, ch 2) across, skip next ch, slip st in last ch; finish off.

Holding four strands of corresponding color yarn together, each 18" (45.5" cm) long, add additional fringe across short edges of Afghan *(Figs. 22b & d, page 142)*.

CHRISTMAS CANDIES

Like an old-fashioned candy store, this cheery afghan is full of colorful striped discs. The festive border and pattern are ideal for a child's room.

Finished Size: 49" x 68" (124.5 cm x 172.5 cm)

MATERIALS
Worsted Weight Yarn:
 Black - 40 ounces, 2,260 yards
  (1,140 grams, 2,066.5 meters)
 Tan - 8¹/₂ ounces, 480 yards
  (240 grams, 439 meters)
 Teal, Blue, Green, Plum, Brown, Bronze,
  Burgundy, and Copper - 4 ounces,
   225 yards (110 grams, 205.5 meters) **each**
Crochet hook, size K (6.5 mm) **or** size needed
 for gauge
Yarn needle

Note: Afghan is worked holding two strands of yarn together.

GAUGE SWATCH: 4³/₄" (12 cm) square
Work same as Square.

SQUARE (Make 117)

Make the number of Squares indicated, working through Rnd 2 in the following colors: 23 Squares holding Teal and Tan together, 23 Squares holding Blue and Green together, 24 Squares holding Plum and Brown together, 23 Squares holding Bronze and Tan together, and 24 Squares holding Burgundy and Copper together.

Holding one strand **each** as indicated, ch 6; join with slip st to form a ring.
Rnd 1 (Right side): Ch 3 **(counts as first dc)**, 15 dc in ring; join with slip st to first dc: 16 dc.
Note: Loop a short piece of yarn around any stitch to mark Rnd 1 as **right** side.
Rnd 2: Ch 1, (sc in next dc, ch 1) 15 times, sc in joining slip st, ch 1; join with slip st to first sc, finish off: 16 sc and 16 ch-1 sps.
Rnd 3: With **right** side facing, join Black with sc in any ch-1 sp *(see Joining With Sc, page 140)*; ch 1, (sc in next ch-1 sp, ch 1) around; join with slip st to first sc.

Rnd 4: Ch 1, sc in same st, ch 1, (dc, ch 3, dc) in next sc, ch 1, sc in next sc, ch 1, slip st in next sc, ch 1, ★ sc in next sc, ch 1, (dc, ch 3, dc) in next sc, ch 1, sc in next sc, ch 1, slip st in next sc, ch 1; repeat from ★ 2 times **more**; join with slip st to first sc, finish off: 20 sts and 20 sps.

ASSEMBLY

With one strand of Black and working in both loops, whipstitch Squares together in desired order *(Fig. 21b, page 142)*, forming 9 vertical strips of 13 Squares each, beginning in center ch of first corner ch-3 and ending in center ch of next corner ch-3; whipstitch strips together in same manner.

EDGING

Rnd 1: With **right** side facing and holding two strands of Black together, join yarn with sc in any corner ch-3 sp; ch 2, sc in same sp, ch 1, ★ (sc in next sp, ch 1) across to next corner ch-3 sp, (sc, ch 2, sc) in corner ch-3 sp, ch 1; repeat from ★ 2 times **more**, (sc in next sp, ch 1) across; join with slip st to first sc: 264 sc and 264 sps.
Rnd 2: Ch 1, (sc, ch 2, sc) in first corner ch-2 sp, ch 1, ★ (sc in next ch-1 sp, ch 1) across to next corner ch-2 sp, (sc, ch 2, sc) in corner ch-2 sp, ch 1; repeat from ★ 2 times **more**, (sc in next ch-1 sp, ch 1) across; join with slip st to first sc, finish off: 268 sc and 268 sps.
Rnd 3: With **wrong** side facing and holding one strand of Teal and one strand of Tan together, join yarn with sc in any corner ch-2 sp; ch 2, sc in same sp, sc in next sc, ★ (ch 1, sc in next sc) across to next corner ch-2 sp, (sc, ch 2, sc) in corner ch-2 sp, sc in next sc; repeat from ★ 2 times **more**, (ch 1, sc in next sc) across; join with slip st to first sc, finish off: 276 sc and 268 sps.
Rnd 4: With **right** side facing and holding one strand of Blue and one strand of Green together, join yarn with sc in any corner ch-2 sp; ch 2, sc in same sp, ch 1, ★ skip next sc, (sc in next sc, ch 1) across to within one sc of next corner ch-2 sp, skip next sc, (sc, ch 2, sc) in next corner ch-2 sp, ch 1; repeat from ★ 2 times **more**, skip next sc, (sc in next sc, ch 1) across to last sc, skip last sc; join with slip st to first sc, finish off: 276 sc and 276 sps.

Rnd 5: Holding one strand of Plum and one strand of Brown together, repeat Rnd 3: 284 sc and 276 sps.

Rnd 6: Holding one strand of Bronze and one strand of Tan together, repeat Rnd 4: 284 sc and 284 sps.

Rnd 7: Holding one strand of Burgundy and one strand of Copper together, repeat Rnd 3: 292 sc and 284 sps.

Rnd 8: With **right** side facing and holding two strands of Black together, join yarn with sc in any corner ch-2 sp; ch 2, sc in same sp, ch 1, ★ skip next sc, (sc in next sc, ch 1) across to within one sc of next corner ch-2 sp, skip next sc, (sc, ch 2, sc) in next corner ch-2 sp, ch 1; repeat from ★ 2 times **more**, skip next sc, (sc in next sc, ch 1) across to last sc, skip last sc; join with slip st to first sc, do **not** finish off: 292 sc and 292 sps.

Rnd 9: (Slip st, ch 2, slip st) in first corner ch-2 sp, ch 1, ★ (slip st in next ch-1 sp, ch 1) across to next corner ch-2 sp, (slip st, ch 2, slip st) in corner ch-2 sp, ch 1; repeat from ★ 2 times **more**, (slip st in next ch-1 sp, ch 1) across; join with slip st to first slip st, finish off.

ABBREVIATIONS

BPdc	Back Post double crochet(s)	FPsc	Front Post single crochet(s)
BPdtr	Back Post double treble crochet(s)	FPtr	Front Post treble crochet(s)
BPtr	Back Post treble crochet(s)	hdc	half double crochet(s)
ch(s)	chain(s)	Lt	Light
cm	centimeters	mm	millimeters
dc	double crochet(s)	Rnd(s)	Round(s)
Dk	Dark	sc	single crochet(s)
dtr	double treble crochet(s)	sp(s)	space(s)
FP	Front Post	st(s)	stitch(es)
FPdc	Front Post double crochet(s)	tr	treble crochet(s)
FPdtr	Front Post double treble crochet(s)	YO	yarn over

★ — work instructions following ★ as many **more** times as indicated in addition to the first time.

† to † or ♥ to ♥ — work all instructions from first † to second † or from first ♥ to second ♥ **as many** times as specified.

( ) or [ ] — work enclosed instructions **as many** times as specified by the number immediately following **or** work all enclosed instructions in the stitch or space indicated **or** contains explanatory remarks.

colon (:) — the number(s) given after a colon at the end of a row or round denote(s) the number of stitches you should have on that row or round.

TERMS

chain loosely — work the chain **only** loose enough for the hook to pass through the chain easily when working the next row or round into the chain.

leg — the first or second part of a pattern stitch.

post — the vertical shaft of a stitch.

right side vs. wrong side — the right side of your work is the side that will show when the piece is finished.

work across or around — continue working in the established pattern.

GAUGE

Gauge is the number of stitches and rows or rounds per inch and is used to determine the finished size of an Afghan. All patterns in this book specify the gauge that you must match to ensure proper size and to ensure that you will have enough yarn to complete your Afghan.

Hook size given in instructions is merely a guide. Because everyone crochets differently — loosely, tightly, or somewhere in between — the finished size can vary, even when crocheters use the very same pattern, yarn, and hook.

Before beginning your Afghan, it is absolutely necessary for you to crochet a gauge swatch in the pattern stitch indicated and with the weight of yarn and hook size suggested. Your swatch must be large enough to measure your gauge. Lay your swatch on a hard, smooth, flat surface. Then measure it, counting your stitches and rows or rounds carefully. If your swatch is smaller than specified or you have too many stitches per inch, try again with a larger size hook; if your swatch is larger than specified or you don't have enough stitches per inch, try again with a smaller size hook. Keep trying until you find the size that will give you the specified gauge. **DO NOT HESITATE TO CHANGE HOOK SIZE TO OBTAIN CORRECT GAUGE.** Once proper gauge is obtained, measure the width of the Afghan approximately every 3" to be sure gauge remains consistent.

BASIC STITCH GUIDE

CHAIN (abbreviated ch)

To work a chain stitch, begin with a slip knot on the hook. Bring the yarn **over** the hook from **back** to **front**, catching the yarn with the hook and turning the hook slightly toward you to keep the yarn from slipping off. Draw the yarn through the slip knot *(Fig. 1)*.

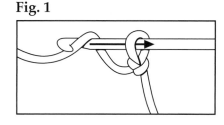

Fig. 1

WORKING INTO THE CHAIN

When beginning a first row of crochet in a chain, always skip the first chain from the hook and work into the second chain from hook (for single crochet), third chain from hook (for half double crochet), or fourth chain from hook (for double crochet), etc. *(Fig. 2a)*.

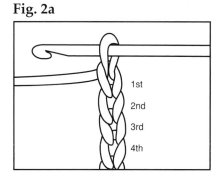

Fig. 2a

1st
2nd
3rd
4th

Method 1: Insert hook into back ridge of each chain indicated *(Fig. 2b)*.
Method 2: Insert hook under top loop **and** the back ridge of each chain indicated *(Fig. 2c)*.

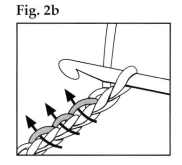
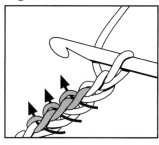

Fig. 2b   Fig. 2c

SLIP STITCH (abbreviated slip st)

This stitch is used to attach new yarn, to join work, or to move the yarn across a group of stitches without adding height.
Insert hook in stitch or space indicated, YO and draw through stitch **and** loop on hook *(Fig. 3)*.

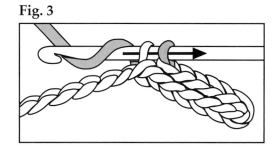

Fig. 3

SINGLE CROCHET (abbreviated sc)

Insert hook in stitch or space indicated, YO and pull up a loop, YO and draw through both loops on hook (*Fig. 4*).

Fig. 4

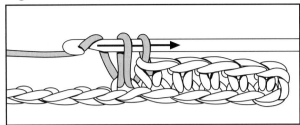

HALF DOUBLE CROCHET

(abbreviated hdc)

YO, insert hook in stitch or space indicated, YO and pull up a loop, YO and draw through all 3 loops on hook (*Fig. 5*).

Fig. 5

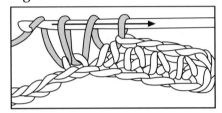

DOUBLE CROCHET (abbreviated dc)

YO, insert hook in stitch or space indicated, YO and pull up a loop (3 loops on hook), YO and draw through 2 loops on hook (*Fig. 6a*), YO and draw through remaining 2 loops on hook (*Fig. 6b*).

Fig. 6a

Fig. 6b

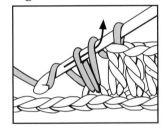

TREBLE CROCHET (abbreviated tr)

YO twice, insert hook in stitch or space indicated, YO and pull up a loop (4 loops on hook) (*Fig. 7a*), (YO and draw through 2 loops on hook) 3 times (*Fig. 7b*).

Fig. 7a

Fig. 7b

DOUBLE TREBLE CROCHET

(abbreviated dtr)

YO 3 times, insert hook in stitch or space indicated, YO and pull up a loop (5 loops on hook) (*Fig. 8a*), (YO and draw through 2 loops on hook) 4 times (*Fig. 8b*).

Fig. 8a

Fig. 8b

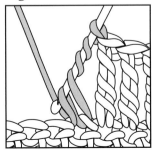
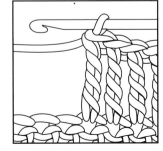

PATTERN STITCHES

POST STITCH
Work around post of stitch indicated, inserting hook in direction of arrow (*Fig. 9*).

Fig. 9

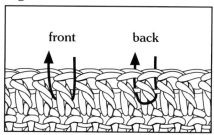

CLUSTER
A Cluster can be worked all in the same stitch or space (*Figs. 10a & b*), **or** across several stitches (*Figs. 11a & b*).

Fig. 10a

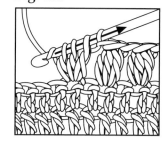

Fig. 10b

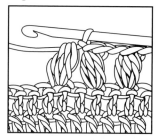

Fig. 11a

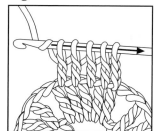

Fig. 11b

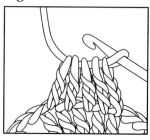

PUFF STITCH
★ YO, insert hook in stitch or space indicated, YO and pull up a loop even with loop on hook; repeat from ★ as many times as specified, YO and draw through all loops on hook (*Fig. 12*).

Fig. 12

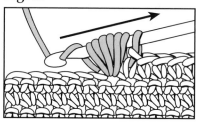

POPCORN
Work specified number of dc in stitch or space indicated, drop loop from hook, insert hook in first dc of dc group, hook dropped loop and draw through (*Fig. 13*).

Fig. 13

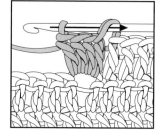

REVERSE SINGLE CROCHET

(abbreviated reverse sc)
Working from **left** to **right**, insert hook in stitch to right of hook *(Fig. 14a)*, YO and draw through, under and to left of loop on hook (2 loops on hook) *(Fig. 14b)*. YO and draw through both loops on hook *(Fig. 14c) (reverse sc made, Fig. 14d)*.

Fig. 14a
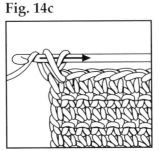

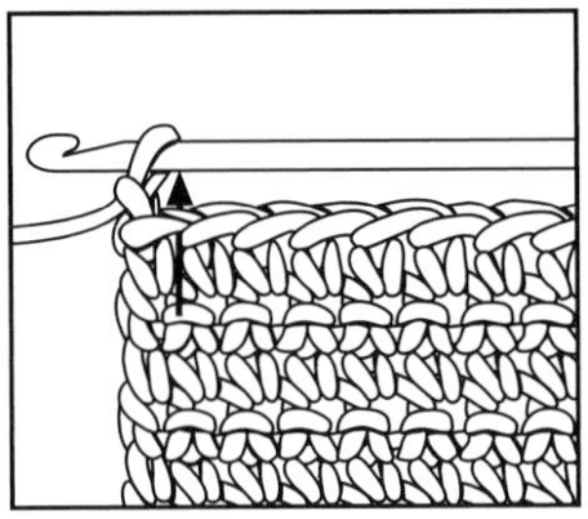

Fig. 14b
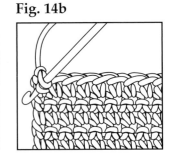

Fig. 14c

Fig. 14d

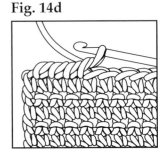

STITCHING TIPS

MARKERS
Markers are used to help distinguish the right side of the Afghan **or** to identify a specific stitch to be worked into later. Place a 2" (5 cm) scrap piece of yarn around a stitch on the row or round indicated, removing the marker after the Afghan is completed **or** as indicated in the instructions.

JOINING WITH SC
When instructed to join with sc, begin with a slip knot on hook. Insert hook in stitch or space indicated, YO and pull up a loop, YO and draw through both loops on hook.

JOINING WITH DC
When instructed to join with dc, begin with a slip knot on hook. YO, holding loop on hook, insert hook in stitch or space indicated, YO and pull up a loop (3 loops on hook), (YO and draw through 2 loops on hook) twice.

BACK OR FRONT LOOP ONLY
Work only in loop(s) indicated by arrow *(Fig. 15)*.

Fig. 15
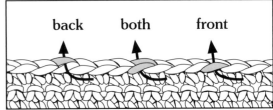

SIDE TWO LEGS OF A STITCH

When instructed to work in **side** of two legs of a stitch, insert hook in two loops on side of base of stitch specified in direction indicated by arrow *(Fig. 16)*.

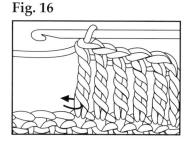
Fig. 16

FREE LOOPS

After working in Back or Front Loops Only on a row or round, there will be a ridge of unused loops. These are called the free loops. Later, when instructed to work in the free loops of the same row or round, work in these loops *(Fig. 17a)*.

When instructed to work in a free loop of a beginning chain, work in loop indicated by arrow *(Fig. 17b)*.

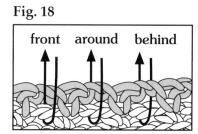
Fig. 17a   Fig. 17b

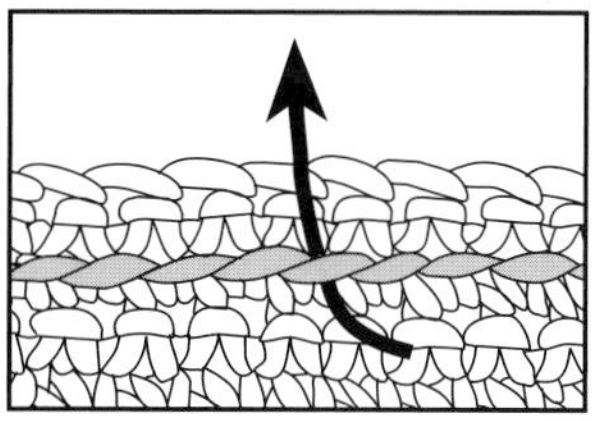

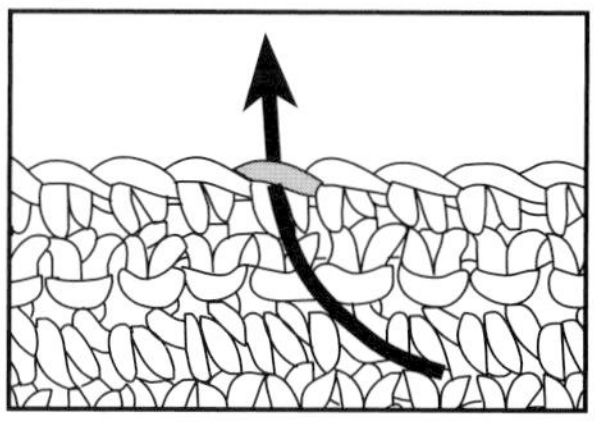

WORKING IN FRONT OF, AROUND, OR BEHIND A STITCH

Work in stitch or space indicated, inserting hook in direction of arrow *(Fig. 18)*.

Fig. 18

front   around   behind

CHANGING COLORS

Work the last stitch to within one step of completion, hook new yarn *(Fig. 19)* and draw through loops on hook.

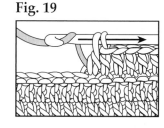
Fig. 19

WORKING IN SPACE BEFORE STITCH

When instructed to work in space **before** a stitch or in spaces **between** stitches, insert hook in space indicated by arrow *(Fig. 20)*.

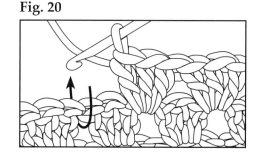
Fig. 20

FINISHING

WHIPSTITCH

With **wrong** sides together and beginning in corner stitch, sew through both pieces once to secure the beginning of the seam, leaving an ample yarn end to weave in later. Insert needle from **front** to **back** through **inside** loops of **each** piece (*Fig. 21a*) or through **both** loops (*Fig. 21b*). Bring needle around and insert it from **front** to **back** through the next loops of **both** pieces. Continue in this manner across to next corner, keeping the sewing yarn fairly loose.

Fig. 21a
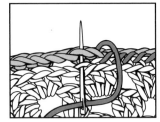

Fig. 21b

FRINGE

Cut a piece of cardboard 8" (20.5 cm) wide and half as long as strands indicated in individual instructions. Wind the yarn **loosely** and **evenly** around the length of the cardboard until the card is filled, then cut across one end; repeat as needed. Align the number of strands desired and fold in half. With **wrong** side facing and using a crochet hook, draw the folded end up through a stitch, row, or loop, and pull the loose ends through the folded end (*Figs. 22a & b*); draw the knot up **tightly** (*Figs. 22c & d*). Repeat, spacing as specified. Lay flat on a hard surface and trim the ends.

Fig. 22a
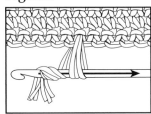

Fig. 22b

Fig. 22c
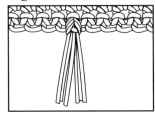

Fig. 22d
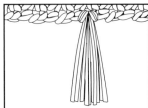

TASSEL (Make 4)

Cut a piece of cardboard 3" (7.5 cm) wide and 10" (25.5 cm) long. Wind a double strand of yarn around the length of the cardboard approximately 21 times; cut yarn end. Cut an 18"(45.5 cm) length of yarn and insert it under all of the strands at the top of the cardboard; pull **tightly** and tie securely. Leave the yarn ends long enough to attach the tassel. Cut the yarn at the opposite end of the cardboard (*Fig. 23a*) and then remove it. Cut a 6" (15 cm) length of yarn and wrap it **tightly** around the tassel twice, $1^1/_4$ " (3 cm) below the top (*Fig. 23b*); tie securely.

Fig. 23a
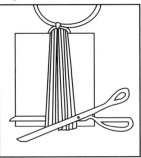

Fig. 23b